HARD MEN

Hard Men

The English and Violence since 1750

Clive Emsley

Hambledon and London

London and New York

Hambledon and London

102 Gloucester Avenue
London, NW1 8HX

175 Fifth Avenue
New York, NY 10010
USA

First Published 2005

ISBN 1 85285 408 1

A description of this book is available from the
British Library and from the Library of Congress.

Typeset by Carnegie Publishing, Lancaster,

Distributed in the United States and Canada
exclusively by Palgrave Macmillan,
a division of St Martin's Press.

Contents

Illustrations

Tables

For Sam and Toby

Preface

Between 1955 and 1963 I went to a boys' grammar school in south-east London. The education that I received there contained vestiges of that of the Victorian public school. The terms 'plucky chap' and 'hard man' were used amongst us boys generally with a satirical smirk. The former was considered old-fashioned, though probably all of us recognised the virtues of the plucky chap: courageous, reticent, prepared to stand up for his principles whatever the odds. The hard man, in contrast, was not really respectable. It was expected, at least among the school masters, that those of us from working-class backgrounds had left the aspiration of being a hard man behind with success in the eleven plus exam. The hard man oozed toughness and violence. The plucky chap was violent only in the last resort; he did not carry his toughness around for all to see and had no air of menace. The plucky chap and the hard man were, and remain, ideal types of masculinity and particularly, I think, of English masculinity. In many respects, like so much else in perceptions of Englishness, they come with the baggage of social class. They also represent different attitudes towards violence.

   The aim of this book is to explore what appears to be the popularly held assumption that English society became increasingly less violent during the nineteenth century and that it remained essentially non-violent up until the middle of the twentieth century at least. I must stress that the focus of the book is English society. All of the primary research was in English archives and, while the Welsh are often subsumed within English society in histories, I am consciously omitting Scottish and Irish society. That said, I acknowledge that when I come to discuss the state and its attitude towards and deployment of violence, then 'British' is the more accurate description. Violence is a catch-all category and can be used to cover a variety of behaviour. My principal concern in what follows is physical, inter-personal violence. I am not concerned with violence against animals, though it could be argued that part of the perception of English people's non-violence rests on them supposedly being lovers of animals. Nor am I using violence in the passive sense that appears to have become popular in some circles as a synonym for the non-physical, sometimes structural oppression of, for example, a social class or a minority ethnic group. Yet, even with the subject restricted to inter-personal violence, there remain difficulties of definition and the range and variety of incidents remains vast.

In preparing this book I have benefited enormously from talking to many colleagues and from reading the work of many more. In particular I want to thank John Archer, Andy Davies, Peter King and Chris A. Williams, who generously read and commented on drafts. Jim Whitfield, Martin Wiener and Stefan Slater generously passed references to me. Nick Hiley gave me the run of the Centre for Cartoons and Caricature at the University of Kent at Canterbury. The author and publishers are grateful to the Lowe Estate and Associated Newspapers for permission to reproduce the cartoons on pages 53 and 129. The errors that remain are mine. Thanks also to Tim Brown, who, as readers who persevere will see, permitted me to write of a terrifying experience. Last but not least, I must thank my wife, Jennifer, for her love, help and support. The dedication is to our youngest grandsons.

Abbreviations

CBOA	Charles Booth Online Archive (http://www.booth.lse.ac.uk)
CCCSP	Central Criminal Court Sessions Papers
MPA	Metropolitan Police Archive, Charlton
OBSP	Old Bailey Sessions Papers (http://www.oldbaileyonline.org)
OUPA	Open University Police Archive
PRO	Public Records Office, the National Archives, Kew
RO	Records Office, as in Bedfordshire RO

1

A Violent Society?

On the evening of 28 February 1938 Troopers Andrew Vanderberg and Reginald Eddie Kaye of the 12th Royal Lancers, armed with revolvers, deserted their barracks at Tidworth in Hampshire and walked into the town of Andover. They held up two police officers from the Hampshire Constabulary and stole their car. After two miles the car broke down. They then waved down a car driven by Squadron Leader Raymond Costa of the RAF. Costa, believing that these were policemen in trouble, stopped to assist; for his pains he was forced, at gunpoint, to drive the deserters to London. Costa was let out of the car when it reached the East End. The deserters took his raincoat and overcoat, and left their own greatcoats. On 1 March, briefly in company with a young man 'well known' to the police, the deserters carried out some small thefts, at gunpoint. Much later that evening the two deserters reached the Woolwich Ferry, where they hijacked another car and driver. What they did not know was that this driver was an off-duty police constable. Constable Elliott Pillar drove the car as instructed but, seeing the lights of Barking Police Station in front of him, jammed on the brakes and the car skidded into a lamp-post. Pillar then grappled with the deserters until the car door gave way and the three men tumbled on to the pavement. A cinema attendant, who had witnessed the crash, ran into the police station, and three detectives and a uniformed officer ran out to assist Pillar. The deserters ran off, striking Pillar across the head with the butt of a revolver as they did so. A chase ensued, down a cul-de-sac and into the garden of the local vicarage. Detective Sergeant Cecil Rackham was shot in the left side. Detective Sergeant George Hemley was shot in the left wrist. But the police officers continued the pursuit and eventually over-powered the two deserters. In the struggle Vanderberg's head was pushed through a glass panel in the vicarage door, at which he dropped his gun and surrendered with the lines that all criminals used when caught by a British Bobby: 'All right guv'nor. I give in' (at least, that was how the *Police Review* reported it). At the Central Criminal Court on 1 April 1938 Trooper Vanderberg, aged thirty-seven, and Trooper Kaye, aged sixteen, were sentenced respectively to ten years' penal servitude and three years Borstal detention.[1]

The story of the deserters, with its hijackings and gunshots, does not fit readily with the traditional image of England, or English crime, during the 1930s. The English image is rather more Agatha Christie than Bonnie and Clyde. In his summing up before passing sentence on Vanderberg and Kaye, Judge Asquith declared: 'It cannot be too clearly understood in this country that the methods of the gangster and the gunman are not going to be tolerated.' Gangsters and gunmen were perceived as North American phenomena, and, indeed, there was a North American angle to the story. Vanderberg had been born in the East End where, in 1938, his parents were still living, occasionally in receipt of assistance from the Jewish Board of Guardians. He had left school at fourteen, in 1914, and had worked his passage to Canada as a deckhand. On the outbreak of war, though underage, he had volunteered for the Canadian Expeditionary Force. While serving in France he had twice been a casualty: in November 1917 he was diagnosed with trench foot; and in June 1918 he was concussed and buried by shellfire. On his return to Canada after the war, he received two suspended sentences for theft in June 1919 and August 1920. In September 1921 he was sentenced to life imprisonment for shooting with attempt to murder during a bank raid in Saskatoon. He had been released, with an order for deportation back to England, early in 1937. While the notion that war brutalises the men who fight has long been popular, it seems unlikely that Vanderberg's violent spree in 1938 can be attributed to brutalisation in the trenches. His military record, with a string of offences including insubordination and going absent without leave, was poor long before he reached the Western Front. A habit picked up in North America, however, was suggested as a reason for his violent behaviour in 1938. His counsel argued that he was acting under the influence of marijuana, which 'produced an effect of exhilaration, excitement and hallucination'. 'It is almost unknown in this country but a curse in Mexico and the lower States of America.' The drug had been sent to him, allegedly, by friends in Canada and the United States. 'Drug said to have made soldier turn gunman', declared a sub-headline of the *Daily Telegraph* reporting the trial. *The Times* settled for 'Took a Drug'.

Kaye had been born in Cheshire and had no North American connections. But he did have two previous convictions for shopbreaking, and a school report quoted in court declared him 'unsatisfactory and untrustworthy, and it had been found that corporal punishment touched him most'. He had started well in the army, but had become disgruntled when punished for a minor offence; after this, it was said, he had fallen under Vanderberg's influence. There was other evidence, notably his diary, to suggest a young man fascinated by guns, girls, adventure and speed. His corporal remembered him reading 'thriller stories and Western magazines'. It was alleged in court that, during one of his first jobs after leaving school, he had tried to bore the barrel of a dummy pistol to make it serviceable. Constable Pillar quoted Kaye as talking about 'plugging' him, and a district inspector of the Metropolitan Police, in a final report on the case, considered that Kaye had done himself no favours in court by his 'bragging role ... He alleged he aimed his revolver to miss the pursuing officers, stating he was so good a shot as to be able to fire at a distance of fifteen to twenty yards and purposely miss by two feet'. A rather different picture emerged from Kaye's distraught and apparently respectable parents. They believed that it was bullying by his corporal that had led the youth to desert. The evidence from Kaye's diary suggests an intense dislike of the corporal. 'I'll swipe Macaulay out of this world before long', declared one such entry less than a week before his desertion.

The conflicting and partial evidence makes it difficult to assess why Kaye and Vanderberg acted as they did. But conflicting and partial evidence is a common problem for the historian. Many of the elements in the story might be pulled out as representative of different, but traditional forms of behaviour – the older man, Vanderberg, with a history of violence and insubordination, possibly aggravated by his war experience and drugs, influencing an impressionable young man, possibly unhappy under the command of a tough, no nonsense NCO. The courageous English Bobbies, who, unarmed, took on gunmen and, though wounded, got their men. The judge's assertion that gangsters and gunmen were alien encroachments on English criminality; and if the story of Kaye and Vanderberg does not appear 'typical' of the criminality or the violence of inter-war England, then what was 'typical'? And why were some things considered 'typical' and others not?

In the years both immediately before and after Kaye and Vanderberg embarked on their criminal spree the English were congratulating themselves on their gentleness and non-violence. The nineteenth century had ended in the warm glow of the 'English miracle' of declining, or at least levelling out, crime statistics. Crime appeared to have been falling since the middle of the century.[2] During the period between the two world wars crime was rarely perceived as a serious problem; the prison population declined to the extent that it was possible for the state to close twenty-four of the fifty local prisons. Neither comment on the English miracle nor the optimism of penologists in the inter-war years saw much reflection on the question of criminal violence; and it was much the same with other commentators on English life.

Writing during the 1930s and 1940s, George Orwell, one of the most acute journalists and critics of the period, presented what might be considered as some of the best, warts and all, accounts of England in the inter-war and Second World War years. Orwell's work was profoundly influenced by a loathing of authoritarian regimes of both the left and the right, and he was intent on contrasting England with the countries of such regimes, especially so when the country went to war with Nazi Germany. Physical violence does not much figure in Orwell's picture of England. His English were, essentially, a 'gentle' people – and he was fond of the word 'gentle' in this context – who loved their animals and their gardens, whose crowds were orderly and who were always willing to form queues. The recent past had known violence, when 'it was impossible for a smartly dressed person to walk down Ratcliff Highway without being assaulted, and an eminent jurist, asked to name a typically English crime, could answer: "Kicking your wife to death".' There might be the occasional 'hanging judge'; by 1945 the traditional, almost domesticated form of English murder might have been in decline as a result of war and American influences. But, unlike their continental neighbours, the English did not kill each other for political motives and their policemen were not armed.[3]

A decade later Geoffrey Gorer, a social psychologist, could describe the development of the English character from an aggressive pugnacity in the eighteenth century to gentleness in the twentieth. And at the close

of the 1960s a senior home office official and historian of the English
police could write of England's 'conquest of violence', at least in its public forms. 'The prime causes of public violence in Britain had', declared
T. A. Critchley, 'by about the year 1900, been largely (though not wholly)
eliminated.'[4] Orwell's, Gorer's and Critchley's England is, consciously or
not, the model of the past by which many contemporary critics examine
the present and assess the state of violence within the country.

Many contemporary commentators write or speak confidently about
violence with very little recognition of the complexities of the term or
of the multitude of incidents, some serious but many more minor, that
need to be considered in any assessment of the issue. A violent incident
can involve one individual, infuriated by a very petty matter, lashing out
at another. Shortly after Christmas 1921, for example, a Chingford
woman scratched a ticket collector in a dispute over a ticket at a station
barrier.[5] Such an offender is unlikely to be stigmatised in the popular
mind as a criminal, though the police might record their offence. There
are other individuals, who could never be conveniently categorised as
'professional criminals', who can be found to have had long careers of
petty offending and petty violence. It is possible, though it might be
difficult to substantiate, that, on occasions, the police or some other
public authority, exasperated by such troublemakers, opted to press
more serious charges so as to have the opportunity for the imposition
of more severe punishment. The case of grievous bodily harm brought
against Jonathan Gwyer Beard, variously described as a shop-blind
maker and a sail maker of Dunstable, and his wife Annie at the Bedfordshire quarter sessions in January 1918 could be one such example.
Annie, aged thirty-eight, who appeared in court holding a baby, had
accumulated eight convictions between 4 April 1916 and 28 August 1917
for a range of petty offences including drunkenness, indecent language,
fighting and assault. Her husband, aged fifty-six, had a record of thirty-
five convictions going back forty years; these had ranged up and down
the country from Brighton to Yorkshire, nine involved assault and in
five of these instances policemen were the victims.[6] The Beards appear
to have been pests whose behaviour might best be characterised under
the popular, contemporary label of 'anti-social'.

Ernest Jeffs also collected a string of convictions before both petty
sessions and quarter sessions, and many of his offences had a violent,

sexual element. When he appeared before the magistrates of Luton district in June 1914 he was aged forty-two and had a criminal record going back twenty-one years. The local police superintendent described him as 'a nuisance to the police and the public'. He had been sent to a Salvation Army home, and then turned out because he was simply too difficult. In June 1914 he was charged with the indecent assault of an eleven-year-old girl; the case was forwarded to the midsummer quarter sessions where he was found guilty and sentenced to two years with hard labour. In August 1919 he was back before the petty sessions charged with attempted rape and assault. The victim, possibly because of embarrassment, offered no evidence on the first charge, and the justices, 'not of opinion that there was aggravation in this case', sentenced him to two months' hard labour. At the end of October he was again before the Luton magistrates charged with assaulting and beating another woman; and he received another two month sentence. At Easter 1925 the quarter sessions sentenced him to three years' penal servitude for attempting to set fire to a stack of barley.[7]

The offences described above were all violent in some measure and were all categorised under a judicial heading relating to violence. The problem is complicated further in that such headings could be changed as a case progressed through the criminal justice system, while in themselves categories do not help to explain important details and circumstances. Thus, for example, in April 1920 the Bedfordshire Police charged Thomas Shanagan with the malicious wounding of Edward King. But when Shanagan appeared before the magistrates at the Luton district petty sessions, the charge had been changed to common assault, for which he was sentenced to fourteen days' imprisonment with hard labour.[8] If the incident itself had not changed, the categorisation had, but the reasons for this are obscure.

Elsewhere an individual's violent behaviour on a single occasion could result in several charges involving several separate victims. At the Nottinghamshire quarter sessions in April 1906, for example, Walter Holgate was indicted for, and found guilty of assaulting seven-year-old Amelia Augusta Lindsey with intent to ravish, and of common assault on Helenor May Lindsay and PC Henry Button.[9] A single violent incident against a single victim could, in contrast, result in several separate charges; a man accused of attempted rape could thus find himself facing three charges: assault with intent to ravish and carnally know; indecent assault; and common assault. Where such a battery of assault charges of this sort were preferred it seems that juries at quarter sessions, at least in Nottinghamshire, were commonly inclined to find a man guilty only on the common assault charge.[10] The *Judicial Statistics* for 1923 suggested that much of the increase in indecent assaults on women 'may be attributed to the growing practice ... of reducing charges of sexual crimes triable only at the Assizes to offences cognisable summarily'.[11] But courts also sometimes directed juries to reject the more serious charge of indecent assault in preference to the less serious common assault, and sometimes the courts simply amended the initial charge before trial.[12] There were instances of men charged with indecent assault who, probably in the hope of a lighter sentence, pleaded guilty in court to common assault.[13] What this means, quite simply, is that a violent offence as severe as rape might finally appear in the legal and historical record as a mere common assault.

These cases came to court and consequently left a trace in the legal records. In contrast with the legal and broad statistical records, few police Occurrence Books or Refused Charge Books have survived. These reveal cases that never came to court and provide the reason why, or at least an inkling of it. In some instances it was simply that suspects could not be picked out at identification parades.[14] Some men may have been reluctant to press charges of assault against others because of a male code of honour that meant a settling of the matter later, by violence; but there may also have been a determination to ignore a fight or to look forward to some other form of settlement. If a police officer did not actually witness men fighting, he could not charge them with doing so. In 1903, for example, the police in the small village of Brill, Buckinghamshire, recorded a case of wounding in the station Occurrence Book. A navvy, working on a new railway line, had been stabbed in the thigh and buttock, but he declined to take proceedings against two others with whom he and his brother were known to have been fighting.[15] In August 1935 William Hills was taken to Poplar Hospital in an LCC ambulance with a cut on his cheek and a bruise over his left eye. Initially, he claimed that he had been attacked with a knife and named an individual to the police. When the police apprehended the accused, however, Hills refused to press charges and both men denied that any weapon had been used.[16] Family links and, perhaps, embarrassment may also have discouraged victims from prosecuting. Henry Mansfield refused to prosecute his son for striking him with a fire grate. John McKay refused to prosecute a woman, probably his wife from the name, for hitting him over the head with a bottle. While a Chingford woman, found injured by a constable in the debris of her smashed up kitchen, declined to prosecute her fifteen-year-old son and said that she would report matters to the probation officer at the local petty sessions.[17]

Recent research by criminologists has revealed a considerable degree of violence, especially drink-fuelled violence, in the modern records of Accident and Emergency Departments. Much of this violence never becomes public in subsequent court cases.[18] Scattered journalistic evidence suggests that it is probable that a systematic survey of any equivalent historical records would provide a similar picture.[19] Unfortunately such hospital records have yet to be tracked down, and those records that do exist often supply little information to the historian; they note details of the injury and sometimes how it was inflicted, but leave everything else to speculation. On 30 August 1930, for example, two men were admitted to Bedford General Hospital. One, a farm labourer, had two black eyes, cuts on his face and was unconscious. The other, a moulder, had lacerations to his arm and concussion. They were both kept in the hospital for about a week. A fight may have been the cause, and similarly with a man admitted at around midnight almost exactly fifteen years later with injuries to his right thigh and left loin. He discharged himself, against medical advice, early the following morning. At roughly the same time a fifty-one-year-old woman was admitted with bruising and abdominal pains having been thrown from her bed by her husband. She remained in hospital for two weeks, but no criminal proceedings appear to have followed.[20]

The surviving evidence from the legal record, from police reports and even from hospital files often provide only the barest details of violent incidents. There are other sources, most obviously the media. Whereas the official record is often terse, media reporting of violence often tends towards the lurid and sensational. Nevertheless, media accounts, sensational or not, provide a window onto contemporary attitudes and understandings. It has been long been popular with the media, and with other commentators, to link acts of extreme, appalling violence with the

broader development of society, and to seek to understand such an incident as part of a national malaise or national problem. The murders of
Jack the Ripper were used by some commentators to criticise the social
conditions of the East End of London and to urge social reform. 'Surely
"JACK the Ripper" is not to be our modern JOHN the Baptist',
protested one London newspaper. 'The brutalisation of nine tenths of
our population is too heavy a price to pay for the culture and refinement of the other tenth.'[21] In the 1970s Stuart Hall and a group of
colleagues at the University of Birmingham argued forcefully that an old
offence, street robbery, with a new name, 'mugging', was being used to
condense a range of race, crime and youth issues and to articulate the
decline of the British way of life and the need for tough law and order
policies.[22] The murder of a Liverpool toddler, Jamie Bulger, by two ten-
year-old boys in 1993 led to a series of newspaper articles seeking
explanations and remedies. An ex-Home Secretary criticised society –
'all of us' – for not seeking to fill a 'moral vacuum' in the nation; a journalist criticised modern politicians, in comparison with the Victorian
counterparts, for becoming too remote from the people and having
nothing to say about the murder; another made a tortuous link between
the little boy's murder and football hooligans, both sullying 'the perception of Britain abroad'; and a novelist used the boy's funeral as a way
into a lament for everything that appeared to have gone wrong in the
country in the preceding decade or so.[23] Yet while the Ripper murders,
most muggings and the kidnap and murder of Jamie Bulger occurred in
public space, these were, essentially, personal acts by private individuals. It is the repercussions and the attempt to invest them with 'meaning'
that relates them to the public sphere.

Some violent private acts can be very public. A suicide, for example,
committed by throwing oneself in front of a train is a very public act. A
suicide by cutting wrists in a hot bath, however, remains a private act in
private space. Murder is rarely as public as the former suicide, so what
makes a private, generally personal act symptomatic of a national
malaise? What happens here is rather an attempt to make sense of an
act, probably perfectly rational and private at the time to the person or
persons who committed it, but which, by its very enormity appears to
need some deeper explanation.

My starting point in this book is the assumption to be found in much

of the contemporary English media as well as elsewhere that, in the not
too distant past, English society has been less violent than others, but
that things are changing for the worst.[24] Put in this way we are presented
with what is essentially a statistical issue: English society is moving from
a time of little violence to one of increasing violence.[25] Marshalling statistics to prove, or to disprove, the case is, however, no simple task. As
has already been explained, violent behaviour and inter-personal violence cover a range of activities both public and private. It is only violent
behaviour that is categorised as criminal for which there are long runs
of statistics, and there are problems with the validity, meaning and
interpretation of such statistics.

There is a general acknowledgement of an increasing intolerance and
general decline of violent behaviour in Europe since the late medieval
period. The conclusion is underpinned by such homicide statistics as
have been found or reconstructed for Europe over several centuries.[26]
Homicide is, of course, a particular and extreme form of inter-personal
violence. It may not be a precise reflection of the scale of violence within
a society, and broad national rates do not differentiate between social
classes, different ethnic groups or geographical regions. Nevertheless, it
is one measure and, many would argue, the best that there is. Even so,
if we accept murder as a measure, there is a further problem: it is one
thing to indicate a trend; it is quite another to explain it.

The most influential and popular theory deployed to explain the
decline in violence in Europe is Norbert Elias's concept of 'a civilising
process'.[27] Elias described the warrior-knight society of the middle ages
giving way to the court society of the sixteenth and seventeenth centuries. The rise of the absolutist ruler led to the old virtues of warrior
bellicosity being replaced by an elite which prided itself on refined,
civilised manners. This refined culture involved an overall shift in
the structure of personality, with new inhibitions on spontaneous
emotions and a distancing from, and disapproval of, displays of aggression. The new culture was initially spread among the elite by the
sanction of ridicule among social equals. It spread down the social scale
by the force of emulation. It is important not to think of the civilising
process as a simple linear progression, and Elias himself was fully conscious that societies do not evolve in tandem with one another, and

that the internal elements of the kind of long-term process that he was describing would not all function together in the same ways and at the same rates. In addition, he was keen to distance himself from any absolute notion of civilisation. His perception was always that, while people in the nineteenth and twentieth centuries might consider themselves to be 'civilised', and while they had grown more 'civilised' than their medieval forebears, there never was an absolutely civilised society. What interested Elias were, essentially, the intergenerational transmissions of learned experiences. Other historians and social scientists, in contrast, have stressed the significance of social disciplining by agencies, such as the church, the law, the military and educational institutions, that enforced self-control and provided the cultural and social framework for a more orderly, pacific and internalised way of life.[28]

England has probably the best range of homicide statistics over centuries and for large geographical areas. The homicide rates in England over the period from the late middle ages to the twentieth century show one of the earliest declines and one of the sharpest.[29] England, like the Netherlands, where there was a similarly sharp decline in the seventeenth century, was a state in which the absolutist project was defeated and which was at the forefront of capitalist development. Equally interesting, and not sitting entirely comfortably with a simple reading of Elias's paradigm, the English did not stand out to their European neighbours in the seventeenth and eighteenth centuries as either non-violent or particularly civilised. The common impression of the Englishman on continental Europe was of an uncouth, ruddy-faced, beef-eating rough, and the English seem to have had little interest in dispelling this image. A change appears to have occurred over the course of the eighteenth century. There was the emergence of an English sensibility and an increasing focus, apparently across all classes in England and picked up on by foreign visitors, on concepts such as 'fair play'. These were contrasted with the barbarity of the crowds of the French Revolution and contributed to the image of a new kind of Englishman. By the time of the French Revolution even the English soldier engaged in battle could be seen as domesticated. According to William Hazlitt:

> The reason why the English are the bravest nation on earth is, that the thought of blood or a delight in cruelty is not the chief excitement with them.

Where it is, there is necessarily a *reaction*; for though it may add to our eager-
ness and savage ferocity in inflicting wounds, it does not enable us to endure
them with greater patience. The English are led to the attack or sustain it
equally well, because they fight as they box, not out of malice, but to show
pluck and manhood. *Fair play and old England forever!* This is the only brav-
ery that will stand the test.[30]

It was in the early nineteenth century that violence began to be
described in England as a social problem. Two broad understandings
of violent behaviour have been described as contesting with each other
in the early years of the century.[31] On the one hand, there was the
traditional perspective of custom that legitimised direct physical confrontation as a means of maintaining personal authority and of solving
personal and public wrongs. On the other hand, there was a new perspective, rooted in rationality, sensibility and political fears aggravated
by the French Revolution. This perspective championed personal control, self-restraint and propriety. It came to dominate the thinking of
the elite and of the growing middle classes. These groups saw crowd
violence and inter-personal violence as primitive behaviour and as
something aberrant and abhorrent to civilised, rational beings. They
identified the problem as one situated among the working classes. As
the century wore on, however, they acknowledged the emergence of a
respectable working class that shared their aspirations. The setting of
the problem of violence, in consequence, was shifted to the poorest
areas of the cities and towns and to the social group that began to be
stigmatised as the residuum. These shifts in perspective were linked
with the concept of the English gentleman that was to dominate the
image of Englishness from the second half of the nineteenth century for
a hundred years.

The concept of the English gentleman, and the overall English view
of themselves, was central to English people's understanding of violence
within their society.[32] Englishness was gendered. As with other European
societies in the nineteenth century, women were not expected to be
physical, except in the sense of the physicality of bringing children into
the world and nurturing them. The ideal English male might be physical when engaged in sporting activity, or in defending his family and his
country, but his physicality was supposedly reined in by notions of fairness and openness. An aggressive determination to win at all costs was

alien to his creed in sport, while in war it was expected that somehow his ideas of fairness and chivalrous behaviour would combine with the undoubted justice of the British cause to ensure victory. Wickedness should be punished, and this might require the use of physical force to chastise the guilty. But, above all, Englishness required reserve and restraint; striking the first blow was wrong. Many of these elements are to be found in what the individuals of other nations understood as their own national characteristics. Yet English difference, as perceived by both English people and others, centred significantly on a characteristic reserve and restraint. All of this constituted the construction of an ideal type, and both English people and others recognised that there were exceptions, often very major exceptions, to the type. What the following pages attempt to do is to explain the inter-relationship of this stereotype with the evidence of violence among the English. What sort of violence was to be found within English society within this age of respectability and restraint? In what ways might this violence be said to have been controlled? In what ways did it change? And how did the English explain the violence within their society that, in many respects, appeared to contradict some of their most cherished perceptions of themselves?

2

Garotters, Gangsters and Perverts

James Pilkington, a cotton merchant and manufacturer, was first elected MP for Blackburn, Lancashire, in 1847. He was never a significant figure in the Commons but, throughout the 1850s, he supported radical reforms such as voting by ballot and a redistribution of parliamentary seats. Around 1 a.m. on the morning of 17 July 1862 Pilkington left the Commons. He was, he recalled, initially undecided as to whether he should call at the Reform Club or proceed directly to his lodgings through Waterloo Place. He determined on the latter but, having crossed Pall Mall, he was attacked, knocked to the ground and robbed of his watch and chain. In their haste, possibly disturbed by some of Pilkington's colleagues taking the same route behind him, the robbers missed the money in his pockets. Pilkington came round covered in blood, with contusions on his head and a severe gash in his jaw. On the following day the assault was discussed by an outraged House of Commons. Sir George Grey, the Home Secretary, reported that Pilkington had not been the only victim of street robbery on the night in question. A few hours earlier the son of a gentleman connected with the British Museum had been attacked and robbed of his watch and his money in Piccadilly.[1]

The attack on Pilkington, which later served as the model for the attack on Mr Kennedy in Anthony Trollope's *Phineas Finn*, was the most celebrated incident in a series of crime panics during the mid nineteenth century about 'garotting'. The perpetrators of the attacks were generally described in the press as hardened professional criminals often recently released from prison on licence – the so-called ticket-of-leave men. Their *modus operandi* was described by one commentator as a 'science', with the victim being pinioned across the throat by one assailant – hence 'garotting' – while a second rifled his pockets.[2] For some contemporaries garotting probably also conjured pictures of the cult of

Thuggee, a sect in India, supposedly followers of the goddess Kali, who had, allegedly, strangled and robbed thousands of travellers and who had been stamped out only a generation before by the British. These killers had been 'discovered' by Captain W. H. Sleeman in the early 1830s and immortalised in Colonel Philip Meadows Taylor's popular novel *Confessions of a Thug*, which went through several editions following its first publication in 1839.[3] Correspondence in *The Times* about street robbery in London a decade before the attack on Pilkington appeared under the headings of 'English Thuggism' and 'Thuggee in London'.[4] During the panics, entrepreneurs with an eye to profit began to market anti-garotting collars and various small clubs and bludgeons called 'life-preservers' to discourage, or to fight back against, such attacks.

The idea of a criminal class, a social group lurking in the rookeries (as the tenement slums of Victorian cities were termed) and preferring idleness and moments of adventure to a fair day's work for a fair day's pay, had become popular in Victorian England. In the panic that followed the murder of Revd G. E. Hollest, the vicar of Frimley in Surrey, during a bungled burglary a dozen years before the attack on Pilkington, *The Times* had written of 'a criminal population dispersed throughout the length and breadth of the land – a caste apart that is most idle, dissolute and unprincipled among us'. An exotic, 'barbaric' comparison was made, but this time not with Indian Thugs but with 'Bedouin hordes'.[5] Such a professional criminal class was a useful way of categorising and stigmatising offenders, but probably bore little relation to the individuals who committed either burglaries or street robberies. Street robbers in particular do not appear to have bothered with the careful planning and sophistication implied by notions of a 'science of garotting'. Any method of incapacitating the victim seems to have been favoured, while, according to a police constable giving evidence at the Old Bailey, the thieves themselves preferred the word 'mug' to 'garotte'.[6] The press, in its enthusiasm during the panic, appears to have applied the term 'garotting' to a variety of incidents of attack and injury even when robbery was not involved, and the public saw garotters everywhere.

Four months after the attack on Pilkington two dozen alleged 'garotters' appeared for trial at the Old Bailey. Several were indeed ticket-of-leave men, which strengthened the assertion that the outbreak of garotting was the work of professional criminals impervious to any existing programmes of reform in use in the prisons. The police testified that some among the accused were known to associate with known thieves. But several of the accused claimed that the police had fitted them up. 'The evidence is got up', protested George Roberts. 'There is not a robbery that [the police] do not get up, especially for garotting.' Samuel Anderson, in the dock with Roberts, declared 'I am innocent, but I am known to the police as a convicted thief, therefore they do not care what they say to bring the charge against me'.[7] The November trials brought the panic to an end, but a virulent press campaign against street robbers and demands for tough sentences prompted Parliament to respond with the Security from Violence Act, which authorised flogging for men convicted of the offence. The Act received the royal assent on 13 July 1863, almost exactly one year after the attack on Pilkington. It was not until 1948 that the punishment of flogging for street robbery was removed from the statute book.

The panic following the attack on Pilkington is one of the best known and best researched of such crime panics in the nineteenth and early twentieth centuries. Statistically, however, the number of attacks was small: only ninety-seven in London in 1862, two-thirds of them after the attack on Pilkington. Violent offences like street robbery made, and still make, good headlines and thrilling stories. They sold and sell newspapers and books; indeed, on at least one occasion during the eighteenth century, a panic appears to have been constructed by one provincial newspaper so as to enhance its sales in a new district.[8] A high percentage of crime panics arose out of offences that involved the infliction of pain and suffering on victims: the Ratcliffe Highway murders of 1811, in which two families were battered to death; the garotting panics of the 1850s and 1862; the Liverpool Cornermen of the 1870s and the same city's High Rip gang of the 1880s; Jack the Ripper; London's Hooligans, Birmingham's Peaky Blinders and Manchester's Scuttlers at the turn of the century; razor gangs and bag-snatchers in the inter-war period; cosh boys, teddy boys, mods, rockers and muggers after the Second World War. But while the form of the panic, and the outrage in the press, among the public and in Parliament, may have been similar, the events that gave rise to the panics could be very different. Street robbery is

generally stranger on stranger violence and different from a fight
between street gangs. Street gangs knew each other, and, while their violence frightened other people, individuals who were not involved with
the gangs were unlikely to become involved or to be attacked. Such distinctions between different forms of criminal violence were, and often
are, lost in press and popular outrage. It is stranger on stranger violence,
in which the victims are 'innocent', that was, and is, the particularly
frightening form of criminal violence for the public.

The offence of robbery links theft and violence. It has been popularly
described as garotting, mugging and bag-snatching, and as perpetrated
variously by footpads, garotters, cosh-boys, depending on the terms in
vogue. Legally, it was clearly defined in the early modern period. It was
the felonious taking of goods or money from a person either by violence
or by putting the victim in fear of violence. It generally involved stranger
on stranger violence. Pilkington, like many other victims, could not
identify his assailants; it was the police who claimed to be able to do
this.[9] Recent research has suggested important parallels in the moral
panics that have erupted over street robberies during the last two and a
half centuries. A specific incident provokes media attention. The media
exaggerate the threat and build on popular fears; it is significant that
most of the panics occur as the nights draw in and concerns are raised
about the safety of the streets after dark. The panics tend to continue for
about two months, though there can be a long tail. There are invariably
interested actors keen to profit financially from selling their newspapers
and holding their audience, or keen to use the panic to press for penal
or policing reforms. These actors play a crucial role in the dynamics of
the panic.[10] None of this is to deny the initial incident of robbery that
sparked the panic, or the violence and fear to which the victim was subjected. But key questions remain. Beyond the exaggerations of the panic,
it is crucial to assess how common the event was that sparked it. Does
the evidence, rather than the shrill exclamations of press, politicians and
others, suggest that the pattern of violent offences was indeed going up
at moments of panic? Similarly, there is the key issue of how much
criminal violence there was over any extended period of time. What
kinds of individuals were responsible for criminal violence? Was such
violence a natural tendency of a criminal class? Most of these questions involve some form of measurement. In any assessment of criminal

violence it is therefore essential to have some engagement with the statistical evidence.

Crime statistics constitute a template by which the state of crime in a country is assessed by politicians, senior police officers, journalists and, ultimately, by the general public. There is considerable debate over their value, as will be evident from what follows here.[11] But the statistics provide a starting point for the pattern of crime. More importantly, perhaps, politicians, senior police officers and journalists based and base their arguments and their policies on their reading of these statistics. The official statistics for England and Wales go back to the early nineteenth century, but they only began to be collected extensively by the police with some broad conformity from 1857. They were collated within the Home Office and then published annually as the *Judicial Statistics*, with an introduction and analysis. The statistics reveal property crime to have been far more significant than violent crime in Victorian and Edwardian England. They also show a general decline in both theft and violence from the mid nineteenth century to the First World War. There were occasional panics about forms of violent crime and violent behaviour, such as 'garotting' in the 1850s and early 1860s and young 'hooligans' at the turn of the century. The appalling but isolated murders attributed to Jack the Ripper in the autumn of 1888 also created a nationwide scare, thanks, according to a head of the Metropolitan Police CID, to 'the sensation-mongers of the newspaper press [who] fostered the belief that life in London was no longer safe, and that no woman ought to venture abroad in the streets after nightfall'.[12] But generally contemporary Victorian and Edwardian commentators thought that things were getting better,[13] and two leading criminologists could subsequently reflect on the years of diminishing crime before the First World War under the heading 'The English Miracle'.[14]

In the aftermath of the war, the statistics of crime for England and Wales began to rise steadily (Table 1), yet violent offences did not figure significantly in the statistics during the first half of the twentieth century. In his centenary history of the Metropolitan Police, Sir John Moylan, the force's financial Receiver, commented:

> The criminal statistics of England and Wales, ever since reliable statistics were available, show that offences against property account for about 90 per

Table 1

Annual averages of selected indictable crimes of violence known to the police, 1897–1959

	1897–1901	1902–06	1907–11	1912–16	1915–19
Murder (victim aged one or over)	86	97	99	92	90
Murder (victim aged under one)	51	53	50	57	52
Attempted murder	75	91	109	81	62
Threats and conspiracy to murder	12	15	20	17	13
Manslaughter	184	152	146	140	110
Felonious wounding	274	242	279	191	119
Malicious wounding	1016	931	1021	772	446
Assault	52	46	66	38	17
Rape	239	199	172	146	99
Indecent assault on female	759	708	902	199	879
Robbery	288	246	236	136	127

	1920–24	1925–29	1930–34	1935–39	1940–44
Murder (victim aged one or over)	103	108	103	107	138
Murder (victim aged under one)	49	37	31	23	25
Attempted murder	103	91	79	76	97
Threats and conspiracy to murder	15	14	14	18	20
Manslaughter	113	136	162	173	140
Felonious wounding	167	152	176	286	304
Malicious wounding	490	938	1232	1639	1836
Assault	42	33	34	26	23
Rape	120	105	82	104	233
Indecent assault on female	1575	1844	1793	2347	2931
Robbery	177	132	240	227	612

	1945–49	1950–54	1955–59	1960–64	1965–69
Murder (victim aged one or over)	141	130	138	144	185
Murder (victim aged under one)	29	11	11	12	(incorporated in above figure)
Attempted murder	179	154	169	202	266
Threats and conspiracy to murder	32	47	56	71	101
Manslaughter	155	176	122	114	177
Felonious wounding	577	1022	1395	1913	2436
Malicious wounding	3081	4811	8210	15,239	25,479
Assault	23	93	182	357	494
Rape	271	299	396	486	732
Indecent assault on female	5093	7258	8538	9630	11,293
Robbery	1005	923	1315	2486	(recategorised)

cent of the indictable offences known to the police. Crimes of violence, in particular homicides, are very few.

Sensational, violent offences like 'hold-ups', 'motor bandits', 'smash and grab' raids and 'bag-snatching' made good headlines, yet such incidents were relatively rare. The number of indictable crimes of robbery known to the police remained at less than 200 a year from shortly before the First World War until the 1930s; during the 1930s it hovered at a little less than 250. Moylan admitted that robberies and assaults with intent to rob in the Metropolitan Police District had roughly tripled from about forty a year during the early 1920s to 120 and more in the early 1930s. But, he pointed out, this was in an area of 700 square miles with a population of around eight and a quarter million.[15] The press carried stories of a 'crime wave' at the end of the First World War.[16] The sociologist Thorsten Sellin concluded that the upheaval of war led to a rising murder rate across the whole of Europe.[17] Across Britain there were widespread fears that civilisation was in danger from the brutalising effects of war and the return of men whose experiences had led them to develop a callous regard for human life. The worst of these fears had subsided by the mid 1920s, yet

a decade after the war Detective Inspector Charles Leach expressed his
belief that the war had produced potential, and particularly dangerous,
criminals among 'the War veterans, many still young in years, but old in
experience, accustomed to looking on life in the raw, unafraid of battle,
murder and sudden death'.[18] Other 'experts' approached the matter differently and, significantly, the statistics do not bear out the concerns that
a brutalised soldiery had returned from the trenches to follow a life of
violent crime.[19] In the introduction to the *Judicial Statistics* for 1924 it
was concluded that:

> Crimes of violence against the person … are fewer than formerly. The aver-
> age number of such crimes which became known to the police during each
> of the five years 1909 to 1913 was 2062; the annual average for the period 1919
> to 1923 was 1389; in 1923 the number was 1269; and in 1924 it was 1259. There
> is a corresponding falling off in the minor offences of violence which are
> tried summarily as assaults. The annual averages for the four quinquennial
> periods 1899–1903, 1904–8, 1909–13 and 1919–23 were respectively 64,186,
> 51,495, 43,320 and 37,908. The figures for 1924 were 34,897. So far as such
> crimes are concerned experience of warfare has not led to any increase of
> crime.[20]

The number of non-indictable common assaults prosecuted in the
magistrates' courts (Table 2) fell steadily during the inter-war period
from around 32,000 a year in the early 1920s to about half that on the
eve of the Second World War. The number of aggravated assaults also
fell, from about 500 a year to less than 200. The number of assaults on
police officers dropped a little, but continued to hover around the 3000
mark.

At the end of the Second World War there were, once again, concerns
that the training of young men for war, especially commando training,
and the brutalising experience of war, would encourage some young men
to employ violence on their return to civilian life. Demobbed servicemen coming to terms with civvy street in which the non-combatant
racketeer had made handsome profits figured significantly in post-war
crime films. The ex-commando could be found quite literally on both
sides of the law in these films, perhaps most notably in *Night Beat*
(1947). For a brief period in the aftermath of the war the British cinema
was permitted by the censor to make films that portrayed a new level of
criminal violence. Among these were *They Made Me a Fugitive* (1947)

Table 2
Annual averages of persons dealt with summarily at magistrates' courts for assaults

	1915–19	1920–24	1925–29	1930–34	1935–39
Aggravated	354	512	347	214	154
On constables	3556	4894	3564	2912	3856
Common	24,118	32,589	25,089	18,389	14,663

	1940–44	1945–49	1950–54	1955–59	1960–64
Aggravated	156	131	92	62	37
On constables	2845	2525	3645	5218	6182
Common	13,593	17,094	15,266	12,107	11,130

and *Mine Own Executioner* (1947). The central character of the former is an ex-serviceman who, finding peace dull, is attracted to a life of crime by a vicious black marketeer. *Mine Own Executioner* showed a disturbed former prisoner-of-war strangling his wife in the belief that she is a Japanese soldier. Sir Harold Scott, Commissioner of the Metropolitan Police in the post-war decade, dismissed the fears about commando training. He conceded that the war may have led to an increase in dishonesty, but considered that 'a large part of post-war crime has been the work ... of men too young to have served in the war'.[21] The *Judicial Statistics* for 1948 appeared to bear this out. Violence against the person was up 27 per cent on the previous year, but 'among persons under twenty-one the increase from 1947 to 1948 was 36 per cent'.[22]

Overall for the two decades after the outbreak of the Second World War the statistics for violent crime are, once again, complicated (Tables 1 and 2). The indictable crimes of felonious wounding and malicious wounding known to the police soared in the 1950s. The reported incidence of robbery increased similarly. The number of aggravated assaults tried in the magistrates' courts continued to fall, however, running at less than a hundred a year in the 1950s. Similarly, the number of common assaults, after rising in the late 1940s, dropped away to just over

12,000 a year. It seems possible that the marked increase in the
indictable offences of felonious and malicious wounding absorbed some
of this decline. It is also possible that the decision to prosecute an
increased number of violent offences on indictment, rather than summarily before magistrates, reflects a growing intolerance of violent
behaviour. It has also been argued that from the beginning of the twentieth century there was a modernisation of policing that involved less
emphasis on the enforcement of municipal regulations and a much
greater stress on targeting motorists, who provided money for the
Exchequer, and indictable offenders, who made the police role appear
more important.[23] It would, however, be difficult to prove any of these
propositions positively. Finally, and in contrast to the overall decrease
in the non-indictable assaults, it is worth noting that the number of
assaults on police officers increased steadily from a low of around 2500
a year in the late 1940s to 3600 in the early 1950s and to over 6000 by
the mid 1960s. This may reflect a genuine increase; but it may also reflect police officers increasingly choosing to prosecute assaults rather than
handling potentially violent situations individually and responding to
violence with violence of their own.

    Across England and Wales as a whole the statistics for crimes involv-
ing interpersonal violence during the nineteenth century and in the
first half of the twentieth followed a pattern broadly similar to that of
other crimes. Things looked to be getting better up until the First World
War. After the war the statistics for crime as a whole began a gradual
rise. This rise became much steeper after the middle of the 1950s. There
is an important contrast that is worth underlining here and one that
challenges simple, popular explanations of crime being caused by
poverty, desperation and need. The statistics for both theft and violence
show a decline during the Victorian and Edwardian periods when, overall, the population of England and Wales experienced a general
improvement in prosperity and living standards. The economic depression of the inter-war period saw little more than a gradual increase in
the statistics. Rather it was in the period of affluence after the Second
World War that the statistics began to soar. Broadly, even though non-
violent property crime was and remains much more significant
statistically than the varieties of violent crime, the patterns look similar.
The statistical pattern in England and Wales is also broadly similar to

that of other developed western countries, but it is unwise to go much beyond broad patterns in any cross-national comparisons, since offences are defined and categorised in different ways in different legal systems. In 1940, for example, the German-born, London-based criminologist Hermann Mannheim warned that it would be 'utterly misleading ... to compare the bare figures for convictions of murder in England and Germany without taking into account that the English conception "murder" is much wider than the German *Mord*'.[24]

Murder seems commonly to be taken as a measure of violence, though whether it should be might be disputed, and the figures given in Tables 1 and 2 give some reason to wonder. The number of homicides recorded in the *Judicial Statistics*, that is the number of both murder and manslaughter cases returned by the police, fell from around one case per 100,000 of the population at the beginning of the twentieth century to around 0.8 or 0.9 per 100,000 just before 1914. Between 1920 and 1938 the number rose very slightly. It may well be, as has forcibly been argued, that the statistics were created principally as a result of police discretion and tight fiscal controls exerted over the criminal justice system by the Treasury.[25] But while murder figures remained low and common assaults continued to decline slightly after the First World War, sexual assaults increased. Mannheim suggested that the latter might have been 'purely statistical' (whatever that may mean) or perhaps partly the result of 'increased mental instability due to the war – a view which draws some support from the fact that similar increases have become noticeable throughout Europe after 1919'. Unfortunately, Mannheim offered no empirical evidence for the suggestion about increased mental instability, merely noting that more research was needed into the subject.[26] In the immediate aftermath of the war, sexual assaults on women and assaults on children were described by some commentators and by some sections of the press as linked to 'insanity', 'moods' or 'passions' caused by the war.[27] While it is possible that some war veterans did express themselves violently against their families, or against women whom they blamed for 'stealing' their jobs in wartime, the statistics for the years immediately following the war do not demonstrate the significant increase in assaults that these descriptions imply.

An important point missed by Mannheim, but picked up by those in the Home Office who were responsible for the analyses which accompanied the *Judicial Statistics*, was the large number of 'sexual offences' committed by persons under the age of twenty-one. This tends to contradict Mannheim's attempt to link such offences with the First World War. The statistics of indictable sexual assaults against women moved in different directions during the first half of the twentieth century. Instances of rape reported to the police began to decline shortly before the First World War and did not reach the levels of the turn of the century again until the Second World War. After 1945 they began to rise significantly. Reported incidents of indecent assaults on women, however, rose steadily during the inter-war years, increasingly markedly in the late 1930s, and soaringly from the late 1940s. The number of men found guilty of sexual offences who were aged twenty-one and over increased marginally in the years immediately after 1945. But, overall, throughout the middle third of the twentieth century just under one half of these offenders annually were aged over thirty years and roughly a third were twenty-one and under. Some, but clearly not all, of these sexual offences can be attributed to young males deciding to exercise their developing sexuality aggressively on unwilling or underage victims.[28] But if the impact of war is difficult to assess, so too is the preparedness of victims to come forward and report violent sexual offences.

Throughout the nineteenth and twentieth centuries social attitudes and embarrassment constituted major disincentives to report instances, let alone to proceed with charges in cases of sexual assault and rape. Judges and juries in the Victorian period were all male and were often reluctant to convict, especially in rape cases where there were rarely witnesses and where consent was often assumed if the victim and the accused were acquainted, even if only slightly. Even marks of violence on the victim were not always sufficient to convince magistrates, judge and jury of an offence. As one historian has concluded:

> Rape victims [in Victorian England] were suspect on at least three counts: they were female, they had been at least temporarily outside the supervision of male guardians (it was unthinkable that their guardians might have been their assailants), and they were publicly announcing their loss of sexual innocence. Judges and jurors frequently concluded that no man should lose his respectability, let alone his freedom, for the mere seduction of such unworthy creatures.[29]

Matters had changed little in the early twentieth century. In consequence it was, for example, quite probably embarrassment, rather than
the possibility of not getting a conviction, that dissuaded eighteen-year-
old Rose Mary Bird from proceeding with a prosecution against three
young men for indecent assault in July 1928.[30]

There may have been some marginal improvements in the conclud-
ing decades of the twentieth century, but evidence in cases of rape,
attempted rape and sexual assault remained notoriously difficult to
present and, especially in court, cross-examination was probably a much
greater ordeal for the victim than for the offender. The local magistrates
dismissed two of the four cases of rape reported in the Brill Occurrence
Book between 1900 and 1932. The victim in another instance, a seventy-
one-year-old woman, declined to proceed with the case against a tramp
who had broken into her house. Only one case reached the county
assizes; it resulted in a sentence of nine months' hard labour for a nineteen-year-old youth found guilty of attempted rape and a sentence of
twelve months hard labour for a twenty year old who had aided and
abetted.[31] Even when a victim was prepared to bring a charge, an incident could still end up in the Refused Charge Book. A young married
woman, 'distressed and hysterical', appeared at Sidcup Police Station in
September 1933 accusing a taxi driver and a commercial traveller of
indecent assault in the back of the former's cab. Another young woman
had also been present and insisted that nothing 'untoward' had
occurred. It may have been that the complainant was unsure how she
would be able to explain a lively evening out to her husband; or it may
have been that the second young woman was in league with the accused.
The station sergeant noted that 'all the parties had evidently been drinking [and] in view of all the circumstances including the doctor's
examination, no police action was taken and [the] complainant was
referred to civil remedies'.[32]

Cases of indecent assaults on children did not necessarily involve
additional physical violence and parents often declined to prosecute.[33]
There may also have been some confusion about the legal definition of
some sexual assaults as when, for example, a fourteen-year-old girl
accused a seventy-two-year-old man of carnal knowledge. Examined by
the police surgeon the girl was found to be *virgo intacta* and the girl
explained that the man had, in fact, only 'touched' her. The police

appear to have accepted her story but decided that they could not proceed with the case because of a lapse of some two years since the
incident, making a charge of indecent assault unsustainable.[34] Some
cases of assault on children were difficult to classify. During the inter-
war period there was, for example, a series of incidents in which young
girls had their long hair cut off and these left both the police and solicitors puzzled as to what charge to prefer. 'It is not too clear', explained
the solicitors of the Metropolitan Police, 'as to whether growing hair is
the subject matter of larceny.' The general assumption was that the
offenders in such cases were suffering from some form of 'sexual aber-
ration', but the charges preferred varied from 'larceny of hair' to
grievous bodily harm, and even to being simply 'a suspect person'.[35]

Assaults on children commonly excited, and still excite, anxiety and
anger, but they did not always result in prosecution or a trace in the
legal record. Many such assaults fell within the remit of social work
organisations such as the National Society for the Prevention of Cruelty
to Children (NSPCC). Founded in 1884 as the London Society for the
Prevention of Cruelty to Children, and becoming a 'national' society five
years later, the society's aim was to prevent rather than prosecute. It
conducted some notable and high profile prosecutions, such as that of a
Baptist minister in 1905 for assaulting three girls in his Brixton chapel.
But the society pursued a policy of prosecuting only as a last resort,
except 'in gross cases of brutality or defilement'. In 1933–34 it dealt
with 44,356 cases, but only 472 prosecutions were brought as opposed to
33,235 individuals being warned and another 8495 being 'advised'.[36]
Albert Baynard, an NSPCC inspector based in Mansfield, for example,
spent over two years working with a family before bringing such a case
before the Nottinghamshire quarter sessions in June 1933. Here the problem was not so much one of violence, though the girl in question had
been struck by her unemployed war veteran father, but more one of neglect and the fact that the child was required to take responsibility for her
eight siblings.[37] The dark figure of unreported and therefore unknown
offences is also a problem with the NSPCC's statistics. Robert Roberts's
parents ran a small shop in Edwardian Salford. Whenever she heard of
a case of serious child beating, 'as with the woman who boasted in the
shop, "My master [husband] allus flogs 'em till the blood runs down
their back!" [Roberts's mother] quietly "put the Cruelty man on".'

The point is that she did it 'quietly' and Roberts went on that the society's 'gallant' work 'hardly touched the fringe of the problem'.[38] While some women and children, and some concerned neighbours, sought assistance in cases of child abuse, there remained a culture of resistance to NSPCC inspectors in many working-class districts. No matter how severe the abuse, some such communities continued to see child protection as too closely linked with stigmatising forms of welfare such as the Poor Law.[39] The point to underline is that the great majority of instances of violence against children that were known to the society were never incorporated into the *Judicial Statistics* and this leaves a large gap in the official statistics of violence.

Criminal violence against women and children is not popularly understood as the kind of activity associated with ordinary criminals committing ordinary crimes. To this extent it emphasises some of the definitional problems inherent in terms such as crime, criminal and criminal violence. Abusive sexual behaviour towards young girls by a Baptist minister in his Brixton chapel was, and was perceived as, rather different from the attack on James Pilkington. The minister was never understood to be a member of the criminal class. Yet the use of violence by more conventional criminals could also be downplayed as much as overemphasised. Having addressed some of the issues surrounding the statistics of violent crime, it is necessary now to shift the focus to individuals and types of violent offender.

Eighteenth-century highwaymen have acquired a romantic air; indeed, an aura of romance surrounded some of them during their own lives. It has been argued that the cult of the robber was part of an English national myth going back to the middle ages. Within this myth robbery was justified when it could be portrayed as just punishment or revenge, and as such it fills the stories of Robin Hood and others. Alongside this, it was often considered that a man of courage and strength was entitled to what he could get, providing certain rules were observed. Thus the highwayman was a 'gentleman' or even a 'knight of the road'. He often assumed a military title such as 'captain'. He faced death on the gallows with courage and bravado. Above all, though armed with sword and pistol, he was supposed to treat his victims with civility and humanity.[40] The highwaymen of Stuart and Hanoverian England rarely measured up to the romantic myth. They could be violent; a few even adopted a shoot first attitude, though this may have been as much out of panic as out of viciousness.[41] But the highwayman, mounted on his horse, could tower above his victims and also make a fast escape. Both of these advantages may have militated against his use of violence. The footpad, in contrast, like the Victorian garotter, attacked his victim on foot, and in consequence he may have considered it important to incapacitate his victim with a blow or blows. Some footpads carried large staves and were prepared to attack men on horses. Even so, during the seventeenth and eighteenth centuries there were proud assertions, often accepted by foreign visitors, that English street robbers and highwaymen were not as violent as those elsewhere in Europe. And at the beginning of the nineteenth century, when plans were presented for establishing the Metropolitan Police, there were those who argued that London remained safe, especially in contrast to the supposedly highly policed city of Paris.[42]

How any contrast between English highwaymen and robbers and those on continental Europe might seriously be measured remains an open question. One significant and measurable difference was that eighteenth-century England did not have the large bodies of bandits that infested border regions and mountain districts of much of continental Europe. It did, however, have large smuggling gangs. Like the highwaymen, these have been romanticised. Often they had a degree of local support; they might provide some additional money, or payment in kind, to anyone prepared to help off load their ships or move their cargoes inland. But they could also be brutal and ruthless, winning support by terror as much as by generosity.[43]

The eighteenth-century criminals who achieved notoriety and a mythic status were often involved in very different forms of criminality. The most notable English examples, Jack Sheppard and Dick Turpin, were far from romantic heroes to their victims and, outside the ballads and story books, they showed little in the way of civility and humanity. Sheppard was a petty thief whose notoriety stemmed from his ability to break out of prison. Turpin was a burglar, horse-thief and murderer as well as a highway robber. The most celebrated of their continental counterparts were Cartouche, Mandrin, and Schinderhannes. Cartouche was allegedly the leader of a gang of Parisian thieves, tried and executed in 1721. It is possible that the prosecution of Cartouche's gang, which fostered the creation of the Cartouche myth, was as much concerned with re-establishing confidence in the city authorities and stability in a city hit by financial scandal as it was with suppressing a major criminal gang. Louis Mandrin was the leader of a large, well-organised gang of smugglers that brought their contraband into France from Switzerland. Johannes Bückler, better known as Schinderhannes, led a gang that rustled livestock, committed highway robbery, burglary and extortion. But he gained a popular reputation in his own lifetime since, with a degree of what has been called 'escapist wish-fulfilment', people on the left bank of the Rhine saw him as selecting his victims from among soldiers of the French army of occupation or Jews.[44] With the exception of Sheppard, who seems never to have been put in the situation, these men did not shirk from killing. But the killing did not detract from the myths that grew up around them. The myths of romantic criminals continued into the nineteenth century. Sheppard and Turpin reached the apex of their mythical appeal in the works of the early Victorian novelist Harrison Ainsworth. But, writing at the same time, Charles Dickens constructed an alternative criminal stereo-type in Bill Sikes, and it was Sikes – a burglar and murderer – who fitted better with respectable Victorian society's fears of the criminal class.

The Victorian reading public was fascinated by the 'dangerous classes' and the 'criminal classes'. A succession of investigators, including Dickens himself, went on patrol with officers of the new police exploring the rookeries of the poor; they wrote up their adventures and what they had seen, for the vicarious delight of the respectable reader. 'Criminals' were seen as a group in the lowest strata of the working classes. In the first half of the nineteenth century they were generally seen as idle, rejecting the concept of a fair day's wage for a fair day's work in preference for an easy life of luxury financed by preying on others. With developments in medical science and the advent of Darwinist perspectives, criminality became less a vice caused by lack of morality and began to be understood more as a problem rooted in heredity or psychological defects. But crime remained something committed by 'criminals', people who belonged to the 'criminal class', a class situated in the lowest, disreputable segment of the working class, the residuum.[45]

There were periodic scares about violent criminals following the garotting panics. Street robbery continued to generate press outrage and angry letters to the newspapers about police ineffectiveness.[46] There were also local scares, sometimes linked with concerns about working-class youths loitering on street corners.[47] In the 1880s concerns about armed burglars resulted in some police officers being armed with revolvers on isolated beats (Figure 1).[48] The first decade of the twentieth century witnessed a series of violent incidents involving foreign-born anarchists. In January 1909 a police constable and a ten-year-old boy were killed during the Tottenham outrage, which involved a wages snatch followed by the police chase of a hijacked tram.[49] Nearly two years later three policemen were shot dead and two others wounded when they confronted armed burglars at a jewellers' shop in Houndsditch. The shooting was the prelude to the celebrated siege of Sidney Street, and to another debate about the extent to which English police officers should be armed.[50] The inter-war years witnessed concerns about violent bag-snatchers and motor bandits. In one of the most notable of these incidents four robbers in a car stole a bag containing just under £1000, the takings from several pubs, that was being carried by a brewer's collector. The robbers were unaware that the collector, Rupert Wagner, also carried an automatic pistol. Wagner opened fire on the robbers' car, mortally wounding one of his assailants, sparking a lively discussion in the press about firearms, and various threats from individuals claiming to be 'criminals' and thus sympathetic to the dead robber.[51]

While there was probably more robbery and other violent crime than the traditional picture of Victorian, Edwardian and inter-war England implies, statistically, as has been noted above, the figure was never high and never significant in the annual *Judicial Statistics*. It also seems likely that a high proportion of the violence committed by those who might be labelled as 'criminal', in as much as they had police and prison records, was often committed amongst themselves. Billy Hill, styled as 'Boss of Britain's Underworld' for his autobiography, rationalised the professional criminal's use of violence in terms of masculine assertiveness typical of the hard man image. He also claimed a degree of care, even restraint, in the way such violence was inflicted. The first individual that Hill 'chivved' was a soldier who 'took a liberty' with him when

WELL MATCHED AT LAST.

TOO long did BOB-
    BY pace the
    streets
With nothing but
    his truncheon,
That wooden pot-
    stick only fit
BILL SYKES'S
    head to punch
    on ;
The burglar his re-
    volver seized,
And cocking it
    demurely,
Derided ROBERT'S
    weapon weak
And shot him
    down securely.
Now ROBERT has
    a pistol just
Like WILLIAM
    SYKES'S hob-
    by,
So BOBBY is a match for BILL—
And ten to one on BOBBY.

A GOOD deal was made of the fact that the Premier recently drove from Chester to Hawarden in an open carriage, "notwithstanding a thick fog." JUDY fails to see anything remarkable in this, insomuch that the right honourable gentleman had, during his absence, been so much mist.

MUCH surprise, without reason, we apprehend, has been expressed because Mr. IRVING is taking even a deal table with him to America. We think little of it. The actor's living is precarious, and audiences are fickle. So long as Mr. IRVING and his company possess a deal table, they will always have something to *feed on.*

---

1. 'Well Matched at Last', from *Judy*, 10 October 1883. This is one of a number of cartoons, published in various journals, commenting on the issue of revolvers to London police officers. The issue followed a series of armed burglaries in the early 1880s.

he was aged fourteen. Hill developed a reputation as a gang leader in London from the late 1920s. He claimed to administer a trade mark wound with his knife, slicing a cross or more often a 'V' on his victim's cheek.

> They remember that, and wherever you saw anyone wearing one you knew that it was Billy Hill who had done it. But I never chivved anyone unless I had to. There's no point in cutting up people if it's not necessary. And would stand for plenty of liberties before I eventually did use the knife. I think the villains respected me too because after I chivved a bloke I did not put the boot in or anything like that. I was always careful to draw my knife down the face, never across or upwards. Always down. So that if the knife slips you don't cut an artery. After all, chivving is chivving, but cutting an artery is murder. Only mugs do murder.[52]

The victims of Hill's knife did not go to the police; and if they were called in for an identity parade after an attack, then they did not point him out. This was a very different kind of violence and a very different kind of victim to the violence and the victims of street robbery.

At the beginning of the twentieth century this kind of inter-criminal violence could be seen best in the ferocious confrontations between race-course gangs as bookies deployed strong-arm men to defend their own turf or to encroach on that of others. The Sabini gang based in Clerkenwell, fought an extensive campaign against the Brummagen Boys; fists, feet, knives, iron bars and pistols were all employed by the combatants. Among the Sabini thugs was Arthur Harding, a petty gangster from 'The Jago' who had graduated from a youthful career as a pickpocket to providing muscle for protection rackets and bookies. Harding never aspired to Billy Hill's criminal heights, but he left an equally vivid memoir of his violent career.[53] The police records are equally vivid. In June 1921, for example, Metropolitan Police Sergeant Joseph Dawson courageously arrested twenty-seven members of a Birmingham gang in a pub on Kingston Hill. The gang, returning from a violent day at the races, contained individuals with a string of convictions ranging from assaulting the police to housebreaking and from wounding to manslaughter.[54] In August 1925 the Metropolitan Police identified a 'race gang affray' in an incident in Waterloo Road involving the pursuit of Arthur Flatman from the Royal Victoria Tavern by Thomas Benneworth. Flatman took refuge in a barber's shop.

Benneworth smashed the shop window with a bar stool before being arrested by two police officers. Both Benneworth and Flatman had criminal records involving theft, receiving and forgery. Benneworth's record included a charge of wounding that collapsed 'owing to the fact that the civilian witnesses, the only witnesses in the case, were in such a state of fear that they went back on the statements'. The barber whose shop window was smashed also appears to have been tampered with before the trial and refused to identify Benneworth in court.[55]

Sheffield bookmakers and entrepreneurial criminals also employed strong-arm men in the early twentieth century. These men fought the Sheffield 'gang wars' to control turf in horseracing, races between men, bare-knuckle fist fights, and the tossing-rings where large numbers gathered on open ground to bet on pitch and toss games.[56] But there were other forms of gang that were not tied to criminal entrepreneurs. During the late nineteenth century newspapers gave considerable space to reporting gangs of youths assaulting police officers and respectable citizens but, above all, fighting among themselves. Young 'Hooligans', 'Peaky Blinders', 'Larrikins', and 'Scuttlers' fought over 'sweethearts', and over strategic territory – 'their' street corners, 'their' public houses. They fought with fists and with anything that they could lay their hands on, and occasionally this meant pistols. Gang members wore distinctive clothing, some of which – brass-tipped clogs and belts with heavy buckles – was sported both for ostentation and for fighting. They had their girls, and some of these girls fought as viciously as the boys, but overwhelmingly the youthful fighting gangs of British cities in the late Victorian, Edwardian and inter-war years were male.[57]

The offenders discussed so far have been overwhelmingly male; crime is generally recognised as an activity that is engaged in predominantly by young men. The fighting gangs were not 'criminal' in the sense that the word is often understood, in the sense, for example, that Dick Turpin, Bill Sikes or Victorian 'garotters' were criminal. It has been suggested that the fighting gangs were showing youthful rebelliousness, and, indeed, contemporary youth gangs are often portrayed as rejecting society's norms. Yet a more recent and more penetrating analysis of late nineteenth-century gangs has led to the conclusion that, rather than rejecting society, they were 'archly conservative'. They embodied a working-class ideal of the hard man. They considered standing up for

one's self and toughness to be core masculine virtues.[58] The law, the
police, the press and elite commentators speaking for the national community might label this behaviour as violent crime, but for the
participants it was a way of gaining respect and position in what they
perceived to be a tough, man's world. Their role models were tough
adults of their neighbourhood, the hard men who were not to be
crossed. If they took role models from the media, in the early nineteenth
century these could be the highwayman Macheath from John Gay's *Beg-
gar's Opera*, or the popularised images of Jack Sheppard, Dick Turpin,
and similar outlaws. By the early twentieth century they were finding
role models in the heroes of Hollywood films. Within this genre was a
male role model who was tough, energetic, often defiant, and who survived and succeeded by his own efforts, sometimes in opposition to the
law. In the 1930s the cloth cap and muffler of the hard man, even to be
found among men like the Darby Sabini gang, was being replaced by the
suit and fedora of George Raft and Edward G. Robinson.[59] The clothes
may have been equally smart, but this role model was quite different
from the ideal English gentleman who was not a product of vibrant
modernity, who exuded home counties' pastoralism and the London
club, and who always, fairly and modestly, obeyed the rules and played
the game.

3

Play the Game

Towards the end of the eighteenth century the shopkeepers and many other inhabitants of Kingston-upon-Thames grew anxious as the annual holiday of Shrove Tuesday approached. It was customary for a football match to be played in the town on that day. The game had rules, at least as far as the participants were concerned. But for those who did not wish to participate, and who did not wish the game to be played, it all seemed little more than an excuse for rowdy, violent behaviour in which heads and windows, and anything else that got in the way, were broken or otherwise roughly handled. In 1797 the town magistrates attempted to prevent the game. A handbill was circulated. But the game went ahead. The following year, at the county assizes, several participants in the game were prosecuted for their riotous behaviour and found guilty. Sentence was respited, however; the judge appeared to believe that no one would attempt to play the game again after the warning that he issued. He was wrong.

Anxious about what would happen on Shrove Tuesday 1799 the magistrates again circulated a handbill. They also took the precaution of advising the officer commanding the cavalry unit stationed at Hampton Court Palace that they might require his assistance to suppress any tumult. The day came and the game began in the market place. The magistrates had three players taken into custody and read the proclamation of the Riot Act. The Act stipulated that, following the reading of the proclamation, those on the street had one hour to leave the scene. When the hour expired anyone remaining was considered to be guilty of riot, which was a felony, and rioters could be dispersed by force. On this occasion the crowd, rather than beginning to disperse, threatened to rescue the three players who had been arrested. The magistrates sent a message to the troops at Hampton Court. The crowd still did not disperse and no troops arrived. One of the magistrates rode to Hampton

Court, but he was told that the officer had gone away and, to add insult to injury, he found the cavalrymen kicking a football on the green at the palace. Meanwhile, the crowd in Kingston rescued their three comrades, violently assaulting the keeper of the local prison in the process. In a letter to the Home Secretary, the three magistrates expressed their fears for the future. 'The Game will be carried on to a greater height than it ever has been the Mob conceiving they have got the better of us and that the Military would not attend.'[1] The Home Office considered that the magistrates might have handled the situation better. The magistrates' concern that the game would continue, however, proved to be correct.

A gentleman travelling to Kingston on a coach from Hampton Court on Shrove Tuesday 1815 found the inhabitants of Teddington, Twicken-ham, Bushy and Hampton Wick, as well as Kingston, boarding up their windows in preparation for the football match. He was informed that recent attempts by town worthies to suppress the game had been rejected by a legal ruling confirming the right to play. So the game – which in 1815 lasted for about four hours, involved several teams playing with several balls, and ended in drinking sessions in the town's public houses – con-tinued, 'to the no small annoyance of some of the inhabitants, besides the expense and trouble they are put to in securing all their windows'.[2] A generation later petitions were presented to the town council urging, once again, that the game be suppressed. In 1840 a similar match was being played in nearby Richmond where, according to *The Times*,

> the place appears as one besieged, the shops being shut and the windows of the houses barricaded with hurdles to prevent them being destroyed, which very often occurs. Numerous accidents happen, no person while walking the streets being free from danger.[3]

There were other matches elsewhere across the country, played in similar ways and with origins claimed in the distant past. They were increasingly condemned for their rowdy, violent behaviour, for the interruption to trade and for the danger to passers-by. Yet the games continued to find supporters even among respectable gentlemen. During the nineteenth century such gentlemen provided fields for the games adjacent to the towns, so as to allow the customs to continue but with the danger to non-participants and to private property removed. These games, these gentry maintained, were character building and helped to foster and sustain the 'bull-dog courage' of Englishmen.[4] The emphasis was on the 'men' since, while gender distinctions became more sharply defined and differentiated during the nineteenth century, it was overwhelmingly young males who had always participated in such games. The attempt to prevent the football match played in Kingston on Shrove Tuesday 1799, and the ensuing disorder, was one incident that highlights a process of attempts to establish a greater control over, and regulation of violent sports, and of young men in general. This process was part and parcel of a reconfiguration of masculinity as well as the development of the archetypal English gentleman.

The kind of football played in Kingston on Shrove Tuesday was just one example of the 'vulgar sports' enjoyed by many eighteenth- and early nineteenth-century Englishmen. Some of these sports involved animals bred to fight, such as bear-baiting, bull-baiting and cock-fighting; though, with the exception of the bull-running festivities in towns such as Stamford and Tutbury, the sports involving animals rarely required young men to show their mettle. Other sports, however, were contests between men and tested their prowess and courage with fists, cudgels or single sticks (also known as back-swords). Such violent behaviour was not unique to England. In rural France village fêtes and feast days could degenerate into mass brawls (*rixes*) between the young men from different villages or parishes. Any gendarmes or local police who sought to interfere commonly found both sides likely to stop fighting each other and to unite against them. At the same time savage battles were fought between the different workers' brotherhoods (*campagnonnages*) that helped find and regulate work for young artisans as they tramped their *Tour de France* at the outset of their career. 'In each brotherhood', recalled Agricole Perdiguer

> members learned how to handle a walking staff and quarterstaff, and how to subdue a man quickly. The strongest, the most terrifying, the most daring were also the most famous and beloved of our *compagnons*. To kill your peer, as long as he was not a member of your own little brotherhood, was not a crime but an act of courage. The Tour of France was completely belligerent. *Compagnons* were warriors, and their brotherhoods were enemy armies, rival nations that dreamed only of crushing one another.[5]

What marked out the English was the degree of elite tolerance that accompanied certain English forms of violence and the way in which such forms were perceived as a distinctive and laudable element within English behaviour.

Many believed, for example, that the practice of such physical contact sports had given Englishmen the edge in war. The author of *Wrestliana*, a short book in praise of northern counties' wrestling, and particularly Cumberland's variant of it, asserted that such physical activities had contributed significantly to the victories of Agincourt, Trafalgar and Waterloo.

> It cannot we think be denied that it is the most noble and manly, and we venture to say the most English-like manner of coping with an antagonist, to meet him breast to breast, and brave at once his united powers and science. It is comparatively like the courageous bulldog which goes at once to the head of the bull; and the cowardly cur which nibbles at his heels.[6]

Much more significant than wrestling was pugilism, and the author of *Wrestliana* clearly drew the inspiration for his title from Pierce Egan's celebrated *Boxiana*, which began publication towards the end of the Regency period. Egan waxed lyrical on the superiority of the Englishman's manner of settling disputes in contrast to the behaviour of foreigners. Englishmen might get a black eye or a broken nose in a fight, but they could shake hands and be friends afterwards:

> We have long witnessed the good effects of this manly spirit in England; and, we trust, it will never be extinguished. Prejudice does much in favour of our native soil; but, upon a dispassionate review of those countries where Pugilism is unknown, we find, that, upon the most trifling misunderstanding, the life of the individual is in danger. In Holland the long knife decides too frequently; scarcely any person in Italy is without the stiletto; and France and Germany are not particular in using stones, sticks, etc. to gratify revenge; but, in England, the FIST only is used, where malice is not suffered to engender and poison the composition, and induce the inhabitants to the commission of deeds which their souls abhor and shudder at – but an immediate appeal to Boxing – the bystanders make a ring, and where no unfair advantage is suffered to be taken of each other. The fight done, the hand is given, in token of peace; resentment vanishes; and the cause generally buried in oblivion. This generous mode of conduct is not owing to any particular rule laid down by education – it is an inherent principle – the impulse of the moment – acted upon by the most ignorant and inferior ranks of the people. Foreigners may sneer at us for our rudeness of customs and barbarity of

manners; but, we trust, that Englishmen will ever wish to be admired for their genuine honesty and rough sincerity than for an assumed and affected politeness.[7]

Some foreigners did sneer; and many visitors from continental Europe in the eighteenth and early nineteenth centuries commented on the aggressive physicality of the English and their propensity to settle quarrels with a fist fight in a ring made by bystanders.[8] It is unlikely that every such fight was as gentlemanly as Egan suggested, and men sometimes died as a result of their injuries. In eighteenth-century London the single most common form of death that brought about a coroner's inquest was one that resulted from kicks or punches inflicted in a fight, sometimes spontaneous, sometimes organised.[9] Many working men also carried knives in the eighteenth and nineteenth centuries; these might be clasp knives used for cutting food or tobacco or tools of a particular trade. Once a fight started, or once men's blood was up, it was a temptation for many to draw the knife. In 1841, for example, Henry Rodgers, a Sheffield shoemaker, believed that William Stringer had insulted his wife and attacked him with 'a knife used in [his] trade with a long handle and a short blade'. The blade may have been short, but it was long enough to kill; for the coroner this was 'a crime of a character ... serious and un-English'.[10] But while there were many exceptions, the concept of the fair fight, and of not taking advantage of an opponent who was injured, seriously winded or knocked to the ground, appears to have played an important part in many fights among working men. A perception of honour may have been instrumental in sparking the fight, and, as part of the ritual of the ensuing contest, it was dishonourable to take an unfair advantage.

The fight that resulted from a quarrel went alongside the organised contest between two men fighting for reward. These contests were especially popular in the late eighteenth and early nineteenth centuries. They attracted all classes, unlike, for example, the similar French systems of fighting known as *savate* and *chausson* or *jeu marseillais* that were shunned by the elite. George IV, as both regent and king, patronised pugilism and had eight champion pugilists decked out as pages at his coronation. But this royal patronage coincided with a growing hostility to the sport in some quarters. There were concerns about the gambling that surrounded the matches, about the enormous numbers of people

that assembled to watch them, and also about the injuries that might be
inflicted. The first two concerns linked with the more general anxieties
about rustic sports that were shared among sections of the ruling elite
and both high church Anglicans and Dissenters. These groups deemed
such sports to be disorderly, indecorous and likely to foster idleness
among the working classes. Their criticisms contributed to the beginning of a concerted effort to domesticate rustic sports during the late
eighteenth and early nineteenth centuries.[11] At the same time there
appears to have been an increasing squeamishness about the public infliction of pain and a growing intolerance of the infliction of physical
injury, let alone death, even in a fair fight.

During the nineteenth century several vulgar sports involving animals
were prohibited, while contact sports such as boxing and football,
which could be very rough and violent, were increasingly bounded by
rules and regulations. Given the context in which these sports were
enjoyed, and often played, at the end of the eighteenth and in the early
nineteenth centuries, these moves to suppress or regulate might be
interpreted as attempts to control and discipline the emerging working
class and to make it more compliant to the demands of the developing
capitalist economy. Yet attempts at control were not new; seventeenth-
century Puritans had also sought to suppress what they considered to be
un-Godly, if traditional sports and pastimes. Norbert Elias's theory has
some useful explanatory value here. The manners, and violence, of
Tudor and Stuart gentry would have been shocking to, and quite out
of place, among their Victorian and Edwardian counterparts. While
more difficult to measure, the same is true for the attitudes of their
respective social inferiors. Seventeenth-century Puritan attempts to
enforce change were ephemeral; the domestication of traditional sports
in the nineteenth century was more lasting, but there were other
elements at work, rather than simply a desire to establish a compliant,
disciplined workforce. These elements were as much, if not more along
the lines of Elias's notion of social constraints merging into individual
restraint among an elite group, and spreading across classes as much by
a desire to emulate as to control.[12]

Henry Fielding's Squire Western, with his love of field sports, his
dislike of the ideas of honour espoused by 'courtiers and Hannoverians',
and his preparedness to use his fists to settle arguments or to ensure a

fair fight, even when he did not recognise the combatants, was fast becoming an anachronism when *Tom Jones* was first published. As the eighteenth century progressed many among the gentry showed themselves increasingly reluctant to indulge in rude jollity and rustic merriment. At same time the sporting clergy was being superseded by men with a sterner Christian outlook who were disinclined to back traditional sports or to grant permission for them to take place on church property and on Sunday. In tandem with this change, the income and social standing of Anglican clergy was also declining, something that became especially apparent in nineteenth century with both Catholic emancipation and the repeal of bars against dissenters. Evangelicalism among the Anglican clergy, the spread of Methodism among the working classes, and the strength of Dissent among both the new industrialists and many of their workforce all combined against traditional vulgar sports. In addition, another slow but steady change whittled away at them. Civic improvements, such as widened, paved streets, the clearing and cleaning of butchers' shambles, new shops and new walks, were accompanied by shifting ideas of who might use the streets and when. Eighteenth-century town worthies began to believe, and hence to decree, that certain spaces should be closed to sport and celebration.[13] The shopkeepers of towns like Kingston were less and less prepared to have their windows broken, their customers frightened and their stock damaged for the sake of tradition, especially when they had to pick up the costs through their rates. The uniform election of borough councils established by the Municipal Corporations Act of 1835 served to strengthen the power of such ratepayers, and Victorian civic pride capped the trends for urban improvement and the control and restriction of urban space.

Yet it was not just the working classes that indulged in the rough and violent behaviour that was increasingly disapproved of, disciplined and regulated in the late eighteenth and early nineteenth centuries. The correspondent who witnessed the Kingston football match in 1815 'observed some persons of respectability following the ball'.[14] It is, of course, possible to juxtapose the gentry's fox-hunting, which was not banned, with the cock-fighting, bull- and bear-baiting that were, and to detect the hand of class interest here. There was, however, also violent aristocratic and gentry behaviour that was stigmatised and controlled. While Englishmen of all social classes boasted of their prowess with their fists, affairs of aristocratic honour had commonly been settled by duels involving swords or, more commonly from the early eighteenth century, pistols. The statistics of duelling are difficult to collect and to assess. On one estimate, it appears that from the middle of the eighteenth century the number of duels in England began to increase. Yet this was at the moment when there seems to have been in England a sea change in elite attitudes to the role of violence, the concept of honour and the understanding of masculinity.[15] Possibly there was a marginal spread in duelling from the nobility, gentry and the military elite to their social inferiors; social emulation was not something confined to the 'civilising process' and some Englishmen may have issued challenges and fought to acquire the patina of gentility. In England, in contrast to continental Europe, duelling seems to have involved a much greater use of pistols. It has been suggested that this led to a larger number of fatalities; yet an unskilled swordsman was always at the mercy of a skilled one. Duelling evoked the same kind of condemnation, and from similar sorts of people, as traditional, violent sports. It declined rapidly from the 1840s; much faster than, but in the midst of, the more gradual decline of traditional 'vulgar' sports and pugilism. The reasons for this are still debated. Men who sought to enhance their social standing by fighting duels, especially when they were caught fighting with pistols loaded only with powder and no ball, arguably brought ridicule on themselves and the activity. The undercharging of duelling pistols with gunpowder, or replacing the shot with something less lethal, had been common among seconds during the aristocratic confrontations of the eighteenth century. The reports of bullies, card cheats and upstarts fighting duels may also have undermined the image of the duel as the preserve of the aristocratic or military man of honour. Lord Campbell's 1843 libel law, which enabled a defendant to plead that he was only speaking the truth, may also have discouraged some recourse to duelling. So too may the army's decision to prosecute duellists more rigorously from the mid 1840s, as did the decision of Sir Robert Peel, as Prime Minister, to refuse the usual army pension to the widow of an officer killed in a duel.[16]

The spread of duelling across the social classes was not just an English phenomenon; but its demise in England during the 1840s was exceptional. English courts began making examples of men who killed in duels and 'fair fights'. In 1838 Charles Mirfin and his two seconds were convicted of murder at the Old Bailey following the death of Francis Eliot in a duel with pistols. All three were sentenced to a year in gaol, with the last month to be in solitary confinement – a humiliating sentence and ordeal for respectable gentlemen. The verdict itself was novel, and the first of its kind for at least eighty years. It made a profound impression and heralded a trend. In the following year Charles Rudge, who had held the stake money during a fair fist fight in Somerset during which a contestant had been killed, was successfully prosecuted for manslaughter. In England in the late seventeenth and early eighteenth centuries the use of lethal violence to defend personal and family honour had been a routine and public ritual. By the mid nineteenth century, both the state's authorities and a growing 'respectable' public, considered such behaviour neither manly nor desirable.[17] Yet in France and Germany the duel, with both swords and pistols, lasted until the end of the First World War, and in Italy it survived into the Fascist period.[18] In each of these states supporters of the duel argued that it fostered manly courage and self-control, attributes respectively labelled republican, militarist, nationalist, but identified as crucial to the societies of republican France, imperial Germany and liberal, nationalist Italy. Arguably the physicality of boxing and rugby fulfilled similar roles in the late nineteenth- and early twentieth-century British context.

It is possible to detect an assault on rough plebeian sports and pastimes inspired by a combination of urbanisation, genteel sensitivity, Evangelicalism, Methodism, and a general concern about popular unruliness. Yet this does not provide a complete explanation for the decline of such sports. The rules that defined boxing, rugby and soccer were also not written simply to domesticate the sports for plebeian players. The first rules for prize-fighting were drawn up by the pugilist Jack Broughton in 1734, after an opponent died in a contest. But the contests continued to be bloody, bruising, limb-breaking affairs, and men continued to die. New regulations were written in the early nineteenth century, but the most significant were those of the Marquis of Queensberry that were issued in 1865. The Queensberry rules were designed to regularise and sanitise the sport,[19] but, by permitting contests on raised platforms, they fostered commercialism and ensured that fight promoters could restrict audiences and more easily collect the entry price. These were not regulations to control plebeian behaviour. As has already been stressed, prize-fighting was not just a plebeian pursuit. The law could be used to break up prize-fights as illegal assemblies; it could also be used to prosecute fighters, their seconds and their promoters for assault, affray and even homicide. The rules drawn up by the Football Association and the Rugby Football Union, established in 1863 and 1871 respectively, were designed to enable gentlemen to continue playing the games that they had enjoyed at school or university. The problem was that different schools and universities had different rules, particularly regarding kicking and handling the ball and bringing down an opponent. The fact that professional teams with loyal working-class followers began to eclipse the amateur gentlemen in soccer was not something that the Football Association had intended; and it was something that the Rugby Football Union's insistence on amateurism limited.

Games continued to be a part of English manliness, as they had been in the eighteenth century and earlier, but the understanding of manliness began to be structured in new ways. It encompassed personal control and, while it might mean physical contact and a degree of violence, that physicality had to be restrained and limited in a way that made it 'fair' to the opponent. For the Victorians this was another element of their civilisation. There were contradictions. While soccer was seen as a way of developing team spirit and manliness, several police forces banned their men from playing the sport at the end of the nineteenth century. The Chief Constable of Halifax, for example, protested to his watch committee about one of his men playing for a professional team. It was 'much too dangerous' and derogatory to the police 'considering the rowdyism and betting that is carried on'. The real concern here, however, was the fact that, if his constable continued to play for the professional team, he might not be fit for duty; and there was the further annoyance that the man 'received nearly as much per match ... as he was receiving per week as a member of the [police] force'.[20] A quarter of a century later the Chief Constable of Sheffield, worried by the number of his men getting injured playing soccer, issued an order condemning and forbidding rough play, which prompted jokes about his men being wrapped in cotton wool.[21]

Chief Constable Sillitoe's injunction was issued only a few years before the notorious 'Bodyline' cricket tour of Australia. Cricket was the ultimate game for English gentleman and one in which, unlike boxing or the various the forms of football, bodily contact was non-existent. But a fast ball, bowled deliberately so as to bounce up at a batsman's unprotected upper body and head, constitutes a dangerous missile and violent intimidation. At the beginning of the twentieth century Surrey had a bowler, Neville Knox, who was very fast and accurate, and who had no compunction about bowling a short ball that rose up to the batsman's body and head. In a match played against Yorkshire in July 1906 *The Times* commented how Yorkshire's top scorer in the game, George Hirst, 'played magnificent cricket, and his pluck was as noticeable as his skill. Three times he received nasty blows from the fast bowling of Mr Knox, but these never unsettled him in the least.' Other batsmen were unsettled, however, and Surrey won by nine wickets.[22] The match prompted one of W. K. Haseldon's cartoons for the *Daily Mail* (Figure 2), though not the controversy surrounding Harold Larwood's bowling during the Bodyline Tour. The extent to which Larwood's bowling, and the tactics under the captaincy of Douglas Jardine, were 'cricket' was debated at the time and has been subsequently; but facing such balls unquestionably required what some would have defined as 'manliness' as well as 'pluck'.[23]

Manliness, involving the participation in rough games but with a measured and controlled use of violent physicality, was something inculcated in boys at the English public schools. There was something of a free for all in the physicality of these schools during the eighteenth and early nineteenth centuries; it was even known for the militia to be called to suppress school mutinies. From the early Victorian period, more to control unruly pupils than deliberately to structure the English male stereotype, these schools began to encourage an idea of manliness rooted in the virtues of rectitude, self-denial and seriousness. Later in the century perseverance, robustness and stoicism became more significant. Team games fostered these virtues and assuaged concerns that a polite, commercial and civilised people would become enfeebled and thus lose out to European and North American rivals. Valour in the ball game also seemed easily to shift into valour in battle; and such ideas can be found in poems written for school magazines years before

2. 'First Aid to the Injured in Cricket', published in the *Daily Mirror* on 30 July 1906, is W. K. Haseldon's comment on Neville Knox's fast bowling for Surrey. Haseldon's pencil notes pasted on the original suggested: 'In future it may be advisable to fit [the] pavilion as a hospital.'

Sir Henry Newbolt's well-known clarion call in *Vitaï Lampada* to 'Play up! Play up! And play the game!'

> Say not 'tis brutal, our noble game
> When it fans our English valour's flame
> How many a charge through the ranks of the foe
> Have been made by a warrior who years ago
> Hurried the leather from hand to hand
> And 'gainst heavy odds made sturdy stand
> 'Neath Old England's banner in every land
> Our football players to guard it, stand.[24]

The manly, Christian Englishman thus fought bravely on the games field, stoically bearing the pain of sports injuries (see Figure 3) and behaved similarly in the rather more dangerous game of battle. But this tended to be a middle-class vision. The glorification of war and of empire-building that characterised much of the fiction intended for boys did not shirk violence and killing. Here the violence was that of battle; this was patriotic, playing for the bigger national team, while the violence of empire building was fundamentally liberal, sweeping away barbarism bringing the advantages of Christian civilisation. Improving adventure magazines and novels for boys, such as those of G. A. Henty, contained plenty of violence in an imperial, civilising setting. Much of this violence and derring-do was little different from that portrayed in the penny dreadfuls. The respectable middle and upper classes approved and legitimated the former, while abhorring the latter and worrying about its impact on youth, especially working-class youth.[25]

An individual's class and gender remained important in an assessment of rough behaviour. The police used their discretion and only involved themselves in a fight if it looked to be getting out of hand and involving too many people. Even factory girls, who sometimes had an inclination to settle differences with fists in rings made by their workmates, were not interfered with by the police.[26] There could also be violence in the working-class spectator sport of professional soccer, and before the end of the nineteenth century voices were raised against rough play on the pitch, violence on the terraces and directed against referees. The number of violent incidents at such matches appears to have been significantly under-reported both in the press and in the correspondence sent to the FA by referees. Yet this violence was generally different from that

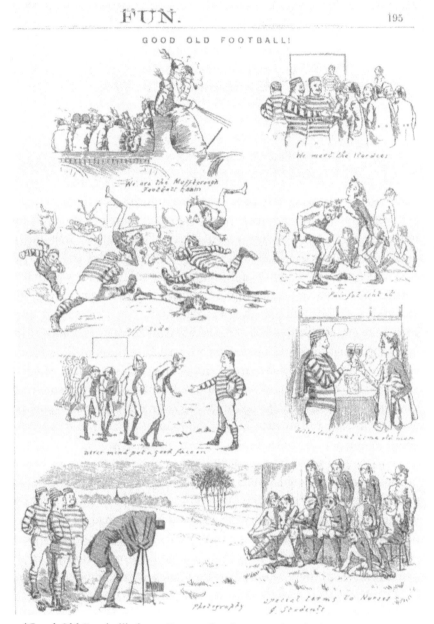

3. 'Good Old Football', from *Fun*, 30 October 1889, is a fairly typical comment on a game of what appears to be soccer played between ill-matched teams.

experienced during the hooligan panics that began to be regularly
reported in the press in the 1960s. The working-class football crowds of
the early twentieth century rarely travelled to away games. They often
attended matches in family groups, with friends or workmates, rather
than in crowds of organised 'supporters'. Individuals in the crowds
might be drunk; they sometimes spat and swore. Their violence, however, when it occurred, tended to be between individuals and was not
necessarily linked to team support.[27] By the early twentieth century the
kind of misrule that had been manifested in Shrove Tuesday football
games could still be found, but its manifestations tended to be primarily
among the respectable classes in annual student rags, or in occasional
confrontations between the young gentlemen of certain amateur sports
teams, or their supporters, after a match.

The Cambridge students' 'rag' took place on 5 November, a day that,
in many towns, had traditionally experienced both misrule and celebration involving all classes.[28] By the close of the nineteenth century the
plebeian misrule elements of the day had been largely tamed in most
towns, but in Cambridge in the inter-war years the students, who were
anything but plebeian, often clashed violently with police. The 'battle'
fought on Market Hill in 1934 resulted in thirty-five defendants appearing at the local magistrates' court; seven of these were charged with
assaulting the police, three for resisting, and four for obstructing the
police.[29]

Nor was it only Cambridge that suffered from the occasional violence
of students. Charles Hanslow began his career in the Metropolitan Police
in the early 1930s and recalled the potential for trouble in London on the
night of the University Boat Race.

> Thousands of students congregated in the Piccadilly Circus vicinity after
> dark and began some silly jokes and pranks after a 'smell of the barmaid's
> apron'. Their victims were often policemen. Parades were briefed by the
> Chief Inspector who 'warned' us that the students usually damaged a theatre
> interior BUT on no account were they to be arrested for this damage! I par-
> ticularly remember that at the Lyric Theatre in Shaftesbury Avenue there was
> a play called I think, *England my England* which was badly mauled by the
> critics. The Boat Race crowd descended on this theatre and eventually myself
> and other policemen were called by the manager. He was frightened, because
> as we all stood together just inside a rear door there was a ghastly uproar.

About a couple of hundred men were smashing all the seating in the stalls. The actors carried on and these were showered with large bits of theatre furniture! The manager calmed down eventually and begged us not to interfere explaining that the Universities always paid for the damage! I think we must have nicked a few students when they left the theatre!! Drunk and disorderly? Insulting behaviour? Perhaps so; they were out of breath by then.[30]

The cartoonist Low captured supposed preparations for this kind of behaviour with his fortified theatre, 'Prepared for the Rag', published in the *Star* in March 1925 (Figure 4). Boys, it seemed, would be boys and would be allowed to be so, providing they could pay for the damage and were, in the aftermath, politely contrite. Occasionally the worst excesses of such behaviour were blamed on 'hooligans who have no sort of connection with any University'. But in stating this the journal *Justice of the Peace* refused to condone student behaviour, dismissed rags as 'silly', and noted the way that contrasts might be made between the behaviour of 'playful' young gentlemen and that of poor lads from the unrespectable East End of London.[31]

Problems with student rags continued after the Second World War until, during the 1960s, student activities on the streets acquired a much more political tone. A London University rag scheduled for 5 November 1953 was the most unruly of these traditional disorders in post-war England. The Metropolitan Police withdrew their permission for the students' bonfire on the 'apprehension of a clash between the local hooligan element and the student body'. The ban prompted clashes between students and the police, the most violent of which involved frustrated students seeking to march on Buckingham Palace and clashing with a police cordon in Aldwych. Mounted police were deployed and the students were reported to have thrown fireworks, toilet rolls, bags of flour and bags of sand at the police. On 6 November 189 individuals appeared at the Bow Street magistrates' court, and students demonstrated outside, linking arms and singing 'Auld Lang Syne', cheering the defendants and carrying them shoulder high as they left the court. A further two students were arrested for obstructing the police outside the court. On 9 November *The Times* carried a leader deploring the behaviour of 'mobs of amateur hooligans', not least because there were 'enough professionals' around.[32] This was a cue for a correspondence about the traditions, and the rights and wrongs of student rags.

4. 'Prepared for the Rag', published in the *Star*, 28 March 1925, is David Low's comment on London theatres' preparations for rowdy student behaviour. (*Low Estate*)

'Have we arrived at a time when a boy cannot throw a bag of flour at a policeman's helmet on a night of licence as, traditionally, Guy Fawkes Night is without being prosecuted and fined by the law for causing a disturbance of the peace?' asked M. E. Cowley of Tunbridge Wells.

> How can we expect our young men and women to have the fortitude and endurance to live out their lives in this mechanical and soulless period of history if they have no opportunity for release of pent-up spirits in the university 'rags' which are their right by custom and which provide relief at the time and a consoling memory for the future? We have become a dry and sensitive race of men indeed when even our policemen cannot deal with a little bad language without dragging in the law to protect them. How the Elizabethans must laugh at us, that robust, boisterous crew we are now so proud of and with whom we try to find some affinity in ourselves at the beginning of this second Elizabethan age. Can we be hoping to be named by posterity as 'the refined Elizabethans'?[33]

Michael Crowther, writing from Cambridge, considered that such 'outbursts' were not 'malicious and relatively little damage is done to property'. Moreover, the 'little inconvenience' of Cambridge student rags was tolerated by the inhabitants 'with good humour'. The recent Cambridge rag manifested 'the old friendly rivalry between gown and town ... and though there was considerable rioting only one arrest was necessary'.[34]

It is always difficult to date and to measure shifts in social attitudes, but, by the early 1950s, it is true to say that the attitude of people like Cowley and Crowther was increasingly that of a minority. The populist conservative *Daily Sketch* had no hesitation about linking violent students with violent working-class youth. On the same day that it reported the 1953 rag it also reported four seventeen-year-old youths and one sixteen-year-old in Liverpool each gaoled for five years for stabbing an eighteen year old who had assisted a girl whom the gang was violently assaulting. The gang was known for wearing zoot suits and 'giving police anxiety' along the West Derby Road. 'We cannot afford to breed hooligans', proclaimed a *Sketch* leader on 7 November, 'whether they wear zoot suits or cap and gown.'[35]

The debates over student rags reflect the kind of arguments over the Shrove Tuesday football games over a hundred years before. But some differences were present, at least by implication. By the period after

Second World War, the participants in student rags were recognised as including women. Nevertheless, the participants were, by definition, from the respectable classes and were future professionals and members of the elite. For some critics, including *The Times*'s leader writer, class did not matter; 'amateur hooligans' from the student body were as bad as the 'professionals' from elsewhere. The defenders of the rags, however, appear to have taken a rather different attitude to class. The English tradition in the rags, in their defenders' perception, did not hearken back to plebeian rustic pastimes but stressed the boisterousness of the first Elizabethans; the men who had taken on the might of Spain and who had begun to carve out an empire. The students were not 'malicious', and their riots were 'tolerated' by those who understood them from long awareness, such as the inhabitants of Cambridge. These young men, and by the 1950s also young women, should be allowed to have their moments of licence as release from the contemporary moment, and to give them lively memories for that period in the future when they shouldered their responsibilities. In the understanding of the defenders of the rags, the disorder was a moment in the rite of passage from being *in statu pupillari* (a term used by *The Times* in its critical leader) to assuming adult responsibility, and the mantle of the respectable Englishman. Yet in the increasingly egalitarian environment of the post-war world it was very difficult to maintain the defenders' distinction between students, who might be permitted licence, and hooligans. The English gentleman as an ideal was in decline, and as a corollary many of the notions about the Englishman's relationship with violence gradually began to be questioned and to disintegrate.

The ideal type of Englishmen varied during the nineteenth and twentieth centuries, and there were disagreements about the importance of different attributes, but strict control of the passions was central. He had enjoyed some licence when young but this had been curbed and controlled by various, well-worn methods, and he had 'got it out of his system'. The English gentleman was expected never to be gratuitously violent, but he needed to know how to defend himself and the weak. Hence boxing, as regulated under the Queensberry Rules, maintained much of the aura given it by Pierce Egan. Fighting was to be fair, face to face, or as Litt had declared with reference to Cumberland wrestling, breast to breast; the heaving of the rugby scrum was a fine model. This tightly regulated physicality was gender specific. It related to manliness and specifically the virtues of the English gentleman; women, or rather 'ladies', were not expected to be physical. The English working man was encouraged to adopt the same forms of behaviour as his social superior. But the idea of the fair fight had never been class specific, while emulation of English gentlemen, and participation in sport under their rules, may even have been encouraged by a degree of class antagonism.

Accidents might happen, and occasionally a sporting contest or a fair fight could result in a fatality. In 1825 the youngest son of the seventh Earl of Shaftesbury died after a fight with another boy. But the Earl refused to prosecute since the fight, even though it was among schoolboys and had lasted over two hours, had been properly arranged with each fighter assisted by seconds.[36] As has been noted, the courts took an increasingly dim view of prize fights, and they took an even dimmer view of the use of weapons in duels and in other fights. Time and again coroners, magistrates, judges and newspapers complained that the use of a knife in a fight was 'cowardly' and simply not English.[37] Even so, the fights among the youth gangs of the late nineteenth and early twentieth centuries, as well as those involving the more mature 'hard men', often saw any chivalric notions rejected from the outset. In the rough street of Campbell Bunk, Islington, between the wars, for example, iron railings were commonly used as weapons and everyone was fearful of Gypsy Jim Hobbs, who allegedly employed 'a big lump of leather with chains on it' for both attack and defence.[38] And while the ideal English gentleman was expected to be controlled, restrained and the protector of women and children, English families could experience persistent, brutal violence.

4

Family and Home

On 24 March 1873 Mary Ann Cotton was executed in Durham Gaol. A little under three weeks earlier she had been found guilty at the Durham assizes of poisoning her seven-year-old stepson, Charles Edward Cotton. She was believed by many to have committed a whole string of other murders – three husbands, a lover, her mother, a sister-in-law, ten of her own children and five stepchildren. But, even when awaiting execution, Mary Ann never admitted any of the murders. She admitted a bigamous marriage, and she suggested that Charles Edward may have died because a chemist had accidentally let arsenic taint some arrowroot that she had purchased, but that was all. The *Newcastle Journal* thought her 'a monster in human shape'. It was surprised 'that a woman could act thus without becoming horrible and repulsive'. It noted also how, maintaining 'a rather kindly manner', she had looked after those she had poisoned as they lay dying in agony. The *Durham County Advertiser* expressed amazement that a person guilty of such hideous offences could 'maintain the quiet decencies of ordinary life. There was no hatred or passion, but a sort of diabolical inhumanity which made the woman absolutely indifferent to everything except the attainment of her own paltry ends'. What those ends were remains a mystery. Possibly, as her most recent biographer has suggested, there was a strong drive for sexual gratification that her successive partners failed to satisfy. Possibly she also sought to gain a little when insurance money was paid out: the unfortunate Charles Edward had been insured for £4 10s. The most respectable of her husbands, a Sunderland shipwright who survived his marriage to her, refused to let her insure him and threw her out of his house when he found her running up debts and misusing his money.[1]

Mary Ann Cotton's notoriety never spread much beyond the north east of England. A melodrama based on her life, however, was still being performed in the region during the inter-war years. She was also a bogey figure used to scare children into good behaviour, and she lived on in children's playground songs.

> Mary Ann Cotton
> She's dead and she's rotten
> She lies in her bed
> With her eyes wide oppen [sic]
> Sing, sing, oh, what can I sing
> Mary Ann Cotton is tied up with string.
> Where, where? Up in the air
> Sellin' black puddens a penny a pair.[2]

Her story is exceptional, but largely because of the number of people that she appears to have killed. There were other instances of women poisoning one or more children for a miserable insurance pay out.[3] Serial killers existed, yet people were not particularly aware of the phenomenon during the nineteenth century. The number of women murderers was always less than the number of men who killed. Yet the fearsome stepmother was a popular stereotype, and not just a stereotype, for murderous stepmothers appeared also in the courts and in the press reports of the courts. Above all, the fact that Mary Ann Cotton's murders were kept within the family is indicative of a much wider experience of inter-personal violence and murder in nineteenth- and twentieth-century England.

Popular anxieties about violence tend to focus on the fear of attack by a stranger. The panics about garotting in the mid nineteenth century and, more recently, about mugging provide good examples. The exceptional panic at the time of the Jack the Ripper murders was similar. This developed partly from what the killer had done. His appalling savagery generated nationwide concerns for the safety of women who would never venture within miles of the courts and alleyways of Whitechapel where the murders took place. But the panic was aggravated by the way that the killings drew attention to the dreadful social conditions in London's East End. The occasional panic about violence on the streets after dark and the threats from strangers contrasted dramatically with the Victorian idealisation of home and family. The ideal home, with everything in its place and every family member knowing their place, provided safety and security. Many, perhaps the majority of, Victorian families may have subscribed to this ideal and sought to live up to it.

Some manifestly fell far short. But the biggest problem was not so much the spouse killer as the violent spouse abuser.

Occasionally, the domestic abuser was the wife. In some northern towns there was a 'hoary folk tale' of a man who returned home drunk, was tied up by his wife and 'beaten into unconsciousness and future sobriety'.[4] Martha Loane, a district nurse who had wide experience working in London, Shropshire, Buxton and Portsmouth during the late Victorian and Edwardian periods, began her account of the poor with a discussion of husband beaters.

> As far as I can gather from the statements of these doughty champions of the supremacy of women, their husbands are beaten for returning home 'more foolish than when they went out', minus an undue proportion of their week's wages.[5]

The women described by Loane appear to have made a habit of such violence. Similar women were to be found in the inter-war years. They not only beat their husbands, sometimes in retaliation for a blow, but some were also prepared to strip to the waist and fight each other in the street like the hard men.[6] On Christmas Day 1929 a Rotherham woman was reported to have prepared the dinner but to have forgotten to boil the potatoes. When her husband allegedly commented, 'Well that's a grand dinner', she responded by giving him a two-inch wound with the carving knife. The wife admitted that she had been drinking, but insisted also that her husband had kicked her. She was bound over to keep the peace and promised to stop drinking.[7]

Domestic violence was provoked by drink, by arguments over money, by differences over domestic chores, and assumptions about the 'duties' of a wife. Most often it was perpetrated by men. In working-class families the man might be the breadwinner but the wife was the home organiser and was responsible for the family budget. Some working-class husbands presented their wives with their weekly wage packets unopened; others handed them over having already taken what they wanted. In the casual labour market of, for example, the Liverpool docks making ends meet could be extremely difficult for a wife. Her failure could be considered demeaning to the husband; so too was any attempt on her part to find work for herself – it implied that her husband was failing to provide. Families might try to keep their problems secret, but the arguments were heard and the bruises were seen.[8] And although the problems may have been more acute, more noticeable and more public in the poorer, overcrowded working-class districts such violence might be inflicted by a man from any social class. Skilled workmen, who might be supposed to have strongly espoused the ideas of Victorian self-improvement and respectability, seem to have constituted as many as one in three of the men prosecuted for wife-beating.[9] Yet the perception in the nineteenth century, and for at least the first half of the twentieth, was that such violence was rooted in one particular class. Baron Bramwell was explicit in this, and in what he saw as the disciplining and moralising role of the courts, when in 1867 he rejected a jury's plea for mercy in the case of John Vickery, a Sussex labourer found guilty of the manslaughter of his wife. Vickery's wife may well have been a spend-thrift and a drunkard but, Bramwell declared, 'it is necessary that people in your class should be taught – what I fear they don't understand – that they have no right to beat their wives'.[10]

Historians have traced an increasing demonisation of the man who assaulted his wife during the Victorian period. In spite of the evidence of skilled men among the assailants, wife beaters were generally seen as coming from the worst sections of the working class. They were men from the residuum, resistant to the advance of civilisation. In 1876 the satirical periodical *Fun*, which commonly joked about corrupt and incompetent policemen, captured this perception in one of its more serious illustrations (Figure 5). And such violence perpetuated itself, as the feminist Mabel Sharman Crawford warned nearly twenty years later:

> The gangs of juvenile scuttlers, who from time to time run riot through the Manchester streets, have doubtless been reared in homes where mothers are subjected to kicks and blows. The boy gangs of Hoxton and Bethnal Green who, armed with knives, go forth from East End courts and slums to assail each other in savage faction fights, have doubtless also been familiarised with the sight of personal violence from their earliest years.[11]

The judicial elite appears to have been more focused on dealing with the problem of the wife-beater than juries; members of the latter were often from a social milieu rather closer than judges and magistrates to such offenders. There could be tension in the courts, and outside, when the men presiding sought greater severity, and the jurors, as in the case of Vickery noted above, considering a wife to have been a 'nag', a drunk-ard, or a failure in her wifely duties, recommended lenient sentences or

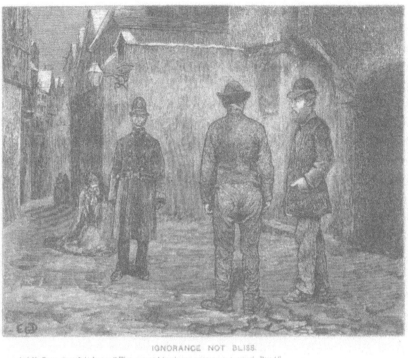

IGNORANCE NOT BLISS.

Amiable Person (to wife kicker) :—" Wot a lark ! 'ere's the pleeceman a comin', Bill !"

Wife Kicker :—" Is he ? Then blow'd if he don't get one too !"

Amiable Person :—" Well, after you knocks 'im on the 'ed into the gutter, Bill, let 'im come to a bit 'afore you begins to kick 'im, or he won't know what you're a doin', and he'll lose half the fun !"

5. 'Ignorance Not Bliss'. *Fun* was often critical of the police. In this cartoon, however, published on 12 April 1876 and reversing the old adage 'ignorance is bliss', a slender constable steps between a 'wife kicker' and his victim. The 'amiable person' clearly expects that the 'wife kicker' will now set about the constable.

sought to downgrade a killing to manslaughter.[12] Such 'extenuating circumstances', however, could still be acknowledged by judges and
magistrates in the late nineteenth and early twentieth centuries. In May
1883, for example, the case against a man in Derby for assaulting his wife
was dismissed following his plea that, after she had joined the Salvation
Army, she was out at meetings until after midnight leaving the home
dirty and the children neglected.[13] A rather more typical defence was
deployed in the case of William Taylor, a forty-four-year-old Bermondsey labourer, tried at the Central Criminal Court in September 1912 for
the manslaughter of his wife. Taylor had a very violent past. He had
received a sentence of three years penal servitude with fifteen strokes of
the cat for highway robbery; he had twenty-three convictions for assault
and others for larceny. He told the judge that he was very sorry and had
not intended to injure his wife when he struck her. Detective Sergeant
Good of the Metropolitan Police spoke up for him. Taylor, according to
Good, 'had a very good character, but was very quarrelsome'. Moreover,
Good added, 'the deceased was partial to other men, and was of a very
irritable and nagging nature'. The judge commented that it would have
been far more serious if Taylor had used any kind of weapon, rather
than his fist, to strike his wife. On conviction Taylor was sentenced to
prison for only six months.[14]

The assault on the wife-beater or killer, however, was not straight-
forward. While judges and magistrates were often keener to punish than
juries, wife-beaters and especially husband-beaters could find themselves the victims of violent community punishment. In 1856 a
correspondent of the *Times* informed readers how, in a small village
near Wakefield, any brutality towards a woman was still punished with
the old folklore tradition of 'rough music'. An effigy of the offender was
carried through the village with a cacophony of banging on kettles, pots
and trays and a blowing of cow horns. The parade finished outside the
offender's door where the effigy was burned.[15] Such 'rough music',
which could be a prelude to local ostracism in shops and at work, was
not confined to small villages in Yorkshire. Indeed, the wife-beater
appears to have become a more predominant target for this kind of
community action from the 1840s. Women, moreover, seem to have
taken a much greater role in these instances of rough music. This might
suggest a growing hostility to attacks on wives among the population at

large, even if this was not necessarily apparent in the courts. It might also suggest that there was an increasing brutality towards wives in the early industrial revolution that was prompting a new level of criticism. This kind of community sanction continued into the twentieth century, even in some urbanised and industrial districts, and it is difficult to know why it happened in one place and not in another. It is also difficult to untangle easily the spur to such action and whether it was genuine 'community' punishment or whether it was the 'community' appropriated by vengeful relatives or aggressive youths.[16] In addition community response could simply be vigilante violence without the folklore paraphernalia of rough music. At the end of 1883 William Henry Stewart of Deptford had been married for three months. His wife had already complained twice to the police about his drunken assaults, but she had declined to press charges. When he attacked her for a third time on Saturday 29 December she fled to a neighbour's house and in the end the police had to take Stewart into custody to protect him from what the local newspaper called a lynching.[17]

There was no steady linear growth of the condemnation of the wife-beater. Indeed, there appears to have been something of a male counter-offensive in the late Victorian and Edwardian periods. A succession of authors, notably the novelists T. W. H. Crossland and George Gissing, drew unflattering portraits of the lower middle class of suburban London. In particular they were contemptuous of the pretensions of the wives in this class who slept late, failed to discipline their servants, were greedy, selfish and pretentious, and were indulged by the weak husbands whom they had emasculated. For the journalist Philip Gibbs, writing on the eve of the First World War, the solution was quite simply that the man needed to employ 'a touch of brutality now and then' to demonstrate that he was the master. The counter-offensive reached a climax in the celebrated case of Dr Crippen in 1910. In the Crippen case, and in the subsequent reporting and revisiting of it, Cora Crippen, the victim, was portrayed as the slatternly suburban housewife who was a poor housekeeper, quite lacking taste. Worse still, while she let the house become dirty and squalid, she gloried in her own appearance. Even the prosecuting counsel was to speculate that 'in another country [Crippen] would ... have been given the benefit of "extenuating circumstances"'. Cora Crippen gradually became the cause of the

respectable but weak doctor's actions, and the roles of victim and murderer were to some extent reversed. The reversal, however, did not save
Crippen from the gallows.[18]

The law and the legal system sometimes impeded the prosecution and
the control of domestic assailants. Women went to police stations to
complain about the violence of a husband or partner, but they declined
to make charges that would lead to a court case. They may have hoped
that the police might warn the offender and that this would be sufficient
to prevent future attacks. After all, a court case could end in the husband being fined or imprisoned. Either outcome could land a
working-class family in financial difficulties; the fine would have to
come out of the family budget, while the removal of the principal breadwinner to prison would seriously effect that budget. The satirical
periodical *Judy* picked up on the working-class wife from the East End
of London who would not prosecute her husband towards the end of
1898 (Figure 6). A dozen years later, in 1910, three assault cases recorded
in the Refused Charge Book for the police station on Isle of Dogs
involved husbands attacking wives. On each occasion the case went no
further than the police station because the wife declined to press
charges. The violence offered in these instances was not restricted to the
use of fists. Eliza Moore, for example, had her sister-in-law's cor-
roborative evidence that her husband had thrown knives and struck her
with a poker.[19] It appears that Lillian Sutherland only went to the police
in April 1932 because her husband's blow had 'glanced off' her forehead
and struck their eight-week-old baby. When a surgeon at the East London Hospital reported the injury to be 'slight', she refused to take the
case any further.[20] At the end of July 1948 a thirty-year-old female cook
called the police to her lodgings. She 'had minor scratches on her throat
but appeared more concerned about any damage that may have been
done to her furniture'. A fifty-three-year-old painter was arrested suspected of aggravated assault and wilful damage; but the cook declined
to press charges. The police could do little more than warn the man who
then

> left the station in quite a good frame of mind explaining that he had had a
> drink or two but had no intention of injuring Miss Fay – he also explained
> that he had been to her room earlier in the evening and in order to let her
> know that he had been there he turned everything upside down.[21]

**IN THE OUT-PATIENT DEPARTMENT OF AN
EAST END HOSPITAL.**

HOUSE SURGEON: *"Come now, tell the officer who
did it. Was it your husband?"*
PATIENT: *"No, he wouldn't a done it—he's more
like a friend than a husband!"*

6. 'In the Out Patient Department of an East End Hospital', published in *Judy*, 14 December 1898. The cartoon provides 'humorous' comment on the reluctance of many wives to give evidence against their husbands for domestic violence.

In addition to the hardening attitude of the courts, new legislation provided more and more avenues for women to take action against husbands who beat them and their children. The Act for the Better Prevention of Aggravated Assaults on Women and Children of 1853 authorised sentences of up to six months or a £20 fine for men found guilty of such assault. Such sanctions, as noted above, were not particularly helpful to a working-class family, but on some occasions women appear to have used the threat of the law, like the threat of the police, as a means to control, shame or warn a violent husband. In many instances the wife dropped charges before the case was heard, or simply did not turn up in court. The problem, of course, is to know how often a wife dropped the case through fear of the husband, rather than because she felt she had made her point.[22] The Summary Jurisdiction (Married Women) Act of 1878 enabled women to go before the courts to seek separation and maintenance from abusive husbands. This may have been a more satisfactory procedure for many wives, but the attitudes of magistrates could undermine the sanctions, and there were problems deeply embedded within this legislation. Most significantly, the Act of 1878 required a woman to have left her husband before action could begin. In 1910 the committee of the Associated Societies for the Protection of Women and Children noted that:

> This condition can only be complied with (1) where the woman herself goes out to work and therefore has regular (though small) income to depend upon, or (2) where relatives or friends (themselves almost invariably poor) have been willing to shelter the wife and children during the pendency [sic] of the proceedings and until the Order is enforceable. In the latter case it frequently means overcrowding and great hardship. Sometimes the woman has to leave the children behind, much to their neglect.[23]

Some police and magistrates appear to have had little sympathy for women complainants. At the turn of the century Superintendent Wyborn of the Southwark Division in London considered that the law went too far in protecting drunken wives. 'A woman of this kind will provoke her husband until he strikes her and will then have him up before the magistrate.' Wyborn thought separation and the separation allowance were too easy for women to get, and that it led some men to give up the struggle and enter the workhouse.[24] A Greenwich magistrate hearing a case for a separation order in 1912 declared himself to be unimpressed with the woman's evidence. He considered the husband 'a rough diamond' but concluded that 'the best punishment he could inflict was that they should continue to live together'. A few months later a magistrate in Lambeth rejected a similar case, finding no evidence of 'persistent cruelty', and showed sympathy for the husband's claim that the wife was always 'nagging'.[25] Since the violence was generally in private, there might be a problem in finding witnesses for the prosecution. In January 1926 Sarah Ward applied to magistrates in Chesterfield for a maintenance order against her husband of twenty years. He had, she complained, recently taken to coming home drunk, dragging her along the floor and beating her with his fists. As a local newspaper explained, however, she had no witnesses 'and the magistrates had no alternative but to dismiss the case'.[26] There was also the problem of emotional coercion and terrorism that always drew back at the point of physical assault. This form of abuse might be terrifying, but it left no physical mark and it was not something easily addressed by the law.[27]

Fun may have portrayed a gallant policeman stepping between the wife and the 'wife-kicker', but others were more critical. A journalist in mid nineteenth-century Liverpool, for example, feared that 'police officers think a husband has a prescriptive right to beat his wife as often as he likes, so long as he does not actually break her limbs or knock her brains out'.[28] The law, however, did not make dealing with domestic violence easy for the police. Whether or not they shared the opinions of Superintendent Wyborn, police officers were reluctant to cross the threshold into the privacy of domestic space even when there was evidence of violence. The fourteenth edition of Sir Howard Vincent's *The Police Code*, published in 1907, instructed officers under the heading 'Husband and Wife':

> The Police should not interfere in domestic quarrels unless there is a ground to fear that actual violence is imminent. If the parties are creating an obstruction, or attracting a crowd of persons, they should be cautioned before the law is enforced.[29]

No clear guidance was given on how a constable was supposed to assess whether 'actual violence' was 'imminent'. At the same time, the suggestion that an obstruction might be created or a crowd attracted implies a public confrontation, whereas domestic violence, by definition, takes

place in a private, domestic sphere. Policemen could not enter such a
private space without a warrant or a very good reason. By 1924 the code
had been revised, though not much more helpfully, to read simply: 'The
Police should not interfere in domestic quarrels, unless there is reason
to fear that violence is likely to result.' At the same time the constable
was urged in the introduction to the code to

> *Beware of being over-zealous or meddlesome.* These are dangerous faults. A
> meddlesome constable who interferes unnecessarily upon every trifling
> occasion stirs up ill-feeling against the force and does more harm than
> good.[30]

Edward Lyscom joined the Metropolitan Police in 1935. His memoirs
give an indication of how some police officers interpreted these regulations and fitted them into their own perceptions of husband and wife,
and male and female relations. As a young constable he was unworried
by a dispute in the early hours of the morning when a husband 'belted
his wife with a frying pan. She wanted him arrested and was not too
satisfied when I referred her to the local court to take out a summons
for "common assault" should she so desire.'[31] A few months later he had
to deal with a fight between a husband and wife in the back of a parked
taxi. He pulled the husband off the wife only to find himself attacked by
both husband and wife; the latter bit his finger. The commotion brought
the arrival of another constable and a sergeant. The latter instructed
Lyscom to let the parties go home, while Lyscom, his pride and his finger
hurt, wanted to prosecute them for assaulting him in the execution of
his duty. 'Look, boy,' he recalled the sergeant saying,

> you may be developing into a useful copper, but you haven't learned about
> women. She does not mind a belting from her old man, but she won't stand
> for a copper pinching him for it. Now take my tip, take their names and for-
> get about your bloody finger.[32]

A rather different incident witnessed by Lyscom, in which a young
widow with two young children was assaulted by her younger brother,
met a different police response. The assailant, who was lodging with his
sister at the time, was immersed several times in a bath of cold water by
a burly, outraged constable. The constable then gave the bedraggled
brother a fierce warning and a lecture on good behaviour.[33]

Overall the evidence about domestic violence in nineteenth- and twentieth-century England suggests a continuing gap between a growing body of legislation designed to assist and to protect women and the fact that widespread violence continued to be prevalent and unpoliced. In this respect, if the English do not appear to have been any worse than their continental neighbours or their North American cousins, they do not appear to have been any better.[34]

Rape and sexual assault, again offences that were and are generally feared as most likely to be committed by a stranger, could also be committed within the family. Marital rape was not something that the law recognised, though, at least from the beginning of the twentieth century, feminist groups were drawing attention to it by their criticism of persistent male demands for conjugal rights.[35] The incidence of such assaults, and of others elsewhere within the family, is impossible to gauge. Many such incidents never reached the courts, and when they did there could be a problem in disentangling contradictory evidence. The Bedfordshire magistrate S. H. Whitbread kept a notebook briefly describing the evidence from some of the cases that he heard in the decade before the First World War. In April 1910 Thomas Pritchett came before him, following an accusation by Pritchett's daughter Lillian that he had made rude suggestions and put his hand up her skirt. Lillian's story was supported by her two sisters and three brothers. Pritchett admitted that his wife had got into debt, and that he had 'smacked her on the head', but he insisted that the accusation by his daughters was part of a conspiracy to get their mother back now that she had gone off with a Mrs Hardy. The court accepted his story and he was acquitted.[36]

There was also the problem of popular perceptions of male and female that could confound the fairness of a trial. The male, it was believed, had a strong, often uncontrollable sexual drive. Any woman who was supposed to have teased a man and led him on made her assailant the victim of both her own stupidity and her failure to behave in accordance with the stereotypical norm of womanhood. Even the social environment could be called upon to alleviate a man's fault. At the West Riding quarter sessions in January 1926, for example, a fifty-five-year-old labourer, Thomas Bembridge, was found guilty of assaulting his daughter-in-law. Bembridge's son and daughter-in-law, with their child, lived with him. The *Sheffield Mail* reported that the jury recommended mercy 'on the grounds that the housing conditions were such as were likely to lead to temptation, the man having to pass through the married couple's bedroom to get to his own'. The magistrates were impressed by this recommendation and by the fact that the convicted man had no previous convictions. As a consequence, they did not inflict the maximum penalty, of two years' imprisonment, but sentenced Bembridge to six months with hard labour.[37]

The crowded living conditions of the poorest members of the working class were feared by many Victorians to foster incest. There is evidence that such fears were greatly exaggerated; nevertheless, there were fathers and stepfathers who forced themselves on daughters and stepdaughters. The statistics of prosecution for incest are no guide to the scale of the problem. Embarrassment and the good name of the family must have been sufficient to stifle charges in many instances. An array of family strategies was also deployed, such as moving the girl to the house of another family member, of a friend or of a neighbour. Community sanctions against an assailant might also be deployed before any resort to the law. When the police and the courts did become involved it appears usually to have been because the man in question had a history of drinking and violence towards his family, and was considered by the family and the community to be too brutal for other sanctions.[38]

The scale of violent assaults on children without any sexual content is also impossible to assess. Assailants were of both sexes. Research into crime in Victorian Kent has shown that here, at least, violent assault was one of the few crimes for which women were represented among the accused in proportion to their numbers in the population. Well into the twentieth century, it was generally accepted that parents had the right to discipline their children with a degree of physical chastisement. Some of the punishment inflicted was ferocious. Children were kicked, punched, beaten with belts, and struck with all manner of household goods used as weapons. A woman who, in the 1870s, beat her stepdaughter with a cat o' nine tails and a pair of tongs was informed in court that parents might inflict punishment with 'a lawful weapon but tongs were unlawful'.[39] Children were beaten for bedwetting, making mistakes in running errands, lying, swearing, stealing and failing to wash properly. Again there was a problem for the police about crossing into domestic space, since a warning from the police to an abusive parent might be sufficient to provoke new beatings and create a fear of making further complaints.[40] Most police forces, like school boards and parochial charities, appear to have passed evidence of serious abuse to child protection societies such as the NSPCC.[41] Many communities also recognised a line of limitation beyond which the degree of punishment should not go. Parents and step parents who crossed that line could face harsher punishment from their community than from the courts. At the same time, if the community, or powerful voices within the community, considered that an individual had given false evidence to the police or had contributed to an unfair court conviction, then uncomfortable gossip, shaming demonstrations or violent abuse and assault could be directed at the informant or witness.[42]

By the last third of the nineteenth century the brutal assailant of children, like the wife-beater, was generally perceived to be a member of the roughest element of the working class. This was not the case in reality. Robert Roberts recalled that in the working-class districts of Edwardian Salford:

> Parents of the most respectable and conformist families were the staunchest upholders of 'discipline', though adults whose standing was suspect or who had in any way transgressed against accepted conduct would often brag about the severity of the chastisement meted out to their erring young, in an effort to restore their tarnished prestige.

He noted also that ex-servicemen often had a reputation for administering severe beatings to their children and he considered that the NSPCC had little impact on the overall problem.[43] The voluntary NSPCC itself stressed its preventative role rather than the instances in which it arranged for the prosecution of offenders. The society declared that its intention was to leave families intact, as far as possible, and to rekindle the natural instincts that humans shared with animals in nurturing children. The cases investigated by the society that could be classified as violent cruelty fell from 45 per cent in 1888–89 to only 7.3 per cent in the year before the First World War. The society's supporters considered this to be an indication of their success in producing a reformation in the bringing up and treatment of children. Yet it is also the case that it was often probably much easier for the society's inspectors and the supporters to expose and explain neglect and fecklessness than to expose and explain parents who violently attacked their children.[44]

Some children died as a result of assaults by mother, father or both parents, but the most vulnerable children were always infants under the age of one year. Probably some of these were killed accidentally by drunk or short-tempered parents because of their crying. But others were killed by their mothers shortly after birth in depression, or in despair and desperation in the hope that the mother might maintain her good name. From the eighteenth century there had been a reluctance on the part of the all-male juries and judges to convict women of infanticide, especially when they faced the prospect of execution. There was also reluctance on the part of police and coroners to investigate dead infants. Tiny bodies were found annually in their hundreds in Victorian London. The work of energetic and determined coroners like Edwin Lankester, appointed as coroner to Middlesex in 1862, drew attention to this appalling situation by insisting on following up many more cases than had been usual. Lankester believed that there were some thousand child murders a year in England and Wales; and this was at a time when the *Judicial Statistics* gave an annual homicide rate, a rate covering both murder and manslaughter, of between 350 and 400 individuals in total.[45] In many instances the failure to follow up the discovery of a baby's or a small child's body was probably because of the lack of leads. In 1873 Frederick Lowndes, a Liverpool police surgeon, explained:

> In all the cases I have had brought to my notice there has been literally no clue by which the police could trace the crime: generally the body has been found wrapped in a rag or piece of sacking; often naked; never in any properly made garment ... Most usually they are found at night or early in the morning, by scavengers, policemen, etc.; more rarely when deposited in fields or pits they are discovered in the daytime by children at play, or labouring men on their way to work. The localities, also, show that all calculations have been made for preserving secrecy, being generally those parts of town which are badly lighted; or, if thoroughfares, those least frequented by passers-by in the night time ...[46]

The cost of autopsies and medical witnesses also militated against the investigation into these deaths. The fees paid in both instances were small and made it unlikely that any of the few experts in pathology were ever used in these cases. Moreover the vagueness of the law about the circumstances in which coroners were required to hold inquests, and the control of local authorities over the award of costs submitted for payment by coroners, tended to limit the number of investigations. Improvements resulting from legislation, such as the Infant Life Protection Act of 1872, from stricter bureaucratic procedures introduced by, for example, the Registrar General, and from a greater awareness of birth control methods in the early twentieth century, all contributed to a decline in the incidence of infanticide. These problems were not unique to England. Infanticide was a well known, and rarely solved, offence in French cities and in the French countryside.[47] Similarly baby farmers, who periodically scandalised Victorian England when they were exposed for taking on the care of children often simply to dispatch them from the world, had their counterparts elsewhere in Europe, in the *Engelmacherinnen* (angel-makers) of Hamburg.[48] Yet the dark figure of infant deaths points, tangentially, to the question of the overall murder rate in England and hence to the exceptionality of the English as, essentially, a non-violent people.

The *Judicial Statistics*, as has been emphasised earlier, are no guide to the level of crime. Recategorisation, periodic clampdowns and panics distorted the pattern presented in the statistics. Murder, however, has been generally considered to be rather different from other crimes and the overall pattern of criminality. Historians and criminologists have long regarded murder as the crime where the statistics are probably the closest to the incidence of the offence. They have also noted that, contrary to much popular opinion and fear about the 'criminal' as 'murderer', a very high percentage of killings have always involved killers and victims who knew each other, being often related by blood or, more likely, by marriage. A recent assessment, however, has challenged the orthodoxy that the murder statistics are more reliable than any other crime figures. Arguably the real reason that the numbers prosecuted for murder from 1880 to the mid 1960s were limited to an average of around 150 a year was tight budgetary control. This control, it has been suggested, limited the facility for open-ended investigations and prosecutions, not only among coroners but also among the police.[49] The financial restrictions on coroners' investigations have already been noted, and concerns about the fallibility of coroners' inquests continued well into the late twentieth century. Quite how far similar restrictions may have limited police investigations into the deaths of adults remains a matter for debate, and there is no clear evidence of mysterious deaths, at least involving adults, being checked because of a shortage of money for the investigation.[50] Yet whether these new suggestions are accepted or not, the sheer scale of infanticide, and the deaths of a smaller number of older children that appear to have been allowed to slip through the coroners' investigations, provides a significant challenge to any general view of the non-violent English that is based on murder statistics.

There could also be violence between families. Sometimes it is difficult to use the fragmentary evidence to piece together a violent incident. At Caddington near Luton, for example, in August 1910 there was an incident involving members of the Bullman and Day families, men, women and children. There were six charges and counter-charges of assault heard at petty sessions and in the local children's court. Half of the charges were then withdrawn and the others were dismissed by the magistrates, with the requirement that the complainant in each case pay 7s. 6d. costs.[51] Even given the fragmentary nature of much of the evidence, it is clear that there were families with a reputation for violence who occasionally conducted feuds. In inter-war London the Phillips and the White families fought savage battles in and around the Caledonian Road. In nearby Campbell Bunk members of the Hume family were viciously attacked on several occasions by at least two members of the Penton family; the Humes eventually left the district. Such families urged their children to stand up for themselves and took a pride in the toughness of their children, encouraging them to fight where the neighbours could see.[52]

Everyone knew about violence in the family and violent families. It was hardly possible to pick up a local newspaper without seeing some reference to such violence at least in the columns reporting on the local courts. Yet this was never perceived as something that created a problem for the concept of the gentle, non-violent English. It was more comfortable to explain such violence as something committed by the residuum, the 'roughs' whom many respectable Victorians deemed not yet ready for assimilation into the political nation. Even after the vote had been extended to all males in the aftermath of the First World War, it was still more comfortable to continue to demonise the wife- and child-beater as someone from the lowest sections of the working class. This is not something that can be written off simply as hypocritical. It was interwoven with an understanding of family, and of reciprocal gender roles, that were, for the most part, strongly and sincerely held, however poorly they fit with the understanding that emerged in the later decades of the twentieth century. The 'rough' from the working class was considered as one manifestation of the 'other' that helped to define genuine English gentleness. Foreigners could be similarly perceived, and foreigners, even if not necessarily violent themselves, could, through their behaviour, propel the respectable, chivalrous Englishman into 'untypical', but ultimately 'necessary', violent action.

5

Foreign Passions, English Laws

At about 7.30 a.m. on 14 August 1917 Lieutenant Douglas Malcolm of the Royal Artillery, on leave from active duty in France, entered the boarding-house room of Anton Baumberg, also known as the Count de Borch, and shot him four times – twice in the chest, once in the front of his neck and once in the temple. Malcolm then coolly walked into the street and gave himself up to a police constable. He handed over his revolver, having first ensured that he had put on the safety-catch. Detective Sergeant Alfred Henry recalled that, shortly before appearing in front of a magistrate, Malcolm confessed:

> Oh! well, it's all over now. I went to give him a good thrashing with the whip. I gave him one before, but he is such a coward. I have done all I can to keep him away from my wife and her from him. He is a white-slave trafficker and a spy. Scotland Yard knows all about him. I have called there. You can imagine how I felt when I saw the coward who was trying to get my wife to go away with him, and me out in France helpless to defend her honour. Can you wonder at what I did on the impulse of the moment, when I saw the cur before me who was luring my wife to dishonour?[1]

In just over a month, the facts of the case were put before two English juries. First, a coroner's jury enquired into the facts surrounding Baumberg's death; and then an Old Bailey jury heard a case of murder. The inquest jury brought in a verdict of 'justifiable homicide'. The Old Bailey jury followed this up by acquitting Malcolm of murder. The portrayal of Lieutenant Malcolm and Anton Baumberg in the press and in the trial presents a vivid example of the construction of the outraged English gentleman and the outrageous foreign 'other'. Malcolm did not give evidence in person in either court. His statement to the police was read out, together with his comment on being charged with murder: 'Very well: I did it for my honour.' The final phrase became a headline for the popular press. Several of Malcolm's letters were read to both courts. He expressed devotion to his wife, commitment to God, and fury at the way that Baumberg had led his wife astray. He warned Baumberg never to speak to, or even to see, his wife again; otherwise, 'wherever I am I will get leave and hunt you out and give you such a sound thrashing that even your own mother will not know you again'. He challenged Baumberg to a duel, giving him the choice of pistols or swords; but received no reply. He insisted that all reports about his wife's infidelity with Baumberg were 'absolutely false'. On the morning of the shooting he wrote a letter to his wife explaining:

> I am going to thrash him until he is unrecognizable. I may shoot him if he has got a gun. I expect he has, as he is too much of a coward to stand a thrashing ... I swear to you that I love you more than any man ever loved a woman before, and if there is any wrong in me it is because I love you too much. You are a brave woman. You are noble, honourable, and an upright, with what a beautiful soul. I believe in God, I said yesterday I did not, but I do. I do, and I thank him from the bottom of my heart for having sent me over in time to save you from the devil incarnate. Your honour is saved. Thank God, oh, thank God ...[2]

The defence counsel acting for Malcolm portrayed him as a shining example of English manhood. It was stressed that he was a member of a successful business, not a soldier by profession, but that he had volunteered on the outbreak of war. His elder brother was the colonel 'who led the London Scottish in their glorious charge'. A witness, Henry St John Oliver, the secretary of the Junior Conservative Club to whom Malcolm had gone seeking Baumberg's address, told the Old Bailey court that 'from first to last his bearing was that of a man'. Sir John Simon, leading for the defence, made reference to Malcolm's 'chivalrous heart', and stressed that he had only been prevented from the duty of taking his wife well away from Baumberg 'by the call of the only other duty he would recognise'. R. D. Muir, who led for the prosecution, recognised that 'a man would be less than human if he did not sympathise with all his manhood for a man like the prisoner trying to defend his wife against a scoundrel'. Two of the popular newspapers, the *Daily Mirror* and the *Daily Sketch*, described the climax of the trial in identical words. These might have been taken from a popular novel of the time describing an idealised, but wrongly accused, English gentleman whose fate had been left to an English jury:

> Malcolm stood impassive throughout. When the foreman announced the verdict a fleeting smile passed over his face and he glanced up at the warder who stood at his side. Then he resumed his grave demeanour, only occasionally raising his eyes to look at the cheering people around.[3]

No one appears to have picked up on the similarity between Count de Borch and 'debauch', but it was hardly needed. Even though Dorothy Malcolm had asked her husband for a divorce and appeared fully prepared to run away with Baumberg, throughout the proceedings it was Baumberg who was portrayed as the villain. He was an illegitimate Jew from Russian Poland. The short-hand notes of an interview conducted at Scotland Yard in March 1917 were first read out in the coroner's court. Baumberg denied calling himself 'Count', though he admitted that this was the term by which friends and intimates knew him. He also admitted living in London and Bournemouth with a woman known as 'the Countess'. Stories circulated, and were stated in both courts, of the Countess having been arrested and shot as a spy by the French. Lieutenant Malcolm's claims that Baumberg was a White Slave trafficker and a spy were also reported, with no corroborating evidence. Detective Sergeant Alexander McHattie told the Old Bailey that he thought Baumberg 'a bad character'. He was about six feet tall, broad-chested, but not athletic. 'He had not much of a leg on him', explained McHattie, 'it was more like a woman's – soft. (Laughter.) He was not muscular.'[4] Nor was he prepared to fight with his fists. When Lieutenant Malcolm first caught his wife with Baumberg, at a cottage in Hampshire, he 'thrashed' him and, according to Muir, the prosecuting counsel, Baumberg took it 'without any attempt to retaliate'. Baumberg subsequently bought a revolver to protect himself from Malcolm, and the defence insisted that it was for this reason that Malcolm had taken his own revolver on the morning of the killing, as well as a riding whip with which to administer a thrashing. The defence was that Malcolm was compelled to use his own revolver since Baumberg was intent on using his weapon. But the defence also played on Baumberg's origins. Sir John Simon used the terms 'Russian nobleman' and 'count' with clear derogatory intent. The *Daily Mirror* described how Simon's 'cutting references to "this cur" or "blackguard" were accompanied by a curl of the lip and a motion with his hand significant of disdain'.[5] The *Daily Sketch* quoted him as declaring:

> Baumberg was one of those species of human refuse carried along in the tide of great cities, living no one knew how, sleeping in cheap lodgings, and carrying on an existence with the help of such women as he had for acquaintances. It was he who threw a black, evil, ugly shadow across Malcolm's house.[6]

In his summing up the judge, Mr Justice McCardie, was at pains to stress that, even though a man was not an Englishman, 'the moment he sets foot on British soil he falls within the King's peace and the shackles of foreign nationality do not prevent him from asking that he shall be protected by the ordinary rules of British justice'. He also stressed under British justice a man could not compel his wife to do anything – 'he cannot imprison her; he cannot chastise her'. The 'unwritten law' by which a man might take chastisement into his own hands in matters like Baumberg's seduction of Dorothy Malcolm did not exist within English law. *The Times* took up the issue in a leader. 'No British jury takes cognizance of the *crime passionnel.*' While the trial and the verdict were 'unusual', the *Times* believed that 'it will be a source of satisfaction that throughout the proceedings no claim was made in favour of any novel development of our criminal law, and no countenance was given to any doctrines which would prejudice and confuse the administration of justice'.[7]

In the Malcolm case all of the violence was committed by an English gentleman. The victim did not resist his thrashing, and while the drawer containing his gun may have been open at the murder scene, the gun was still in its case and there was no clear evidence that he had gone for it in any struggle. Yet Lieutenant Malcolm, and his wife, were portrayed as the victims of a foreign scoundrel. 'Who was the victim?' asked a headline in the *Daily Sketch* reporting the charge of murder against Malcolm.[8] (It has already been noted how Dr Crippen was increasingly portrayed as the victim of his selfish, spendthrift wife.)[9] The portrayal of the chivalrous Malcolm, driven to the end of his tether and thus to violent behaviour, is one of the more extreme examples of violence by Englishmen being portrayed as something forced upon them by the behaviour of foreigners. The situation was also aggravated by the fact that Britain was at war, a time when the threat from the alien other, against whom the national community was defined, appeared greatest.

During the eighteenth century the Freeborn Englishman was defiantly Protestant. He defined himself particularly in contrast to the unfortunate foreigners who lived under the twin tyranny of Catholicism and the rule of absolutist monarchs who employed arbitrary laws and standing armies. Foreigners, both visitors and migrants, often met hostility in London and were commonly and indiscriminately labelled as 'French'. The French were the principal enemies in the wars of the eighteenth century, rivals in trade, in systems of government and in religion. Yet, towards the end of the century, and in spite of the duration and ferocity of the Revolutionary and Napoleonic Wars, the open hostility and aggression appears to have largely disappeared.[10] Hostility to Catholics during the eighteenth century brought about the Gordon Riots of 1780. This, the most serious, violent and prolonged disorder in eighteenth-century London, was provoked by the government's attempt to soften the laws against Catholics.

The Irish were present in England in significant numbers during the eighteenth century. Irish harvesting gangs provoked the ire of English agricultural labourers. Religion may have given an added edge to their confrontations, but, by the end of the century the Irish were reasonably well integrated into the host community. Irish districts were not singled out for attack during the Gordon Riots and Irishmen made up a disproportionate number of the British military during the Revolutionary and Napoleonic Wars; the Duke of Wellington commented that religious divisions were irrelevant within his army. The Irish rebellions of 1798 and 1803, however, created suspicions and led to the creation also of Orange Lodges in England that drew their membership from loyal civilians and from military veterans, many of whom had experience of the troubles in Ireland. The lodges were suspended temporarily in 1825 and permanently in 1836, but they helped to foster anti-Irish and anti-Catholic sentiments, especially in the burgeoning industrial districts of the north.[11] This, together with the influx of Irish immigrants in the wake of the terrible famine of 1846, helped to fuel the fierce and violent Protestantism and anti-Catholicism that resurfaced as a significant element of popular Englishness in the mid nineteenth century. These elements also laid the foundations for the vicious sectarianism that characterised Liverpool, in particular but not uniquely, in the nineteenth century.[12]

English supporters of the aggressive anti-Catholic lecturer William Murphy were as much at fault as the Irish Catholics who attacked them for the violence that surrounded Murphy's lectures in the 1860s and early 1870s. The fighting in Hyde Park on successive Sundays during September and October 1862 involving pro-papal Irish and anti-papal supporters of the Italian Risorgimento hero Giuseppe Garibaldi – supporters who included Englishmen, radical Italians and off-duty soldiers from the Brigade of Guards – similarly cannot be blamed on one side or the other.[13] Yet the Irish districts of English towns and cities were commonly stigmatised as violent and dangerous and singled out for special surveillance by the local police. Surveillance and stigma continued to the end of the century in some districts even when many of the immigrants had been succeeded by their children and grandchildren. The Metropolitan Police spoke to Charles Booth's social investigators of 'Irish cockneys'. Inspector Carter considered a block of streets in Bromley and Bow to be 'worse than almost any district in London ... This block sends more police to hospital than any other in London. [The] men are not human, they are wild beasts.' According to Constable Clyne, taking an investigator around 'the Dust Hole' in and around Plumstead Road:

> No law runs in these streets. The priest is powerless and seldom seen. The police only come when there is a bad row and they are summoned. No man would go alone. When called he waits for at least one other.

Inspector Reid in Whitechapel believed, however, that, while the Cockney Irish in his district were 'still rough', they were 'getting better'.[14]

Local newspapers made much of 'riots' and 'rows' by the 'sons' and 'daughters of Erin' in these districts, behaviour which, the *Chester Chronicle* declared in 1850, was 'disgraceful to any civilized country'. William Murphy's death in Birmingham in 1872 was linked to a beating that he had received from Irish Catholics at Whitehaven during the previous year. According to the editor of the *Belfast News*, quoted with apparent sympathy by the *Whitehaven Chronicle*, if people had not known where Murphy had been assaulted, they 'might have imagined that the outrage had been committed by Kaffirs or Maoris, or some other savage tribe'.[15] The identification of the Irish with violence received a new impetus from the Fenian bombings in the late 1860s and early 1880s. But even before the first bomb exploded, as rumours of Irish American Fenians seeking to cause insurrection circulated, *The Times* published a leader contrasting English politics with those of the Fenians, and also those of continental Europeans.

> Over and over again have we seen in foreign papers the expressive taunt that if England can do nothing else she knows how to suppress a rebellion ... The truth is that we hate rebellion, not only as an offence against law or natural duty, but as a breach of the law of that great game of politics it is our boast to be always playing. We decide our differences by argument, by mutual compromise, by the play of parties, by all the arts of peace, and when men betake themselves to conspiracy and bloodshed we think it foul play. They have all the chances and opportunities that we have, but if they find themselves beaten, they overturn the tables, put out the lights, and make a row. Thus a rebel in this country is not the romantic personage that we imagine in continental politics; he is a mere robber and ruffian.[16]

After the Fenian bombing campaigns, and until the end of the First World War and the creation of the Irish Free State, indiscriminate and lethal violence deployed on mainland Britain for political ends was always assumed to be the fault of an alien 'other', the Irish or some other group. The mob violence against Catholics and Irish had largely faded out by the late Victorian period. Yet violence, intimidation and discrimination remained a feature of the way that some English people treated the Irish in England. This violence did not often take account of any notion of the English idea of the fair fight and, at the same time, the accusations continued of the Irish immigrant being particularly violent.[17] Finally, although the etymology of 'hooligan' is unclear, the Irish flavour and sound of the word that entered the vocabulary at the close of the nineteenth century suited well with prejudices that considered violent behaviour by young men to be 'un-English'.[18]

The Irish were the most significant non-English group in English towns and cities during the eighteenth and nineteenth centuries, but other recognisable groups also experienced hostility. Such groups were not necessarily non-English. The native-born enthusiasts of the

Salvation Army, who employed elements of working-class culture such as songs and dancing to further their cause, could be jeered and pelted at work, and assaulted when they assembled outside pubs or marched in the streets. The Salvationists were described as a 'new papacy'. Their behaviour was labelled un-English and a threat to the national character. Their founder and general, William Booth, was also labelled as a Jew, thus building on an anti-Semitic as well as the anti-papal tradition.[19]

Anti-Semitism was apparent in eighteenth-century London but, along with the hostility towards other foreigners, the more extreme forms of hostility towards Jews appear to have subsided by the beginning of the nineteenth century. It is possible that the success of several prominent Jewish pugilists contributed to this decline though, as has already been noted, there appears to have been a general lessening of public hostility towards foreigners as the Hanoverian period drew to a close.[20] Towards the end of the nineteenth century some English cities experienced a significant influx of Jewish refugees from the Russian Empire. These new Jewish communities, and other Russian immigrants, did not acquire the stigma of their Irish counterparts. The police had difficulty in penetrating their communities, but, generally speaking, the Jewish immigrants at the close of the century did not get drunk in English pubs and did not assault the police.[21] The Jews were not particularly the objects of English crowd violence and much of the most blatant anti-Semitism came from commentators and writers who maintained that Jewish immigration was one of the elements undermining the English way of life. There was hostility among some sections of the working class who feared that Jews were taking their jobs and taking over whole streets. Such concerns were aggravated by the belief that the murders of Jack the Ripper were committed by a Jew. The murders were, declared the *Daily News*, 'foreign to the English style in crime', and the old story was revived that Jewish men ritually killed any gentile woman with whom they had enjoyed sexual relations so as to purify themselves. The police discovered a chalk inscription close to the body of one of the Ripper's victims: 'The Jews shall not be blamed for nothing.' Sections of the press assumed that the Ripper himself had written it. Fearful that it would provoke violence against the Jews, the Commissioner of the Metropolitan Police had it removed – before it could be fully investigated.[22] But, in general, it was more mundane anxieties and prejudices that provoked hostility, and a steady undercurrent of 'Jew-baiting' which might result in acts of violence between individuals.[23]

It was, however, the extremist politics of the few that prompted the most anxiety. This was especially the case when the extremism exploded into gun crime in London shortly before the First World War. In the wake of the Tottenham Outrage of January 1909, in which a policeman and a ten-year-old boy were shot and killed during a violent confrontation involving two members of a Russian revolutionary group, *The Times* expressed relief that 'this type of crime is ... not indigenous'. It was concerned, however, that the 'evil example is potent and the permitted presence in our midst of the worst types of foreign criminality' might encourage 'the low organisation of the [native] criminal brain' to use revolvers when they committed crimes. Nearly two years later, after the Houndsditch shootings, *The Times* reported:

> A consensus of opinion among those who know the Lithuanian immigrants in the East End of London is that many are arrant cowards, as well as most ignorant and vicious. They take no chances; and think very lightly of making away with any one who is likely to betray them.

An article in a parallel column on 'The Alien Immigrant: His "Habitat" and Character', noted that most of these aliens were hard-working and drank only moderately. But they were dirty and gambled, and there were some unsavoury characters whose women worked nightly as prostitutes in the West End, and who had themselves been responsible for the recent brutal murder of a sailor.[24] A similar, but rather more unpleasant, series of articles appeared in *The Standard*. These trusted that 'the bark of the rifles in the Sidney Street battle' had finally alerted to the public to the danger of 'alien immigration'. The articles asserted that 'the alien Jew' was deeply involved in criminality, dishonesty and vice. 'He can never become an Englishman or, indeed, a good English citizen, because he will never be able to share our ideals, to adopt our code of morals, or our standard of honour.'[25] When war came in 1914, Jewish districts were targeted in several cities amid stories that young Jewish men were avoiding service in the armed forces and even assaulting servicemen at home recovering from their wounds.[26]

Some foreigners did engage in notorious and well-publicised criminal activities. Brilliant Chang, deported in 1925, was the best known and

probably the most successful drug dealer in London during and immediately after the First World War. Eddie Manning, a Jamaican-born
jazz-drummer, was Chang's contemporary and, during the 1920s,
received a string of convictions for shootings, the possession of drugs,
harbouring prostitutes and receiving. From the 1930s the five Messina
brothers, the offspring of a Sicilian father and Maltese mother, ran a vice
syndicate in London's Soho that never shirked from violence.[27] Men
who ought to have known better, together with the popular press, made
much of such individuals, suggesting a link between foreigness, violence
and criminality that was alien to English culture. Thus the readers of
Detective Inspector Herbert Fitch's autobiography were informed that
prostitutes were ultimately behind half of all crime and nearly all murders; moreover, Fitch declared, prostitution was largely managed by
'foreign bullies'.[28] The unconnected murders of three foreign pimps in
London's Soho over the space of ten years were, nevertheless, linked
together by the populist *John Bull*.

> To the men who pore over crime statistics at Scotland Yard, Soho is the place
> for its area has a worse record for blood and violence and for darker forms
> of vice than any other in Great Britain … Decent, hardworking, clean-living
> foreigners, as good as any Briton, living cheek by jowl with the scum of con-
> tinental gutters. And now the mixture is getting too strong for anybody's
> taste.[29]

It was similarly convenient to blame foreigners for the gang violence
that surrounded some bookmakers during the interwar years. Thus the
racing correspondent of *The Times*, commenting on the 'feud between
gangs of ruffians' at Alexandra Park in April 1921, identified the two sides
by origin as Italians and 'foreign Jews'.[30] But the Sabinis were born in
England, and the supposed 'real villain' of the family, Joseph, fought in
the British army during the First World War, was invalided out and
pensioned because of his wounds. The Sabinis fought against, but also
linked up with, Jewish bookmakers; their principal opponents were the
Brummagen Boys, the men surrounding Billy Kimber, a Birmingham
bookie. Arthur Harding, the East End gangster, spoke of the Sabinis
bringing some strong-arm support from Sicily, yet the presence of
Harding in the conflicts, in itself, points to a significant native English
presence among the combatants. The Sabinis, apparently, did not
understand Italian; however, the district within Clerkenwell in which

they lived preserved their filtered form of Italian customs. 'It was to them quite natural and reasonable to use a knife … when their passions were aroused', recalled a local stipendiary magistrate commenting on these customs.[31]

According to Superintendent Mulvaney, who commanded the Whitechapel division of the Metropolitan Police at the close of the nineteenth century, the mixed population in his district was not rough towards the police, but they knifed one another. 'Stabbing cases are fairly frequent in the foreign streets.'[32] Many English working men carried knives and used them at work during the nineteenth century, yet they do not appear to have drawn these knives often when involved in an argument or a fight.[33] Magistrates and judges criticised Europeans who brought 'their' forms of violence to England during the nineteenth century. In 1843, during a stabbing case heard at the Old Bailey involving two Italians, the Recorder of London 'warmly reprobated the un-English practice of using such a deadly weapon'.[34] The waterfronts of seaports were often rough places, and sailors commonly carried knives. When a foreign sailor appeared in a Victorian court charged with using a knife to kill or wound an opponent in a fight, the defence counsel might stress the accused's 'foreignness'. On conviction, such seamen might be told by the judge that he would not impose the maximum sentence on account of their being foreign and, presumably, not knowing any better.[35] During the Garibaldi riots concerns were expressed that both the Italian and Irish combatants, but not the English, were making free use of their knives. Only one Italian, however, was apprehended, convicted and imprisoned.[36]

The English press enjoyed praising English institutions at the expense of continental neighbours who had not quite got things right or who appeared, occasionally, to be slipping backwards. Thus the 'special correspondent' of *The Times* in Florence explained that the Italians, 'enamoured of English institutions', had established a jury system, but it did not work as it might since they drew their model from the French variant. Moreover, unified, liberal Italy remained a land of violent brigands, violent police and fearsome homicides, but through 'false sentimentalism' its politicians had abolished capital punishment.[37] France was criticised for being little better. A multiple homicide in Paris at the beginning of 1885 led to *The Times* headline 'Lynch Law in Paris' just a few columns from its report of the trial of Madame Clovis-Hughes for shooting dead a private investigator who had already been imprisoned for defaming her. Her husband, a Radical deputy and the veteran of a duel, had congratulated her on her action. She had proudly proclaimed her premeditation. The jury acquitted her in what *The Times* described as 'a thoroughly immoral and deplorable verdict [that] exposed the law to derision'. The best thing now, the correspondent went on, was for the French to re-enact 'the code of the barbarian tribe from which [they] derive their name'.[38] In the case of Lieutenant Malcolm, of course, it was the virtue of the English legal system that it avoided the recognition of *crime passionnel*, though still coming up with a popular, if highly suspect, verdict.

In the inter-war years there was a new target for English criticism. The people of continental Europe still appeared to have strange ideas linking passion and crime, and they also had more violent politics. But the new threat was the example offered by the United States with its guns and gangsters, particularly as portrayed in the popular cinema. In the case of troopers Vanderberg and Kaye, described at the beginning of this book, the judge had warned that gangsterism and gun law were not English. It was also acknowledged that English gangsters, such as those involved in the turf wars in Sheffield, were not like those of Chicago. Nevertheless there was a need to 'trim their nails' rather than permit the popular cinema to encourage them.[39] Eighteenth- and nineteenth-century England had been relatively free of legislation regarding guns. If an individual could afford it, and wished to purchase a pistol, then there was little or nothing to impede him or her. As has already been described, a scare over the use of guns by burglars led to some arming of some police officers during the 1880s. In Liverpool publicans were known to keep firearms behind the counter, possibly to persuade difficult drunks to go home.[40] Even after the Firearms Act of 1920 restricted their availability and use, some English offenders continued to carry guns in the interwar years, yet English commentators could still claim that it was unusual and alien, and certainly not the commonplace represented in the popular films coming from America. But it was not just the use of firearms that fostered concern about the American other. A succession of commentators feared that English morality, and English youth, was being corrupted by the culture represented in Hollywood cinema. George Orwell described an unpleasant 'Americanised' culture leading 'the decline of the English murder' and a related declining moral atmosphere in the crime literature written for the popular market. The problem, as Orwell and others saw it, was that in American popular culture 'might' was deemed to be 'right'.[41] Orwell could only warn; others could censor.

During the inter-war period the assumption that violent behaviour by gangsters was 'American' permeated the British Board of Film Censors. The censors were, moreover, determined to prevent any controversial issues being presented to the mass working-class cinema audience unless these were set in some overseas setting. The comments of the two censors responsible for vetting scripts, Colonel J. C. Hanna and Miss N. Shortt, the daughter of a former Home Secretary and then President of the Board of Censors, are such as to suggest modern parodies of a crusty, retired army officer and a sheltered middle-class spinster. These two were concerned about attempts to replicate what they perceived as lurid American gangster story lines in a British setting. They opposed any sequences showing police officers carrying firearms and practising what they took to be American 'third degree' interrogations. American gangster films themselves created alarm. *The Public Enemy* (1931) was initially banned and *Scarface* (1932) was only permitted to be shown after major cuts. American social protest films critical of the penal system such as *I Am a Fugitive from a Chain Gang* (1932) and *Each Dawn I Die* (1938) were required to have written prefaces to the effect that such prison or penal systems could never exist in Britain.[42] This was in spite of the fact of the well-publicised Dartmoor Prison mutiny of January 1932 during which prisoners took control of the prison and were only suppressed by the deployment of prison officers carrying rifles loaded with buckshot and local police wielding batons, with two companies of infantry in reserve.[43] Concern about the American other influencing the cinema-going public slid into thinly veiled, and sometimes blatant anti-Semitism as commentators pointed to the presence of Jews among the makers of American films. R. G. Burnett and E. D. Martell, the journalist authors of *The Devil's Camera*, one of the most extreme of such complaints, were concerned that the national strength was being sapped by films that encouraged 'squandermania, promiscuity, crime and idleness'.[44] Concerns were raised again in the aftermath of the Second World War when a cycle of British-made gangster films, notably *Brighton Rock* (1947) and *No Orchids For Miss Blandish* (1948), perturbed cinema critics and politicians alike for their violence, squalor and American echoes.[45]

Throughout the period during which the English criticised their continental neighbours for their legal attitudes to crimes of passion and their violent behaviour, and their American cousins for their guns, gangsters and disagreeable culture, Britain was the centre of a massive empire. The English did not know and rarely met the indigenous peoples of their empire or peoples from the non-European world. Small clusters of Asian, African or Afro-Caribbean seamen might be found in the dock areas of the big seaports, but they were rarely to be found elsewhere. Such peoples were exotic alien 'others' who occasionally could be employed by the Victorians to contrast with the criminal classes of the rookeries and to provide parallels with, or labels for, forms of undesirable behaviour. The early Victorian description of street robbery as 'Thugee' is a case in point. The English, and the British as a whole, saw themselves as bringing civilisation and enlightenment to 'savage' and 'primitive' peoples. J. R. Seeley, for example, Regius Professor of History at Cambridge, confidently declared that liberty had been 'a leading characteristic of England as compared with continental countries' and that these ideas were being spread across the empire. The English had lifted the Hindu from the medieval to the modern world, replacing a cruel, rapacious and violent regime.[46] The use of violence in the creation of empire was glossed over; and the use of violence against rebellion was justified on the grounds of the continuing brutality, ignorance, primitive nature and thanklessness behaviour of the subject peoples. *The Times* declared the Indian Mutiny a 'treacherous revolt'.

> We have indeed been mild, merciful, and liberal rulers compared with the Mogul or the Persian; but we can be quite as energetic and firm on an emergency, and this is what we have to teach the dreamy and vapouring native, and are now teaching him.[47]

The tiny insurrection in Jamaica less than a decade later met with equal surprise and anger:

> Foolish and self-conceited as the negro may be, unscrupulous, wicked and reckless as his remote advisors may be, we cannot yet believe that either he

or they have ever conceived the possibility of defying British Sovereignty in the West Indies. If they have ever harboured this thought, it only shows how necessary it is to keep ever displayed before the eyes of barbarians the signs and symbols of civilized authority. The only motives of such credulity must have been the habitual lenity of the British Government and the rare appearance of British force.[48]

A week later, as stories of atrocities filtered across the Atlantic, the paper lamented that it appeared 'impossible to eradicate the original savageness of the African blood'.[49] There were atrocities on both sides in the Indian Mutiny, but the most sustained violence perpetrated during the Jamaican rebellion was that committed by the British. The initial riot had left eighteen dead and thirty-one wounded. The repression saw 439 men and women shot or executed following a court martial, some six hundred men and women flogged, and a thousand homes – mainly rough cottages – burned.

The English also believed their own rhetoric. The 'superior enlightenment' of an 'educated and civilising race' – the words are those of Seeley – could not be tarnished by copying the brutal behaviour of others. The reports of the repression prompted a backlash from liberal England: questions were asked in Parliament; a Royal Commission was appointed; and the possibility was mooted of prosecuting Edward Eyre, the Governor of Jamaica, for murder. In the event the commission praised Eyre for his prompt action in suppressing the trouble, but it criticised him for allowing excessive severity and for the summary trial and execution of one of the alleged ringleaders. Eyre lost his position.[50] General Reginald Dyer's order to fire on an unarmed crowd in Amritsar in April 1919, killing, according to the official figures, nearly four hundred and wounding more than twelve hundred, brought a similar response. Dyer was to speak of his action in the schoolroom terms of 'teaching a lesson' to naughty boys. There were those who insisted that the general's action had saved the empire; it followed hard on serious rioting and attacks on Europeans, and his apologists wrote of 'frenzied mobs' 'baying for blood'. The Morning Post raised over £26,000 in a public collection for him. But there were also those who condemned his actions and who, in the immediate aftermath of the First World War, feared that such behaviour smacked of the Prussian militarism that had so recently been defeated, and at such a high cost. The Hunter Committee that investigated the massacre was critical of Dyer, but it split on racial grounds with its Indian members issuing a much more critical minority report that, interestingly, referred to 'inhuman and un-British' behaviour and drew parallels with wartime atrocities by the German army.[51]

Belief that the empire was benign was based on assumptions that, in many instances, cause discomfort or condemnation in the modern world. Yet the belief, together with the assumption that the gentlemen who administered the empire were fair and restrained in the best English tradition, probably did have a moderating effect on behaviour. But racism, based on fear and suspicion of the other undoubtedly existed, and its manifestations could be found at the heart of the empire. In English seaports racism showed itself in occasional attacks on black seamen.[52] Some of the worst trouble occurred in the immediate aftermath of the First World War. Between January and August 1919 rioting swept through several of the largest seaports in Britain. The riots were principally directed at black seamen who were accused of taking the jobs of white Britons. The black seamen, who felt that they were being denied equality, rights and work in spite of their wartime efforts and commitment to the empire, responded in some instances with counter-violence. Lurking within the concerns over work and a prejudice against black people, there were also fears about miscegenation. A magistrate in South Wales was reported in the *Monmouthshire Evening Post* as stating that he 'could understand and sympathise with the feeling of the white men when they saw white women associating with black men, but the men had no right to take the law into their own hands'. Some of the reporting of the rioting came close to using this almost as absolution for the white men who had instigated the violence, and overwhelmingly the press reaction blamed the blacks as instigators of the riots. The response of the government was to encourage the repatriation of black seamen, though no allowance was provided for any white wife and family of a black man.[53]

Rioting and attacks on black and Asian people occurred spasmodically in the 1920s, but the most serious recurrence of race riots came in the aftermath of the Second World War as immigrants, particularly from the West Indies, entered the country with government encouragement to alleviate post-war labour shortages. There were serious riots directed against such immigrants in 1958 in Nottingham and in Notting Hill,

London. Responses to the trouble were often similar to those in 1919. The rioters were condemned, but their actions were also described as 'understandable'. Sections of the press blamed the government for permitting unrestricted immigration. So too did some MPs, notably Cyril Osborne, Conservative MP for Louth, and George Rogers, the Labour MP for North Kensington. Rogers described the violence as the legitimate response of the local community to undesirable elements in the black population. The answer, from this perspective, was immigration control; later, arguments were again made for repatriation.[54]

The story of Lieutenant Malcolm and Anton Baumberg is one of the most extreme examples of the way in which English commentators and the popular media have denied any equivalence between the violence of English people and violence committed by an alien 'other'. Even when the violence was largely one-sided, as in the case of Malcolm, Eyre, Dyer or the Notting Hill rioters, there was a temptation to excuse it on the grounds of extreme provocation or the need to check the unruly, uncivilised behaviour of the 'other'. Similarly in cases of extreme violence, as with Jack the Ripper or the use of firearms during the 1930s, it was tempting to blame an outsider for committing the act or the example of an alien culture for seducing the easily led. Violence that could be identified as the work of outsiders, such as the Fenian bombings or the anarchist outrages at the beginning of the century, served in turn to strengthen the idealised self-perception of the English. The English have not been alone in blaming outsiders and immigrants for crime and violence, though the desire to create and preserve a national role model characterised by restraint and gentility probably accentuated the contradictions recognised by a more critical and less confident age. Not that some of those who lived through individual violent events involving the 'other' did not themselves see contradictions. Governor Eyre and General Dyer were both investigated and both lost their positions, though they were not tried for murder as a few had hoped. Englishmen who attacked foreigners and who rioted against immigrants were brought to court, often convicted and punished. Yet there were still those among the elite, and those among the magistracy, who expressed understanding. The understanding of rioters, and who exactly participated in riots, presents another central issue in the exploration of violence and the English.

6

Violent Protest

At the beginning of the twentieth century Dunstable, a market town to the south of Bedfordshire, had a population of about eight thousand. The town was a centre for the manufacture of straw plait and bonnets, work that mainly involved women. A recent innovation was the manufacture of felt hats. There was also a large printing works, a brewery, a foundry and a chain works. Ernest Mowse was a family grocer, tea dealer and provision merchant with a shop at the north end of the high street. Around 10.30 p.m. on 10 August 1914, just under a week after the outbreak of the First World War, a crowd began to assemble outside Mowse's shop. Mowse had recently raised his prices, partly, perhaps, as some grocers explained to a local newspaper, as a way to check panic bulk buying because of the war and to ensure that regular customers were served;[1] partly, perhaps, because of the opportunity for profit offered by the war as people began panic buying. There had also been rumours in Dunstable: first, that Mowse had been heard to say that 'he could do without the trade of the Poorer Classes'; and, secondly, that he had visited the smaller shopkeepers with whom he did wholesale business and persuaded them to raise their prices also. After about half an hour, when the streetlights were extinguished, the crowd began singing patriotic songs such as 'Rule Britannia' and 'Three Cheers for the Red, White and Blue' and throwing stones at Mowse's shop. The shop window was broken, and so was a window upstairs, the shop's blinds were torn, and the paint and woodwork were damaged. Some pots of jam and the glass on a showcase of biscuits were broken. The small contingent of police in the town could do little. 'It was impossible to stop the stone throwing', reported Inspector Purser. 'All I could do with the four constables, was to prevent the shop from being looted, and Mr Mowse fetched out by the people.'[2]

Major S. J. Green, newly appointed Deputy Lieutenant of Bedfordshire

and commander of the Dunstable squadron of the Bedfordshire
Yeomanry Cavalry, drove up in his motor car. He urged the crowd to
disperse, then thanked them for their kindness towards him and his
men, who were preparing to set off for the war:

> Your Inspector of Police does not want to have any trouble with you fellows
> here, and I am going to ask you quietly to disperse. You know you can do
> no good here, and I ask every man who has got any respect for law and order
> to go quietly to his home.

The crowds cheered him as he drove off, but did not immediately disperse and men continued to mill around in front of Mowse's shop until
1.30 a.m. On the evening of 11 August, in spite of an announcement from
the mayor that rate-payers would have to pay for the damage caused by
such disorders, a crowd assembled at the town's main crossroads. The
street lamps were kept on. Police patrolled alongside borough magistrates. Another shop window was broken, but there was no further
damage.[3] The incident in Dunstable was one of several such disorders,
symptomatic of the anxieties about food and its cost on the outbreak of
the war.[4]

Until the growth of interest in 'history from below' in the late 1950s
and early 1960s, popular disorder was rarely an issue for historians of
England. Popular protest action was only really considered when it
focused on national issues, such as the Gordon Riots, or when it was
related to wider political issues, such as at the Peterloo Massacre and
during various Chartist demonstrations. Protest crowds tended to be
seen as deviant and dangerous, and there was often an implicit assumption that, unlike their continental European counterparts, the English
had increasingly ceased to participate in violent demonstrations.
T. A. Critchley's notion of the conquest of violence has already been
mentioned. Twenty years after Critchley's book Anthony Babington, a
historian and retired circuit court judge, could comment that, by the end
of the First World War, the 'British ... were essentially a law-abiding
people; they prided themselves that they had reached a stage of social
maturity in which disorders prompted by a lust for violence or a criminal impulse were relics of a past age'.[5] For Babington this British (or
English) pride was a reflection of a reality. Political violence will be discussed later.[6] The concern here is what can be termed protest violence,

what caused it, what was its extent, and how far it was overcome by 'social maturity' or anything else. The separate categorisation of 'protest violence' and 'political violence' is, in many respects, an artificial one. Much of the research since the early 1960s has emphasised this. The division used here is a rough and ready one. The intention is to differentiate between violent crowd activity motivated, on the one hand, by bread and butter issues, conditions at the workplace, wage rates and so on, and, on the other, by political principles and hostility to the principles of others. One further point of qualification is obvious but can still benefit from emphasis: while much of the theorising about and research into crowds has concentrated on riots or the crowd as deviant, there were also crowds that celebrated, commemorated and validated constitutional and civic structures throughout the eighteenth, nineteenth and twentieth centuries. These, like some of the rioting crowds, were fun to be with but were not violent or threatening to anyone.[7]

Most of the research into popular protest has explored the seventeenth, eighteenth and early nineteenth centuries. George Rudé's investigations of eighteenth-century crowds showed that even the notorious Gordon rioters who subjected London to a week of violence and terror in the summer of 1780 were not drawn from either the criminal classes or the very poorest sections of the working population. Among those tried for the riots whose occupations were recorded there were an apothecary, several small employers, shopkeepers and independent craftsmen; rather more than two thirds were wage-earners.[8] E. P. Thompson followed up Rudé's work with a seminal essay on the moral economy of the English crowd during the eighteenth century. Thompson argued that

> It is possible to detect in almost every eighteenth-century crowd action some legitimising notion. By the notion of legitimation I mean that the men and women in the crowd were informed by the belief that they were defending traditional rights or customs; and, in general, that they were supported by the wider consensus of the community. On occasion this popular consensus was endorsed by some measure of licence afforded by the authorities. More commonly, the consensus was so strong that it overrode motives of fear and deference.[9]

Thompson's main concern in this essay was the food riot which he showed to have been a complex, but generally highly disciplined, form of popular action. Crowds, often with women as the initiators of the action, entered markets when prices were high, and sold off necessary foodstuffs at what they considered to be fair prices. They also punished farmers, millers and bakers suspected of profiteering at the poor's expense. The crowds were motivated by beliefs in a customary right to food at a fair price and in the injustice of profiteering from the sale and resale of necessities. They appealed to Tudor and Stuart laws that suited their claims; and they put pressure on their social superiors to conciliate, arbitrate and ensure that food was available and fairly priced.

The term 'moral economy' itself is of uncertain origin. Thompson suspected that it came into use in the late eighteenth century, and he found it being used into the 1830s. This half century or so coincided with the time when the moral economy was coming under threat from the new political economy that stressed the importance of the free market and, particularly, of allowing freedom of trade in grain. In a riposte to his critics twenty years after the original essay, Thompson noted how the term that he had picked upon was increasingly being used in other contexts, especially with reference to peasant economies in the Third World. He urged that some redefinition was necessary if its use was to be extended, though he acknowledged its usefulness as an investigative tool in different contexts.[10] This chapter does not attempt a redefinition, but rather stresses how, while violent protest may have declined during the nineteenth century, echoes of Thompson's moral economy with some very broad legitimising notions continued within English society. The attack on Mowse's shop is a clear example, with a local community demonstrating its hostility to an alleged profiteer in foodstuffs. From the evidence available, however, the disorder in Dunstable lacked clear appeals to custom and tradition, and it lacked appeals to the gentry to arbitrate and conciliate, though in the singing of patriotic songs and with the cheers for Major Green the crowd was insisting on its essential loyalty. Something had happened over the previous century, but it seems unlikely that it can be explained by the ending of a lust for violence and criminal propensities. Such desires do not appear to have been much present in the kinds of riots discussed by Thompson in the first place.

Thompson's work has been both challenged and developed by others, but without a return to the old notions of riot being simply the work of

dregs from the slums and of 'criminals' joining in for the sake of plunder and rapine. Nicholas Rogers, in a study of the crisis years of 1756 and
1757 when food shortages combined with political dissatisfaction and
failure in a war with France, has argued that Thompson's perception of
plebeian–patrician polarity in food riots is too simple. In the riots of
these years the crowds were given at least tacit backing by towns that
issued instructions to their MPs and petitioned Parliament to impose
strict controls on food and curb the free market of grain. This was not
just self-serving, but drew on a rhetoric that saw profiting from the grain
supply as part of a deeper problem of political venality and self-interest
that appeared to be hampering the war effort.[11] In a study of riots in the
late eighteenth and early nineteenth centuries focused particularly on
Devon, John Bohstedt concluded that the sites of the classic, and most
successful, crowd actions during this period were medium-sized market
towns. Bohstedt argued that there was a 'protocol' of riot. The rioters
were not drawn from the poor but from artisans and labourers who,
while vulnerable in times of food shortages and high prices, aspired to
some respectability and who would have resented the label pauper. They
were bound by, and acted within, horizontal and vertical bonds of kin,
workplace and social patronage. In times of shortage they drew on these
links, on traditional tactics of behaviour and on calculations of how different magistrates would respond to that behaviour. They rioted in a
relatively restrained manner, avoiding provocative excesses in assaulting
people and destroying property, but acting in sufficiently forceful a
manner to bring their social superiors to an awareness of their immediate and pressing problems. Such rioting, in Bohstedt's estimation, did
not challenge power arrangements but acted within them; it was community politics. While this behaviour, however, was successful in
medium-sized towns where the bonds of community were strong and
clear, it tended to be much less restrained in sparsely populated rural
areas and in the burgeoning industrial cities.[12]

Rioting is a criminal offence that, during the eighteenth century, was
a felony punishable by death. When a members of a crowd fixed prices
in a market place with threats of violence, or scattered flour on the road-
side or in a canal to punish an individual whom they considered to be
a greedy miller, they were committing an act that the authorities might
choose to define and describe as riot. In one reading their 'impulse' may

have been 'criminal', and in any reading their behaviour was terrifying
to their victims. But the members of the crowd are not readily identifiable as members of a social group that regularly participated in
law-breaking, notably violent theft. What the recent research has drawn
attention to here is a system for bringing bread and butter problems to
the attention of social superiors who could do something about them,
and who often accepted that it was their social obligation to do something. At the same time there appear to have been specific contexts in
which this system worked best, where there was acknowledged space for
a community with a problem to make this manifest, and people with
power to acknowledge the manifestation. Much, however, could still
depend on individuals. Some magistrates had a reputation for being
approachable and showing a genuine concern for the poor, and others
appeared to be the opposite.

This kind of protest was not unique to England. The term *taxation
populaire* was used to describe crowds fixing grain prices in the markets
of eighteenth-century France. In 1775 Louis XV's new principal minister,
Turgot, sought to solve the problem of a poor harvest by insisting that
the rules of a free market be left to function. The result was widespread
rioting that became known as the Flour War, *la Guerre des Farines*. The
political agitation of the early months 1789 was widely aggravated by riots
over the price of grain that began in the spring and continued into the
summer.[13] But dearth and high prices have not always fostered riots. A
good example from the British Isles is the terrible Irish potato famine of
the mid 1840s that led to, perhaps, as many as a million deaths. The
starving Irish did not demonstrate. This was possibly simply because
they were too debilitated, but there were also other factors at work. It is
possible that, during the eighteenth century, there was the emergence of
a fledgling moral economy perspective among urban crowds. But by the
late eighteenth century rural protest in Ireland was becoming closely
entwined with sectarianism. Subsequently, in the turbulent economic
and political context of the early and mid nineteenth-century it became
dominated by secretive groups who gathered at night to coerce or to
attack specific individuals or their property. The landowning Anglican
ascendancy, unlike its English equivalent, was unable to exert much
authority over a largely Catholic peasantry, and the government in Westminster had created a paramilitary constabulary to impose and maintain

order. Thus in Ireland, in 1846, the space simply did not exist for moral economy protest and any meaningful response from a paternalist elite.[14]

The food riot declined in nineteenth-century England and a variety of elements contributed to this, none of which necessarily have much to do with either the 'conquest' of violence or 'social maturity'. Perhaps there was, increasingly, a broad acceptance of the market economy, but gradually, and more importantly, bread became less the main staple of life for the poor and there was a greater variety of foodstuffs available and affordable. Much might still depend on the attitude of individual magistrates. There were some who considered their summary courts to be places where the poor man might easily get justice, and there were some who were prepared to use their own court for their own ends.[15] At the same time there seems to have been a broad shift in the attitude of magistrates towards the law and its role in social relations. Paternalists and patricians were always present among the magistracy. It appears, however, that, from the early eighteenth to the early nineteenth century, the paternalist magistrate, who was prepared to arbitrate and do deals with the local population, increasingly gave way to the patrician, who prided himself in imposing the law in a disinterested fashion for the public good as he perceived it.[16] Moreover, from the early nineteenth century the law appears to have been understood much more as embodying national norms rather than as a flexible instrument that might be used, even by magistrates and judges, as a means for establishing or re-establishing local community harmony. Increasingly, too, magistrates began to be drawn from a new elite of men who had made their money in trade, who were local employers and who seem to have been more inclined to use the law in a proactive fashion when trouble threatened. The establishment of permanent police forces meant that crowd action could be either nipped in the bud early on or, if necessary, suppressed without recourse to the deployment of soldiers and their lethal weaponry. Finally, in keeping with the dislike of other manifestations of public rowdiness and violence already discussed, there appears to have been a greater intolerance of disorderly crowd action among the elite. Government insistence that magistrates allow the free circulation of grain and resist moral economy protest during the serious dearths of 1795 to 1796 and 1799 to 1801 coincided with the wars against Revolutionary and Napoleonic France. While the British state triumphed

over Jacobinism and looked on, often smugly, at revolutions in continental Europe in the first half of the nineteenth century, there were
concerns about revolution at home. These concerns involved fears that
the 'dangerous classes' in the rookeries of the big cities were eager for
the opportunity for riot and plunder. Such anxieties confirmed the elision of rioter, revolutionary and member of the dangerous class; an
elision that continued into the twentieth century.[17]

Other forms of crowd action linked to the ideas of the moral economy also declined during the nineteenth century, and again a variety of
elements contributed to this. Violent protest was sometimes directed
against attempts to end customary rights, particularly when common
land was subject to enclosure. Riot appears to have been among the least
successful forms of opposition to enclosure; it also tended to occur only
after all other forms had been tried and failed. The small owner occu-
piers, tenants, cottagers and landless labourers whose way of life and
existence was threatened by enclosure employed a variety of responses.
They counter-petitioned Parliament and they dragged their feet and
failed to comply with the requests of local officials who were seeking to
press ahead with the formalities necessary before legislation. Violent
protest was commonly directed at the enclosure fencing. This might be
by masked men acting under cover of darkness. It might be by more
public crowd action. In 1765 a protest against enclosure at West Had-
don, Northamptonshire, took the form of a two-day football match,
advertised in advance in a local newspaper, the *Northampton Mercury*.
£1500 of new enclosure fencing was damaged during the game.[18] Such
protest could also cut across social classes and, once again, a sharp
plebeian–patrician polarity is too simplistic.

The arguments and disorders over the enclosure of Otmoor in
Oxfordshire continued from the 1780s to the 1830s. They involved members of the gentry supporting plebeian defenders of the community
rights of grazing on the commons. Local parish officials also sided
with their poorer neighbours in rejecting the enclosure, or at least
failed to enforce the laws urged by those engaged in the enclosure.
Farmers, whose land was threatened by drainage for the enclosure,
broke down offending embankments. The judge who heard the case
against them directed the jury to acquit on the grounds that they had
acted 'to *relieve themselves* from the inconvenience of having their own

lands overflowed'. Local magistrates hired Metropolitan Police officers, and equipped them with pistols, to protect the enclosed land. But the magistrates also expressed as much concern over preserving the peace as enforcing and maintaining the rights of the proprietors of enclosed Otmoor.[19] The turbulence around Otmoor coincided with other issues that prompted protest in the early nineteenth-century countryside: the introduction of machinery, most notably the threshing machine; the demands for tithes; low agricultural wages; unemployment; and the introduction of the New Poor Law. The Captain Swing riots that swept across the south of England between 1830 and 1833 are the best known of the disorders. But violent protest in the countryside was not confined to riot. The repression that followed the Swing Riots appears to have made rural populations wary of open mass action. In its place there was a growth of incendiarism and, to a lesser extent, animal maiming, particularly in East Anglia.[20]

This kind of violent rural protest was again not unique to England. In eighteenth-century France, the enclosure of common land was favoured by the Physiocrats, but here concerns about the trouble that such changes might provoke appears to have restricted the process. Legislators during the French Revolution sought to resolve the question of the commons by land divisions and sales. This drew some of the sting by establishing a rural society in which there were many thousands of landowners, even if a high percentage owned insufficient land for a family's subsistence. But legislation during the later stages of the Revolution also sought to limit access to forests. A generation later, the Forest Code of 1827, although it was geared towards the management of royal forests, was also designed to break links between forests and the pastoral economy and to abolish local land-use rights. The new code provoked widespread disorder among those who, as far back as popular memory went, had been accustomed to grazing animals in the forests and gathering kindling and firewood. The trouble was most serious and most protracted in the department of the Ariège. Here local men with blackened faces and long shirt smocks outside their trousers, thus giving them the appearance of women, drove away forest guards and charcoal burners in the so-called *Guerre des Demoiselles.*[21]

During the eighteenth century there were riots against press gangs and military recruiters in England. The legitimising notions here are

relatively easy to appreciate. No one was keen to see young men seized
for the fleet in time of war, but again the polarity of plebeians against
patricians is too simple. Shipowners and businessmen objected to their
crews being pressed by the navy and were even known to sue the Admi-
ralty for loss of trade and cargo. Magistrates and town worthies disliked
having their communities disrupted by press gangs whose activities
pushed at the limits of English liberties, especially in the heady days of
Wilkite radicalism when constitutional questions of arrest and imprisonment were highlighted.[22] Professional seamen appear to have
accepted the fact that large numbers of them would be required to man
the Royal Navy in time of war; it was possible for a sensible naval
recruiting officer to come to an understanding with local magistrates
and local seamen's leaders to fill the recruiting tenders and to keep
trouble to the minimum. The most serious problems occurred when
individual warships sent press gangs ashore to make up their crews
without reference to local recruiting officers or local magistrates. At the
beginning of the war against Revolutionary France the navy's recruiting officer in Liverpool appears to have negotiated all the right,
unofficial agreements. But when, against the recruiting officer's advice,
a frigate sent a press gang ashore, and, in the ensuing disorder, its midshipman commander killed a master mariner, serious rioting ensued.
The local coroner brought in a verdict of murder, the midshipman was
arrested by local magistrates and sent to Manchester, and the magistrates stood by while two naval recruiting offices were destroyed by a
furious crowd of carpenters and seamen. Similarly, while recruiting for
the army was not popular, it was the corrupt practices and kidnapping
of young men by 'crimps' that provoked the most serious trouble. In
the summer of 1794 and again in 1795 rioters swept through London
destroying recruiting houses, incensed by reports of crimps.[23]

The end of the 'Second Hundred Years War' with France in 1815, and
Britain's general avoidance of military action in Europe for a century,
meant that there was no need for a large wartime army. Similarly, while
it was the most powerful navy in the world during the nineteenth
century, the Royal Navy was always the more popular service at home.
In the absence of war, it had no need to make up its numbers with
impressment. Soldiers and sailors might be violent and disorderly
when on leave, or when at a loose end in a garrison or naval town, but

violent community hostility to recruiters was not an element of English life after the war with Napoleon.

Protests over recruiting were not unique to England. Recruiting demands sparked the counter-revolutionary uprising in the Vendée in 1793, and conscription for Napoleon's armies provoked trouble throughout his empire. In France itself protests over the annual demands for young men for the imperial armies gradually declined; the population appears to have been worn down by bureaucratic routine, propaganda, fines and more punitive measures. But, years after Napoleon's final defeat, violent hostility towards the gendarmes responsible for enforcing the Restoration's conscription legislation spluttered on in some of the more remote French departments.[24] The principal states of continental Europe, unlike Great Britain, raised conscript armies throughout the nineteenth century. Submitting to the mechanisms of a conscription system became something of a rite of passage for the young men of these states. Again the bureaucratic inevitability of the procedure, the propaganda of the nation state and, less and less, punitive measures appear to have worn down the hostility of local communities.

Popular protest in the shape of food riots, recruiting riots or enclosure riots tends to be associated with the pre-industrial economy. In an industrial economy like Victorian England it is generally assumed that the most common forms of non-political popular protest were linked with relations at the workplace. As with any shifts detected in social behaviour over a long period of time, the division is not hard and fast. Weavers in eighteenth-century Gloucestershire moved easily from food riots to industrial action and back. In both kinds of protest their actions suggest elements of the thinking associated with the moral economy. There were appeals to custom and the assertion that the wellbeing of the community should take precedence over an individual's right to profit and the workings of the market.[25] The wave of violent protest known as Luddism that swept through Derbyshire, Leicestershire and Nottinghamshire, and then on to Lancashire and Yorkshire, in 1811 and 1812 appears to have been similar. The breaking of machines – some old, like the framework-knitter's loom; some new, like the shearing frame – was mixed with protests over wage rates, food prices and also, at different times and with different emphases, political radicalism.[26] But it is a dilution of the concept of the moral economy to see it regenerating itself as an anti-capitalist critique and as a means of resistance to capitalist development.[27] The moral economy was not anti-capitalist, indeed it might be understood as a system for policing capitalism. Moreover, the English working class needed neither the concepts of the moral economy nor those of Karl Marx to organise and protest at their place of work or about their conditions of work. Violence and the threat of violence were deployed in this protest. There were a few incidents resulting in loss of life, such as the Luddite attack on a steam-loom factory in Middleton in 1812 April during which five of the attackers were killed. But the overall incidence and scale of this protest are difficult to gauge and the official statistics are of little help.

Violence in industrial disorders in eighteenth- and early nineteenth-century England is sometimes put down to the 'immaturity' of early trade unionism. It is important to recognise that violence was not an automatic response to economic change, to new machinery or to changing work patterns. It was only one of many tactics, often deployed simultaneously, by which groups of workers sought to maintain control of their workplace and working practices. The situation varied from region to region and from trade to trade. In some instances there was no trouble; indeed there were trades in which the workforce played an active role in developing innovations.[28] Where there was violent behaviour, or where there were threats, this might be emphasised by one side, especially by the employers, against the other as a means of generating support. When combination by workers was illegal, the stress on the violence, or the potential for violence, among Luddites and other worker activists was a way for employers to claim support from the authorities to maintain public order and protect property. Such support was usually translated into the deployment of troops and, later, police; and it was difficult for such a deployment to appear neutral. But then industrial protest in the eighteenth and early nineteenth centuries was often violent. Luddites smashed machines. Mines had their winding gear sabotaged. In the countryside threshing machines were attacked, barns and ricks were burned, and animals maimed. In the early nineteenth-century rural disorders of Captain Swing, farmers and clergymen were mobbed during demonstrations demanding higher wages and lower tithes. Eric Hobsbawm famously coined the term 'collective bargaining by riot' that was to be echoed later by Bohstedt's view of other riots as 'community politics'.[29] Alongside the attacks on property, and the less common assaults on employers and other social superiors, went violence and threats of violence directed towards fellow workers who were reluctant to join a strike or who acted as blackleg labour. The repeal of the Combination Laws in 1824 coincided with booming trade, high prices and a shortage of labour. The response of the liberated workforce was to embark on a wave of industrial activity, some of it characterised by ferocious violence towards workers who would not join. A parliamentary select committee was rapidly convened and new legislation followed which allowed combination for negotiating hours and wages, but which provided for severe sentences in cases of violence or intimidation. Yet even after trades unions began to be accepted, and, often grudgingly, workers' leaders and employers began to play by new rules of negotiation and conciliation, violence remained a sanction that might be called upon in industrial disputes.

Modern strikes involve the potential for confrontations in three directions. First, and most obviously, there is the opposition between the strikers and their employers. But there is also the potential for conflict between strikers and waverers within their own ranks and between strikers and other workers – blacklegs – recruited by the employers to maintain production and break the strike. Several nineteenth-century commentators chose to ignore the way in which almost any strike contained the possibility of violence. They contrasted what they considered to be the brutality and primitive savagery of strikers with the general progress of civilised society. The passions of strikers were stigmatised as the kind of behaviour that might be found among 'the American Indian or African warrior'.[30] Others, however, politicians among them, sought legislation to control and limit the potential for violence.

During the 1850s Parliament debated Bills on the molestation of workmen, with the questions being raised, regularly, of how the problem of 'quiet and peaceful intimidation' might be solved, and of what precisely 'peaceful' persuasion in the context of a group asking an individual to join them was. The Molestation of Workmen Bill passed into law eventually in 1859. Most Victorian labour leaders appear to have been reconciled to the permanence of capitalism and to have accepted that violence, real and threatened, ought not to be part of industrial relations. But, on the ground, there could be regular, if mundane threats, fights and intimidation at many Victorian workplaces.[31] In the heat of a strike or in a period of tense industrial relations, serious violence could flare towards waverers and strike breakers. Less than a decade after the Molestation of Workmen Act, the country was shocked by the violent 'outrages' that gave rise to the Royal Commission on Trade Unions, notably in the brickmaking trade in the Manchester area and in the cutlery trades of Sheffield. The Sheffield Outrages had climaxed with the destruction of a workman's home by gunpowder.[32] Ten years later, in the spring of 1878, a strike against wage reductions in the north Lancashire cotton industry lasted for nineteen weeks. There was rioting in every major town, including Burnley, Clitheroe and Preston, as well as many smaller ones. Threatening letters were sent and money, food and drink were extorted. Police deployed to maintain order became the specific targets of crowd action, and employers were burned in effigy and had their homes attacked. Ransford Jackson, the hard-nosed chairman of the employers' association, saw his house, Clayton Grange, burned to the ground. Efforts were made to blame vagabonds, roughs and the Irish for the violence. But there seems little doubt that the rioters were drawn largely from the younger members of the factory workers. This was a stable population, conservative and semi-rustic, united by a strong local dialect and by beliefs that they were a key reason for the industry's success and that their cause was just.[33]

Throughout the nineteenth century, and beyond, some trades still depended upon toughness and physicality. The building trades and mining in particular required tough, hard men. So too did many of the trades that were at the centre of the New Unionism involving unskilled labour towards the end of the century. In the mass demonstrations of the Great Dock strike of 1889 the crowds were peaceful, but in the strike of 1912 there was considerable violence deployed on all sides. Strike breakers were armed with pistols and allegedly wounded as many as twenty men in a confrontation on the London docks at the end of July. The Transport Workers' Federation organised their own police from ex-soldiers and sailors whose tasks was to carry out picket duty, and who fought fierce battles with strike breakers. In addition, the Metropolitan Police were deployed in numbers. A Home Office enquiry into police behaviour at an incident in June concluded that they had been guilty of 'some excesses' and that some individuals had 'undoubtedly a right to complain of the treatment they received' from the police.[34]

The violence and the extent of the industrial disorders in the decade before the First World War led some on the employers' side to consider the creation of their own private police organisation. At the inaugural meeting of the Volunteer Police Force, held at Crystal Palace on Trafalgar Day 1911, the body's organising chairman, Arnold Statham, expressed concern about the revolutionary forces within the country:

> The much boasted 'solidarity of labour' is too often a mere cloak for class warfare to extort surrender to unjustifiable demands ... What Britain wants today is not weak-kneed local authorities, but a BISMARCK with a will of iron.

The Home Office, however, was hostile. Sir Edward Troup, the permanent under secretary, considered it impossible 'for a Government which stands for law, order and impartiality and not for punching the heads of strikers, to have anything to do with it'.[35]

In the aftermath of the First World War there were those, particularly among labour leaders, who feared that the war had fostered Prussian militarism among reactionary elements within government circles. These fears were reinforced by the violence of the government's auxiliaries in the war in Ireland. The Black and Tans appeared a potential White Guard or *Freikorps* that might be deployed against workers at home.[36] At the same time, members of successive governments and their civil servants feared that they might well have to prepare for 'punching the heads of strikers'. The conclusion of the war, after all, brought a wave of industrial unrest that was made all the more frightening in many eyes by the success of the Bolshevik Revolution in Russia and the pro-Soviet sentiments of some activists. In 1921 the Home Office contemplated a 'citizen guard' to relieve the military from some internal duties and to act as an auxiliary to the special constabulary. Two years later Lloyd George issued an appeal for volunteers to serve in an armed Defence Force that would be subject to the Army Act and within which members of the Territorial Army were encouraged to participate. The Defence Force rapidly sank into disuse. In 1926, on the eve of the General Strike, the government established the non-military Civil Constabulary Reserve. This reasserted the position that had developed over the preceding hundred years that the main responsibility for the maintenance of public order rested with the civil police.[37]

The General Strike was noteworthy for the peaceable behaviour of the great majority of the strikers. An American reporter observed that he had 'seen more fighting in one night of a local steel strike in Pittsburg than there has been in all England this week'.[38] And English commentators liked to boast about how different their strikes were from those in the United States and on continental Europe. But violence did flare up in several of the post-war strikes.[39] The ferocious 'Battle of Ammanford' was fought on 5 August 1925 between striking colliery workers and Carmarthenshire police assisted by eighty men from the Glamorgan police reserve. Somewhere between fifty and one hundred people were injured.[40] There were clashes during the General Strike, but in several instances it appears that these were provoked by the police or, more often, by young men serving as special constables. The Civil Constabulary Reserve, who wore no uniform but an armband, were particularly resented as 'strike breakers' and were even seen by the police as having a potential for provoking trouble. The union movement lost much of its credibility and support in the aftermath of the General Strike, but when membership revived during the 1930s the incidence of strike activity remained low. At the same time a new tactic evolved on picket lines, shared between police and strikers. Two walls of men, police and strikers, pushed and shoved each other, occasionally exchanging blows, but generally keeping the potential for the stoning of police lines and the drawing and swinging of police batons to a minimum. This tactic survived into the 1970s and in many instances beyond. But from the 1970s there was a new militancy on the part of some trade unions and, at the end of the decade, Margaret Thatcher's government showed a preparedness to confront trades unionism with a new level of aggression and toughness. At the same time the police developed new, tougher tactics and officers equipped with flame-proof overalls, wearing new helmets and body armour, began to confront protesters from behind walls made of long perspex shields, or else to charge into crowds behind smaller, round shields to seize 'ringleaders' and 'troublemakers'. These changes and a return to more violent confrontation became particularly apparent during the miners' strike of 1984 to 1985. The debate continues as to whether the new police tactical behaviour was a response

to more violent behaviour, or whether its adoption was largely unnecessary and served only to ratchet up the scale protest violence in a
society significantly reordering its economic base.[41]

The violence in support of industrial protest was perpetrated by
workers and not by the 'criminal class' or the residuum from the slums.
It was not something that happened every day, every week or even every
year in different English workplaces. It blew up only occasionally, generally when tension in a particular industrial confrontation reached a
peak. That it declined during the nineteenth and early twentieth centuries was due, at least in part, to the growth and acceptance of
institutions for negotiation and compromise, such as the trade unions.
Those on the workers' side who employed violence or the threat of violence would, almost certainly, have been able to provide some sort of
legitimising notion for their actions. But, in the context of England
being perceived as a pacific country, was the scale of violence in this
protest less great than elsewhere?

England did not witness anything on the scale of the great uprisings
that occurred among the silk workers of Lyon in 1831 and 1834, and
which resulted in massive troop deployments and hundreds of casualties. For Marx the Lyon insurrectionaries, fighting under their banner
Vivre en Travaillant ou Mourir en Combattant, were 'the soldiers of
socialism'.[42] But the Lyon insurrections were not common incidents
among the workers of nineteenth-century France, any more than the
insurrection in the ironmaking town of Merthyr Tydfil, also in 1831,
sparked by a heady mix of wage cuts, redundancies and political propaganda for the Great Reform Bill, was typical of nineteenth-century
Britain. Perhaps two dozen died at Merthyr, with another seventy or so
injured when the government in Whitehall sent a Scottish regiment to
put down a rising by Welsh workers.[43] French troops killed nine strikers and wounded many more at Fourmies in 1891; two years later British
troops killed two and wounded fourteen during a strike at Featherstone
Colliery in West Yorkshire. In the former the dead became worker martyrs; but much less so in the latter. For different reasons both the Right
and the Left in France played upon fantasies of violence. The Right,
particularly in the aftermath of the Commune, wanted to emphasise
the violence of workers, while the socialist unions were keen to play up
their revolutionary credentials and potential for violence. There were

revivals of worker militancy in the 1860s and again in the 1890s and the decade before the First World War. It is possible that the general expectations of bloodshed may have lowered the threshold at which it occurred. Yet analyses of French strikes following the Commune and up until the Second World War have concluded that there was remarkably little violence, and that when it did occur it was most often linked with other, specifically political violence or calls for revolution.[44]

In the United States the clashes between capital and labour were particularly violent. Part of the problem was that the National Guard and the police were often in the pockets of employers by virtue of the latter's position in state legislatures and municipalities. Also, unlike their British counterparts, American workers were divided by ethnicity and creed, and did not have demands for political rights as an additional bond to unite them. Moreover, workers' leaders in the United States, again unlike their British counterparts, were never reconciled to the permanence of industrial capitalism. They adopted more violent tactics during the 1870s, and stuck with them, as did their opponents. The results, at times, were appalling: from the Haymarket bombing in 1885, the violent Homestead strike of 1892, the Ludlow Massacre of 1914, to the Memorial Day Massacre at the Republic Steel Factory in Chicago in 1937.[45]

The numbers of fatalities in English protest disorders, at least during the nineteenth and twentieth centuries, were proportionately fewer than in the United States and in some countries on continental Europe – again, the statistics are difficult to draw out and to compare. It is possible that the notions of Englishness militated against extremes of lethal violence on both sides in public protest. While there were significant exceptions, notably in the industrial disorders before and immediately after the First World War, generally the authorities considered that it was un-English to deploy armed men against protesters, and protesters reciprocated. Arms and explosives were available, as the Sheffield Outrages, armed burglars and the shootings in the 1912 docks dispute reveal. The lack of violence was not necessarily an illustration of 'social maturity' among the English or demonstrative of their 'conquest' of violence. Indeed, some English protests could be very violent, though hardly ever taken to the point of killing. Rather it was a cultural assumption that lethal weaponry was simply not something that English people employed when protesting either over economic matters or in political confrontations. England, the English assured themselves, and continental Europeans often agreed with awe, did not have revolutions and, this was generally perceived as a demonstration that the English had eradicated violence from politics. But to what extent was this true?

7

Stones and Fisticuffs

John Thelwall prided himself on being a British Jacobin. In 1794 he was one of the score and more radicals arrested under the suspension of the Habeas Corpus Act and subsequently charged with high treason. In January 1795 he was the last of the three men brought to trial at the Old Bailey on the charge. Like his two predecessors, he was acquitted, and his acquittal led to the government dropping charges against the others still held in custody. The experience of the trial did not dampen Thelwall's commitment to radical politics; and the Gagging Acts of 1795 did not silence him, though they did require that he disguise his lectures on political issues as classical history. In 1796 he embarked on a lecture tour of East Anglia. His first venue was Yarmouth. There were some minor disruptions to the first two lectures on 15 and 17 August. The third lecture, on the evening of Friday 19, began peaceably enough with some two hundred people, both men and women, assembled in the meeting room. But, shortly after the proceedings commenced, they were broken up by the sudden attack of, according to Thelwall, about ninety sailors armed with bludgeons and cutlasses. Lecturer and audience fled, while the assailants 'roaring out "God save the King", with great ardour and exultation, proceeded to plunder and destroy' everything in the lecture room. Thirty to forty people were injured. The local magistrates refused to attempt to suppress the trouble. Undeterred, Thelwall moved on to Lynn Regis. Again his lecture hall and his audience were attacked. Again the local magistrates refused to take any action, even when Thelwall was pursued through the streets and when the house where he had taken refuge was assailed. Eventually, Thelwall believed, the crowds 'were called off by those miscreants who spurred them on'. It was a similar story a few days later at a third lecture venue in Wisbech.[1]

The hostility to enemy aliens during wartime has already been discussed. Attacks on suspected 'traitors' – especially after a government

minister had described one of Thelwall's co-defendants in the two treason trials as 'an acquitted felon' – in the heat of a war might not seem
surprising.[2] If the eighteenth-century English crowd's legitimising
notions could lead to the defence of young men against press gangs and
crimps, so pride in British arms and xenophobia might prompt attacks,
possibly with the encouragement of drink supplied by social superiors,
on those who appeared to support the enemy. Thomas Hardy, a Scottish shoemaker working in London who stood trial for treason with
Thelwall, had his house attacked during the celebrations for the naval
success of the Glorious First of June in 1794. His wife died as a result of
the miscarriage brought on during her escape from the building. Three
years later Hardy refused to put lights in his windows to celebrate the
naval victory of Camperdown. Some supporters from the radical London Corresponding Society defended his house from the loyalists who,
again, attacked his house. Order was finally restored on this occasion
when a party of soldiers was summoned.[3]

One hundred years later, critics of the British campaign against the
Boers in the South African War had their property attacked by jubilant
crowds during celebrations such as those following the announcement
of the relief of Mafeking. At times anti-war protesters were also physically assaulted and had meetings broken up by violent 'jingoes'. A by-
election held in Stratford upon Avon in the summer of 1901, for example,
was the setting for a succession of extremely disorderly meetings. The
Liberal candidate was critical of the behaviour of British troops in South
Africa and the Liberals accused the police of partiality during the disorders. In Birmingham the following December, Lloyd George had to be
rescued from an anti-war meeting disguised in a policeman's coat, while
police baton charges to restore order resulted in one death and some
twenty-seven people being taken to hospital.[4] During the First World
War, meetings of pacifists, and of those dissenting from the war and
from conscription, were attacked. Once again the police and the authorities were accused of partiality. Before one of the more brutal encounters
at a war dissenters' meeting in Cory Hall, Cardiff, in November 1916, the
patriotic South Wales miners' leader, C. B. Stanton, urged his supporters
to 'stop these men by any means short of murder'.[5]

Wars may figure disproportionally on the history shelves of book-
shops, but between the fall of Napoleon in 1815 and the German invasion

of Belgium in 1914 Britain was not involved in any major international conflict on continental Europe, with the exception of the geographically confined Crimean War. The violent attacks described above might, in consequence, be categorised as exceptional incidents in exceptional times. The attacks on Thelwall and Hardy can also be fitted in to the general assault on British Jacobins, labelled by some of its victims as the English or the British 'Reign of Terror'. This was a deliberate, self-dramatising attempt to draw a comparison with the much more extensive, bloody and systematic terror of the Jacobin dictatorship in France. Some of Thelwall's assailants in 1796 were sailors from a warship allegedly egged on by their captain. It has been suggested, however, that, by the end of the Revolutionary and Napoleonic wars, radicals no longer had cause to fear 'the mob'. It had become impossible to recruit loyalist 'Church and King' crowds in London and the major industrial cities as the English working class evolved into a recognisable entity.[6] The leaders of the violent jingoes of the South African War, who made a conscious and rational decision to break up anti-war meetings and attack those protesting against the war, have been identified as principally young men from the middle class.[7] This, together with the critical labelling of those who attacked anti-war meetings during the First World War, almost becomes a mirror image of the labelling of protest crowds as made up of 'criminals' and the dregs of society. It largely excuses the working class, as a class, from any responsibility for reactionary political violence. Loyalist and jingo crowds, by definition, appear reactionary, attacking those adopting a liberal or democratic positions or, like the moderate British Jacobins, apparently moving in that direction. This was not always the perception of contemporaries. Liberals like J. A. Hobson and C. F. G. Masterman both believed that the jingoes were primitives from the working class sweeping out of the urban abyss.[8] It is not the intention here to assess the extent to which the label 'reactionary' can be applied satisfactorily to these violent political crowds. 'Reactionary' and 'progressive' are highly subjective adjectives, and the issue here is rather to assess the extent to which violence was a part of politics in England during the nineteenth and early twentieth centuries rather than to label any particular group as responsible.

Politics in eighteenth-century England contained a significant element of rough and tumble. Candidates were hissed, booed and even pelted when they stood on the hustings. Not every Englishman had the vote, but even those without it were inclined to participate, either to let their opinions be known or simply for the fun of it. Continental European visitors expressed amazement at the turbulence and the lack of deference. 'Shouting speakers, stones and fisticuffs, and all the orgies we witness of English liberty', was how a young French nobleman, Alexis de Tocqueville, described the hustings in 1828.[9] The rough and tumble of the hustings rarely degenerated into serious violence; but there were instances of deliberate attacks on those working for, or those supporting, a candidate, or on the house where a candidate lodged. Such attacks invariably brought retaliation. In some instances gangs of toughs were recruited to protect a candidate and his supporters, or deliberately to terrorise the opposition. Occasionally troops had to be brought in to subdue electoral disorder.[10] William Hogarth captured the mayhem with his series of four illustrations on the election in the mythical constituency of Guzzle-down based on events in Oxfordshire in 1754 and first exhibited between 1755 and 1758. The first in the series (Figure 7), *An Election Entertainment*, shows in the centre foreground a hired tough having a head wound dressed, while to the right an attorney, registering votes, reels back having been struck on the head by a brick thrown through the window. Crowds press at the open door and mill in the street outside.

Political issues other than elections brought crowds on to the streets of eighteenth-century England, and especially of London. These crowds were given considerable latitude in affirming and even questioning the legitimacy of regimes. Their activity was usually synchronised with a calendar of public anniversaries or political events such as a general election or a military victory; they were also found at trials and public punishments. There were debates throughout the century over whether the crowd genuinely demonstrated popular attitudes and sentiment, whether it was a mindless, politically ignorant rabble, or whether it was simply gullible and easily influenced by the malevolent. The positions adopted in these debates commonly reflected a commentator's response to a recent event.[11] The most celebrated street disorders of the period were those that surrounded the colourful self-publicist John Wilkes. Crowds vociferously gave him their support when, following his

7. William Hogarth's 'An Election Entertainment' is one of his series of four illustrations of the election in the constituency of Guzzle-Down. The illustrations were based on events in Oxfordshire in 1754 and were typical of the rowdy events that could occur during contested elections in Georgian England.

criticism of the king's ministers, he challenged the legality of the attempt
to arrest him and his printer on a general warrant and when, after an
enforced exile, he sought re-election to Parliament for the turbulent
urban county of Middlesex. The most notorious of the disorders were
the Gordon Riots, occasioned by fiercely Protestant crowds concerned
about Parliament legislating to remove some of the bars against
Catholics. There were initial attacks on the Catholic chapels, on the most
visible and influential members of the Catholic community, and on
the politicians who sponsored the new toleration. But, as the disorder
progressed, there were also attacks on institutions such as the Bank of
England, the Excise Office and the Customs Office, on prisons, on brew-
eries and distilleries. The magistracy could not cope; and around 10,000
troops were rushed into the metropolis. The traditional view has it that
the crowd was eventually quelled by volley-fire during a final attack on
the Bank of England on the evening of 7 June, though following this
repulse crowds continued to surge through the City attacking houses
with little hindrance. It seems more likely that the riots ran out of steam,
especially as the rioters became aware of the sheer number of troops that
had been mustered in great camps in Hyde Park and St James's Park.[12]

The Gordon Riots witnessed a serious breakdown of law and order,
yet it is difficult to estimate just how anarchic the disorder became. The
press coverage and the comment of contemporaries were generally hostile. Even the political radicals who had encouraged street allies in the
Wilkite disorders were critical and feared the impact of the violence on
their aspirations for reform. Yet the most recent attempt at a serious
assessment of the riots has suggested that the participants are best
understood by being considered more on their own terms. They saw
themselves as the defenders and shock troops of English popular Protestantism drawing on traditional understandings and fears. In fact, they
put less emphasis on Protestant martyrs and Catholic atrocities than had
been common among their predecessors. They were particularly critical
of the kind of cosmopolitan toleration that was rooted in the eighteenth-
century Enlightenment, that was apparent within sections of the ruling
elite and that had fostered the proposed toleration of Catholics. The
attacks on public buildings and the threats to St James's and to Downing
Street appear only to have occurred when the crowd was at its most
exasperated with the forces of authority.[13]

But if England experienced Wilkite disorders and the Gordon Riots, it did not endure a revolution at the close of the eighteenth century or during the nineteenth century. The kind of revolution that engulfed France during the 1790s, and that re-echoed across continental Europe during the nineteenth century especially in France, Austria, Germany and Italy, passed England by. Crowd disorder took on a new dimension as a result of the French Revolution. The street violence of the Revolution was luridly portrayed for contemporaries in the press and in the graphic cartoons of Gillray and others; the Parisian *sans-culottes* who made up the revolutionary crowds became grotesque cannibals. Subsequently, the revolutionary violence was vividly captured for the nineteenth-century reader in Thomas Carlyle's description of the primeval force of the Parisian crowd first published in 1837. 'Sansculottism' was 'waste, wildflowing, as the unfruitful sea'. Moreover, 'to Insurrection you cannot speak; neither can it, hydraheaded, hear'.[14]

Some historians have described England's proximity to revolution during the 1790s, when there were insurrectionary plotters and elements in the political opposition that may have been prepared to seek to ride the tiger of revolution.[15] There was political unrest towards the end of the Napoleonic Wars. Some Luddites had political aspirations and this trouble continued through into the post-war period. Indeed, it was during the thirty or so years following the victory of Waterloo and the end of the wars that popular politics meant radicals organising mass meetings, mass demonstrations and petitions, seriously threatening open constitutional confrontation. This mass platform, underpinned by a radical press and a national network of clubs and societies, was quite different from the informal networks of market pub and workplace that had provided the basis for popular politics in the eighteenth century. Violence flared across the country as Parliament debated the Bill that was to become the Great Reform Act of 1832. Groups among the Chartists were wedded to physical force. Successive governments prepared for violence but, in the generation following the Peterloo Massacre of 1819 when cavalry killed eleven and wounded hundreds at a political meeting in Manchester, they also urged moderation on the forces of order and the importance of not shedding blood. It was probably for similar reasons that the Home Office vigorously resisted the requests of chief constables that their men be given military training and have firearms, even artillery so as to act as auxiliaries to the military in case of invasion.[16] British governments believed their own rhetoric about the virtues of an unarmed, non-military police. Fortunately, and perhaps partly because of the restraint urged by government, serious bloodshed was rare at political meetings. When it did come, such violence did not often result in death; and it never came with the unstoppable fury of Carlyle's *sans-culottes* or the stopping power of General Bonaparte's 'whiff of grapeshot'. Some contemporaries considered that the good sense and moderation of the English had prevented, and would continue to prevent, them from sliding towards revolution. The arrival of several thousand political exiles in Britain in the aftermath of the revolutions of 1848 served to confirm such beliefs. The point has been re-echoed by those historians who put stress on what they see as the generally consensual nature of English politics, with slow but steady improvements being made by men of good sense, and recognised as such by the overwhelming majority.[17]

This is not the place to embark on a theory of revolution. The point to stress is that the violence of a revolution occurs once the process of revolution is underway. Revolutionary violence involves crowds on the streets and mass participation, but it also involves influential political groupings, and sometimes also social and economic blocs, contesting for power and using violence in that contest. Such violence can take the form of purges or civil war. Violence is an integral element of revolutions but not an obvious cause of revolutions. It therefore makes no sense to argue that England avoided revolution because its politicians and people did not employ violence within the political process, or because of something inherent in the English character or the character of English politics. Indeed much of the rough and tumble of eighteenth-century English politics continued into the nineteenth century and beyond.

Political disorder could, on occasions, be closely linked with bread and butter issues and it can be misleading rigidly to seek to categorise protest under separate and distinct headings as, for example, 'political' and 'economic'. Luddism in Lancashire, particularly, linked the political and the economic. There was an element of this in some manifestations of Chartism. In the summer of 1842, for example, the political demands of the People's Charter were often harnessed to the demands of strikers in the disorders surrounding what some have been tempted to label as 'the first general strike' not only in Britain but in any industrial country.[18] Rioting in London in the summer of 1855 protested against new legislation but was moved by the economic restrictions threatened in Lord Robert Grosvenor's Bill against trading on Sundays. Grosvenor and his confederates wished to keep the Sabbath a holy day, but Sunday was a day when many of the weekly-paid working class found it convenient to shop. Moreover, those who took to the streets to demonstrate could also see that, while legislation of the previous year had limited their Sunday drinking hours, no such regulations had been applied to the private clubs of gentlemen in the West End.[19] A decade later rioting around Hyde Park was overtly political, occasioned by government attempts to close the park to a mass meeting summoned in support of parliamentary reform. There were those who feared (and a few like Karl Marx who hoped) that the disorder, the alleged brutality of the police and the stone throwing of the crowds presaged revolution. Some reports described 'the dregs' of the city taking over the streets, but the government kept its head, considered the disorder as, essentially, a problem of policing, and the following year saw the passage of a new Reform Act.[20] Twenty years later the government again appears to have considered serious disorder as a police matter. In February 1886 crowds of unemployed building workers and dockers from the East End assembled for a meeting in Trafalgar Square alongside socialists and anti-socialists. As they moved away from the square towards Pall Mall they were abused from the windows and balconies of gentlemen's clubs. The crowds replied with stones, attacks on carriages and the looting of some shops. On 'Bloody Sunday', 13 November 1887, relying on some equivocal legal recommendations, the police banned a meeting of the unemployed in Trafalgar Square. One person was killed in the ensuing violence as the police enforced the prohibition of the assembly. Again concerns were expressed about violence from the residuum, but much of the argument and protest was centred on the right of assembly and, particularly, of free speech which had, for generations, been hailed as cornerstones of the Englishman's liberty. If the government was relieved by the outcome, and by the ensuing responses of the courts and the judiciary, it remained uneasy about the original police ban.[21]

Victorian working people could make their feelings known on foreign

politics as well as on domestic issues. The Garibaldi riots, described earlier, had traditional anti-Catholic and anti-Irish elements, but they also
reflected a genuine enthusiasm among English working people for the
charismatic Italian hero. The assault on the Austrian General Haynau
and his small party at the Barclay Perkins Brewery in Southwark in
September 1850 reflected a popular hostility towards the government
in Vienna for its suppression of the Hungarian and Italian revolutions in
1848–49. Liberals and Radicals had emphasised the brutality of the Austrian regime towards the Hungarian and Italian struggles for 'liberty',
and 'General Hyena', as he was known in England, had been singled out
for obloquy, accused of hanging men and, worst of all, ordering the
flogging of women. No doubt pelting and roughing up a foreign gentleman appealed both to a rough sense of fun and to the xenophobia
and class perspectives of the brewery's draymen and the crowds in the
surrounding streets. Nevertheless, at least some in the crowd knew precisely who Haynau was and were aware of the Liberal and Radical
interpretations of events in the Austrian Empire.[22]

The Victorians were more riotous than, perhaps, the traditional
image would allow, yet riots were not regular events. Even less well
recognised, and again running contrary to popular received opinion
about the Victorians, there was a continuing element of Hanoverian
licence, disorder, intimidation and violence running through Victorian
electoral politics. Things may have appeared to be improving during
the 1850s, though the lack of disorder in the elections of 1857 and 1859
might better be explained by the fact that many constituencies lacked
contests. In the 1860s contested elections saw the reappearance of serious disturbances and attacks on candidates, on their supporters and on
voters. The 1868 election was particularly violent. In Blackburn, schools
were turned into hospitals to look after the injured. In Bristol, it was
alleged that Liberal agents had come from London and paid several
hundred men to arm themselves with bludgeons to chase Conservative
voters away from the polling places. The Ballot Act of 1872, which introduced vote by secret ballot, abolished public nominations and increased
the number of voting places for constituencies, contributed to the end
of the violence and intimidation especially on election days. But election meetings and the declaration of a poll might still occasion fights
and disorder.[23]

During contested elections in the late nineteenth and early twentieth century candidates gained press and popular approval by holding public meetings that were genuinely open, as opposed to private, 'ticketed' ones. The press commonly described the former as demonstrating a candidate's popular support but also as revealing his 'pluck'. The disruption of a meeting was often portrayed as an example of honest outrage rather than as rowdyism. Some politicians connived at the disruption of their opponents' activities. The code of English manliness pervaded this turbulence. Roughs were hired for both defence and attack; in the early 1920s Arthur Harding, the East End gangster, was recruited to protect the Liberal candidate for St George's in the East from thugs hired by the Labour Party.[24] The roughs' behaviour was sometimes labelled as 'unmanly' and their fighting as 'dirty', but the candidate and his supporters were 'manly' and were praised as such when they responded to provocation and defended their honour.[25] Showing 'pluck' in the face of physical attack during an election became categorised under the same sort of heading as showing 'pluck' in a rugby match or facing a fast bowler in cricket. G. H. Radford, the Liberal MP for East Islington, considered electoral violence to be regrettable, yet, he told the Commons in December 1908, it was something carried on from 'immemorial times [and] a form of sport which was as well recognised as football'. Radford was speaking during the debate on a Bill for the preservation of order at public meeting when arguments for the right of free speech and the freedom to present a case were heard alongside arguments in support of rough and tumble. Will Thorne, the trade union leader and Labour Member for West Ham South, for example, recalled getting 'an awful bashing' at Camborne during the 1906 general election, yet he still would not countenance legislation to 'prevent anyone making interjections at meetings'.[26] The resulting Act of Parliament made the deliberate interference in a public meeting cognizable at law for the first time. In the following year the departmental committee enquiring into the duties of police forces with respect to the preservation of public order at public meetings was informed by several senior policemen that, if politicians wanted to preserve order at their public meetings, then they should hire sufficient tough stewards. Captain the Hon. G. A. Anson, Chief Constable of Staffordhire, when asked what would happen if a small steward was confronted by a large protestor, commented that it was 'the business of the steward to get a big friend to help him eject the big man'.[27] The consensus was that it was not the duty of the police to maintain any 'right' of free speech or to steward political meetings, though some forces allowed policemen to be hired as stewards. In the event of serious trouble and a call for police assistance, the police usually closed the meeting rather than ejecting any trouble-makers. The departmental committee recommended that there should be no national directives for the police and that chief officers should continue to be left to deal with such meetings as they saw fit. Police should be available in case there was a breach of the peace, but the concern was expressed that, if the police were required to steward meetings, they might be resented as infringing the freedom of public meeting.[28]

When suffragettes adopted the tactics of disrupting the public meetings of their opponents they were appropriating male rights and customs, but they were also setting out deliberately to expose the misogyny and brutality within this. The physical violence and intimidation directed against them in response, and which was sometimes overtly sexual, was still little different from the traditional response meted out to men responsible for disruption. Equally there were some male commentators prepared to praise the suffragettes engaged in such actions for their 'pluck'.[29] Similarly, the violence and lack of police action at, for example, Stratford upon Avon in 1901 and Cory Hall in 1916, were both in the tradition of the rough and tumble of public political meetings in Victorian and Edwardian England. Significant change in this broad acceptance of rough, sometimes violent public politics did not occur until the aftermath of the First World War. The arguments for and against such behaviour were highlighted most strongly by the violence at the meeting of the British Union of Fascists (BUF) held at Olympia on 7 June 1934, an event that prompted the authorities to take a much greater role in the control and supervision of political meetings.[30]

The BUF's Olympia meeting was part of Sir Oswald Mosley's drive to enlarge membership of the party by demonstrating its case to be logical and reasonable. About 12,000 people attended; some two thousand of these were Blackshirts, of whom roughly half were stewards. In accordance with recognised practice, there were no police officers inside the hall, but 760 were on duty in the immediate vicinity, since there were fears that anti-Fascists were preparing to disrupt the meeting. Some anti-Fascists succeeded in gaining admission to the meeting. Those who heckled Mosley's speech were ejected and, as the evening wore on, these ejections appear to have become increasingly violent. A small group of police entered a foyer to rescue a group of men from beatings, and the BUF subsequently threatened the police with a court action for trespass. Mosley justified the violence of his Blackshirts. He insisted, moreover, that they responded with fists while 'many of the Communists were armed with razors, stockings filled with broken glass, knuckle-dusters, and iron bars'. He subsequently portrayed the Blackshirsts as the true Englishmen, preserving free speech in the traditional English manner:

> The blackshirt movement in the thirties was the only guarantee of free speech in Britain ... It all began in a characteristically English fashion, we improvised to meet attacks, to meet an existing situation. [After a series of attacks] I began gradually to collect a regular body of stewards, young men in plain clothes who acted as chuckers-out in the traditional English fashion, as I had seen Tories thrown out of Liberal meetings when I was nine years old, and as when I was seventeen I had often been thrown out myself with a merry band of my Sandhurst companions, when making ourselves a nuisance at such a time-honoured English institution as the Empire music hall.[31]

This is special pleading from a long way after the events, yet there were some prepared to put this gloss on the Olympia meeting in its immediate aftermath, including the maverick socialist and former editor of the *Daily Herald*, Hamilton Fyfe, Lloyd George, who wrote to Mosley recalling the violent meetings at the beginning of his own political career, and Douglas Jerrold, the founder and editor of *English Review*. Jerrold couched his sympathy with the sporting comparison: 'you can see nearly as much toughness in a "Rugger" match in the Midlands, or in Wales any Saturday in the autumn or winter'.[32] But the overwhelming response to the meeting and the behaviour of the Blackshirt stewards was critical. 'I am not against interrupters being ejected at a meeting or for that matter seeing a man knocked down in a scuffle', declared William John St Clair Anstruther-Gray, a product of Eton, Oxford and the Coldstream Guards and the Conservative MP for Lanarkshire North, 'but when it comes to seeing eight or ten men kicking and beating a man on the ground then everything British in me swells up on the side of the fellow who is not getting fair play'.[33] The cartoonist Low deployed a sporting image, but one rather different from

that of Jerrold (Figure 8). The day following the Olympia meeting England faced Australia in a test match a Trent Bridge, and Low showed
John Bull castigating Mosley and his Blackshirts from the stand; their
behaviour was clearly 'not cricket' and hence, by definition, not English.

The rejection of the old rough and tumble politics was in no small
measure a result of the violence shown at the Olympia rally.[34] Two years
later, in October 1936, the battle of Cable Street, when Jewish and left-
wing groups prevented a BUF march through the East End, suggested a
serious threat to public order on the streets – violence that was not dis-
similar from that witnessed in France, Germany and Italy. The 'battle'
brought all sides together in Parliament to agree stricter controls on
political meetings, demonstrations and marches. By the end of the 1930s
very few in England could be found prepared to speak up for the old
traditions. After the Second World War there were occasional violent
incidents, notably when meetings of regrouped Fascists were interrupted, heckled and broken up by groups such as the Association of
Jewish Ex-Servicemen. But the turbulence of Georgian and Victorian
street politics and elections was over and, thanks to the Public Order Act
of 1936, the police had wide powers of supervision and authorising what
might take place and where. Political violence re-emerged during the
1960s, but no longer linked with mainstream political parties. Rather the
trouble began as people took to the streets over particular issues – 'Stop
Immigration' on the right; 'Ban the Bomb', 'Anti-Apartheid', 'US out of
Vietnam' on the left. During the 1960s violence at such political protests
was characterised by the pushing and shoving that was also seen on
industrial picket lines. Arguably the protesters became more aggressive,
but so too did the police with their new riot tactics and equipment.

There were no revolutions in late eighteenth- or nineteenth-century
England. There was no Fascist take-over or serious threat of the over-
throw of the constitutional structure by one of the great 'isms' of left
or right during the inter-war period. Revolutions and coups were not
regular occurrences on continental Europe, even though their bloody
and spectacular duration and aftermath figured large in contemporary
literature and subsequent history. But the absence of violent changes of
regime in England does not mean that there was no violence in English politics. On the contrary, for much of the period from the
eighteenth to the beginning of the twentieth centuries, English elections

8. 'The Other Test Match', published in the *Evening Standard*, 13 June 1934, was David Low's comment on the BUF's violent Olympia Meeting. Low plays here with the English concept that something brutal and unfair was 'not cricket'. An irate John Bull rises from his seat in the crowd to protest, while Sir Oswald Mosley, in black uniform and pose that both seem very un-English, exhorts his men from the edge of the pitch. (*Low Estate*)

were consistently physical and rough. The lack of the occasional mass and murderous politics found elsewhere, however, together with the stable balance of the two-party system within a generally accepted and revered constitutional monarchy, enabled the perception to emerge and the assertion to be made that England was different. It also enabled the perception and the assertion that England enjoyed a unique form of non-political and non-violent police.

8

Violent Policemen

In the early hours of Tuesday 21 August 1906 George Gamble, a painter and decorator, was walking through Whitechapel in East London when Ethel Griffiths spoke to him. The two were rather more than acquainted; Gamble admitted at the Old Bailey that he had enjoyed 'immoral relations' with Griffiths. Griffiths, who was separated from her husband in Wales, made ends meet by occasional prostitution and admitted being 'three times convicted for dishonesty', suggested that Gamble might like a 'short time' with her. While they were speaking PC Edwin Ashworth approached. Gamble decided to move on. A few moments later Griffiths caught up with Gamble and informed him that the constable had suggested that she spend a 'short time' with him. Ashworth now approached the couple for a second time and began to taunt Gamble. The taunts turned to blows. 'Do not knock me about', Gamble recalled saying.

> 'If I am doing any wrong take me to the station and charge me.' He [Ashworth] was shoving me, pushing me, trying to make me touch him, trying to tease me to cause me to raise my hand to him. I did not do so because I knew I should be charged with assaulting him. I had no experience of this sort of thing.

Gamble was knocked to the ground by Ashworth and given a brutal kicking. Police Sergeant Thomas Sheedy, who observed the incident, rather than controlling his constable, told Gamble to get up and 'fight like a man'. He eventually told Ashworth to stop as Gamble had 'had enough'.

The kicking ruptured Gamble's uretha; he spent the next three months in hospital, undergoing several major operations. There followed nearly four weeks in a convalescent home. The case was taken up locally. The local petty criminal and thug, Arthur Harding, complained that the police had tried to fit him up on an assault charge for his involvement in seeking to prosecute Ashworth. Then James Timewell, the single-minded head of the Police and Public Vigilance Society, took up Gamble's case and wrote to the Commissioner of the Metropolitan Police. The Commissioner, in turn, wrote to Ashworth's sub-divisional inspector requesting an investigation. Ashworth denied everything. Local shopkeepers had heard nothing and, unfortunately, there was no record of Gamble's admission to hospital, since his name had been written wrongly as 'Pierce' in the casualty register. The case became more public, and notorious, when it was examined by the Royal Commission on the Duties of the Metropolitan Police set up in 1906 and when a succession of witnesses substantiated Gamble's account. The evidence of these witnesses suggests that the investigation by the local inspector was not as thorough as it might have been, or that people in the area were wary of giving evidence to police investigating police. Following the publication of the Royal Commission's report, Ashworth was suspended from the police and charged with assault and causing actual bodily harm. In October 1908, at the Old Bailey, both Ashworth and Sheedy were identified by several witnesses. Ashworth steadfastly denied committing any assault. Sheedy denied seeing one. Ashworth was found guilty and sentenced to nine months with hard labour. He was then dismissed from the police. Sergeant Sheedy, however, appears to have kept both his job and his rank.[1]

The Gamble case presents a very different image of the London Bobby from the usual. The common way that such incidents were, and are, presented by police apologists has been to describe men like Ashworth as 'rotten apples' or, in older parlance, 'black sheep'. But this hardly explains the behaviour of Sergeant Sheedy. If Ashworth was indeed behaving in an exceptional and novel way, why did Sheedy, a man with a good record who had served in the police for nearly thirteen years, not stop him and discipline him? Why, instead, did he tell Gamble to get up and 'fight like a man'?[2] These questions raise a whole clutch of issues about the relations between the police and different elements of English society during the nineteenth and twentieth centuries, and about the way in which relations between police and public have been portrayed, and who has been responsible for the portrayal.

Max Weber famously argued that a defining quality of the state is the way in which it appropriates to itself the legitimate use of violence within a given territory. The policeman is the most obvious functionary able to deploy this legitimate violence in his day-to-day dealings with citizens, and some contemporary sociologists have suggested that 'the application of physical force' is one of the key defining elements of modern police.[3] This is not, of course, to argue that the policemen of liberal democratic societies patrol their beats daily inflicting violence on citizens. Rather, this definition provides a way of differentiating between members of other bodies authorised to enforce laws and regulations and members of the police institution.

The nineteenth-century Bobby had to be tough. His was a hard life which involved patrolling in all weathers and disproportionately during the hours of darkness. Some working-class districts were particularly hostile to the policeman. Middlesbrough was a rough, booming industrial town in the mid nineteenth century, with a large number of young, unattached men, many of them Irish, who had moved in to work in the iron-making, engineering and shipbuilding trades. They thought nothing of a rough-house when the pubs closed, and woe betide any police officer who got in their way or who tried to arrest a mate. During the 1860s the recorded assaults on Middlesbrough police were running at about sixty a year, while the police force itself averaged only about thirty men.[4] Other towns could be as bad. 'The other day in Birmingham we had a man killed', explained the Chief Constable of Staffordshire, an ex-military man, to a Parliamentary Select Committee in 1875.

> Not a week passes in the Black Country but what a man is almost killed: a soldier may be in the army for twenty years and never be hurt, but the policemen in the Black Country are liable to be hurt every day: certainly they would not go five years without being hurt.[5]

Victorian policemen probably did not always report assaults. Indeed it was probably seen as part of the job's masculinity that they should be able to take care of themselves without necessarily resorting to the law. On occasions the policeman responded to provocation with physical toughness and aggression and even by getting his retaliation in first.[6] At times this could provoke severe criticism, though having criticised rough policemen in November 1873 the *Illustrated London News* went on: 'we perpetually read of attacks on the police without reading also of that wholesome chastisement which we should like to find following such outrage'. In the following year an article in the *Westminster Review* suggested punishing all attacks on the police with a flogging. This, it was asserted, would deter offenders and 'with the cessation of violent assaults on the police, police violence will also disappear. For it will be unnecessary and inexcusable'.[7] Violent behaviour by policemen could result in prosecution and conviction. Alfred Bowes Barugh was killed when PC John Norman stuck him on the head during disorders at the Malton Steeplechase in 1870. In sentencing Norman to nine months with hard labour at the York Assizes the judge declared:

> Persons intrusted with power must be careful how they exercise it. There appears, however, to be no malice against the deceased, and no doubt there was great provocation and the police was badly used. The prisoner had been ordered to draw his staff and to use it if necessary. In some respects the prisoner was unfortunate in having caused the death of the young man.[8]

But police officers were not always 'unfortunate' in this way, as in the case, for example, of two constables from the Metropolitan Police charged with assaulting John Brosnan. In the early hours of a winter's morning in 1884, Brosnan challenged the constables while they were lashing together three vehicles. The conclusion to this incident prefigured the assault on Gamble. A third constable appeared on the scene and suggested, in words like those of Sergeant Sheedy thirty years later: 'Don't hit him any more, I think you have given him enough.'[9]

It is possible that such tough police behaviour changed as assaults on police officers declined towards the end of the Victorian period. The situation was often stated to be significantly different in the early twentieth century. A correspondent of *The Times*, writing at length about the Metropolitan Police in 1908, noted such a change:

> A constable who said to me once, 'I like night duty best – you can give it to 'em (the hooligans) hotter than by day', would shake his head, now that of a very old man, over this change perhaps, though in his case the liberty of action he enjoyed was put to good use.[10]

Proving, rather than simply asserting this change, however, is difficult. There were still respectable commentators who considered that policemen in the East End of London felt 'like a mercenary force in a strange and alien land' and feared the kindness and courtesy they exercised in the West End of London would be thought of as weakness in the East End.[11] It is probable that the glowing picture presented of the Metropolitan Police in *The Times* was penned to counter the uncomfortable reading about the behaviour of a few police officers, including Ashworth and Sheedy, revealed in the 1908 Report of the Royal Commission on the Duties of the Metropolitan Police. Fourteen years later, in a tone similar to that of *The Times*, the *Justice of the Peace* declared:

> Incredible as it may seem in these days, there are still retired police officers, hardly yet old men, who can recall the days when, rattle in one hand and truncheon in the other, they fought many a fight with local ruffians, vanquished them, and established their authority and reputation in their own district by the strength of their own right arms.[12]

Yet the system of beat patrolling was not much changed in the first half of the twentieth century, and there continued to be districts that were hostile to policemen. Three years after its expression of belief that things had improved, the *Justice of the Peace* discussed the law relating to assaults on the police. It also explained how in 'populous districts the constable constantly finds himself in the presence of a hostile crowd, hampered by obstruction when dealing with a troublesome prisoner.'[13] In 1927 it reported a series of assaults on police officers, and the angry comments of magistrates hearing the cases. 'Some people go in for parson-baiting and others go in for baiting the police', declared one such outraged magistrate.

> It is a form of big-game hunting. I hold no brief for the police, but it is dirty and cowardly for a gang to set upon one or two men. It is not English or decent. The people of this district [the Thames Police Court] must be taught to find some amusement other than knocking the police about – there are always the pictures.[14]

Wilmer Gardens in Hoxton was known as 'Kill Copper Row'. It was one of the streets in working-class London said to be the site of the urban myth of the policeman stuffed into a drain and later dying of his injuries. Campbell Bunk, Islington, was similar; between the wars it had a reputation for hostility and occasional violence towards the police.[15] But it also had some tough policemen, working-class hard men in the sense of those discussed earlier. PC Ginger Mullins, for example, broke up fights in Campbell Bunk with his own fists and boots, always placing his helmet and belt on a carefully folded tunic beforehand – and no one would ever touch 'Mister' Mullins's uniform during the ensuing fight. Mullins, 'of great physique and as strong as an ox', was not unique.[16] Fred Hall, who began his police service in Birmingham between the wars, recalled a toughness and feeling of superiority among his comrades, fostered in part, he thought, by their training in self-defence and their experience as new recruits in the boxing ring.

> Although our training manual said that we should only use sufficient force as a necessary, we had been well bloodied in the ring and knew that speed and the first good blow would always do the trick ... If ever we did come unstuck and came off second best, we never complained of assault but would usually put our injuries down to having fallen or walked into a wall because it was looked upon as a sign of weakness to be beaten, whatever the odds were.[17]

Veterans of the Liverpool Police of the inter-war period had similar stories of rough streets and equally rough policemen. 'Policemen in those days, particularly like me who had been away to sea, were a bit rough. We didn't carry batons for ornaments.'[18] Commenting on the law regarding assaults on the police in 1925, the *Justice of the Peace* conceded that a few police were 'brutal'.[19] The problem here is to disentangle 'brutality' and the English notion of the 'fair fight'. When Sergeant Sheedy told Gamble to get up and fight like a man, was he urging him simply to act like a proper Englishman and commit himself to a 'fair fight'? Similarly, when Ginger Mullins placed his helmet, belt and folded jacket on the pavement, were these actions a part of the ritual of a hard man confronting other hard men in a 'fair' contest?

Tough beats continued to exist long after the Second World War. In some instances capable hard men like Ginger Mullins were chosen to police them. But in some instances too it appears that officers could be posted to them for breaking the rules or for offending a senior officer. John Wainwright wrote of his posting to such a beat in West Yorkshire in the late 1950s and early 1960s.

> It was a 'punishment beat' and, regardless of any disclaimer made by official-dom, they do exist. They are recognised and earmarked as beats with which to tame stroppy coppers and, having crossed [Detective Chief Superinten-dent] Metcalfe ... I was due to be chopped down to size ... You name it, and short of murder, some bastard at Toll Bar had committed it. The emphasis

was on violence, with theft running a close second and, more often than not, going hand-in-hand.

Wainwright's difficulties were probably aggravated by the fact that his was a rural beat where he was the only officer, with his police 'station' doubling as home for himself and his wife. Not all police officers were hard men and the pressures of such a beat could have a deleterious effect on a man, on his family, and on his attitude towards his career.[20]

Looking back on the late 1920s and the beginning of his police career, Victor Meek, who appears to have revelled in such nicknames as 'Old Bastardface', recalled an unwritten rule in dealing with 'customers'. 'If they started it they were naturally charged with assault. If I felt that I had been the aggressive one, then the most they had to fear was a charge of obstructing an officer in the execution of his duty.'[21] Harry Daley, who joined the Metropolitan Police in 1925, recalled that prisoners were 'occasionally' struck, but considered that 'violent policemen were in the minority even among the old-timers'. He thought that police violence began to decline as better men were recruited and subsequently promoted. Yet he also describes the very violent arrest of a man whose offence was that, having been prevented from getting on a tram by the conductor, he waved two fingers and blew a raspberry. The other arresting officer with Daley twisted the man's arm painfully behind him as they marched him to the police station; and, at the station, the other officer threw the man on the floor and then deliberately banged his head on it. Shortly before the man appeared in court charged with insulting behaviour, Daley had a 'menacingly short' interview with the station inspector who advised him: 'Be careful what you say to the magistrate – that's all'. 'I plead guilty to moral cowardice over this and similar cases,' explained Daley, 'but ordinary men with dependent mothers [and, he might have added, with wives and children] were not at this period in a position to be martyrs.'[22] This was no fair fight, and here the police closed ranks to protect their own in a fashion that they had been accused of in previous generations.[23] But violent police officers did not always get away with it, as the prosecutions arising out of the assaults on Brosnan and Gamble reveal.

A few policemen were disciplined and dismissed or ordered to resign for violence towards members of the public; some were disciplined and dismissed or ordered to resign for violence towards their comrades, superior officers, or wives.[24] But concern was occasionally expressed about the difficulty of bringing a case of assault against a police officer. In 1868, for example, the satirical magazine *Tomahawk* expressed fears about what it saw as the increasing power of the police. It appeared impossible, even for a respectable man assaulted by a police officer, to have his case properly investigated and to see the officer disciplined. The English, the magazine fretted, 'may in attempting to preserve our public safety, jeopardise our public liberty, and become only in a less degree, than the French, the slaves of those who should be our protectors'.[25] There is also a considerable amount of evidence to suggest that, from the Victorian period at least up until the end of the Second World War, many, and perhaps most, magistrates favoured police evidence in instances involving violence. The satirical magazine *Fun* was regularly critical of this in the mid nineteenth century. 'The invariable support which the authorities give to the constables has encouraged and tempted them to exercise their power most tyrannically.'[26] The cartoon, 'Nupkin's Justice', is a good example of *Fun's* attitude (Figure 9). George McAdoo, former Commissioner of the New York City Police, was surprised, at the beginning of the twentieth century, to see how the magistrate's court treated the police

> as part of the machinery of the law, and as partners with it in the doing of substantial justice ... Not a single policeman was reprimanded or criticized in any case, even when the court made prompt acquittals as against the charge of the constables.[27]

Magistrates hearing cases from the East End of London appear commonly to have accepted police stories uncritically and to have admired the constables who patrolled the area, given the 'class' of individuals who lived there.[28] One reason why George Gamble did not fight back may have been a concern that he could then have been accused of assaulting Ashworth and that most magistrates would have accepted the constable's story in preference to his own. In February 1929, following a charge of assault brought by a costermonger against a police constable in Islington, the magistrate concluded that the constable made a mistake 'thinking that the complainant was deliberately trying to carry on his business in the middle of the road'. But he also went out of his way to

NUPKINS'S JUSTICE.

Learned Magistrate:—"HEAR THE EVIDENCE FOR THE DEFENCE? NONSENSE! I WON'T HEAR A WORD OF IT! WHAT'S THE USE?—I COULD NOT THINK OF DOUBTING A POLICEMAN'S WORD."

9. 'Nupkins's Justice', from *Fun*, 13 October 1866. The 'learned magistrate' refuses to hear any defence evidence from the ragged boy on the grounds that it is not possible for him to doubt a policeman's word. The cartoon reflects what appears to have been a widespread belief among sections of the working class during the nineteenth and early twentieth centuries.

portray the incident in a light favourable to the policeman. He recognised the bitterness and tension between police officers and
costermongers brought about by the police attempting to move on illegal street sellers. The constable, he believed, 'got "rattled" and acted
without his customary discretion', partly because of a hostile crowd. He
did not think that the constable had kicked the costermonger. '[The
constable] no doubt caught [the costermonger's] arm and moved away
with him some little distance.' The case was dismissed.[29]

It was in dealing with disorder that the police most clearly manifested their ability to deploy violence on behalf of the state. A variety
of contingencies and pressures could influence the nature of that violence. It was alleged, for example, that Irish sympathy for the Boers and
the head constable's predilection for former members of the Royal Irish
Constabulary gave an additional edge to a police baton charge during
the Lloyd George riot in Birmingham in 1901. Policemen were commonly accused of aggression towards strikers during the Victorian
period, before the First World War and during the inter-war years. This
was occasionally picked up by sections of the press or by individuals
writing in the press, such as the north-eastern poet who, following a
police baton charge against a crowd of strikers and their families,
penned a pastiche of Tennyson's *Charge of the Light Brigade.*[30] The more
radical labour journals emphasised police violence.[31] But this was not
something ever taken up and much stressed by the Labour Party, which
did not share the strong oppositional culture of its continental European counterparts. Moreover, police violence was generally played down
in the expanding popular media, first in the mass press and then in the
cinema.

'Hunger Trek Ends', *British Paramount News*'s account of the National
Unemployed Workers' Movement meeting in Hyde Park on 27 October
1932, showed mounted police riding hard into a crowd swinging their
batons. But the commentary, without supporting pictures, stressed that
'extremist speeches', 'the hooligan element' and 'ruffians' were to blame
for the trouble, while 'the most humane force in the world ... by firm-
ness and great courage ... averted bloodshed and serious disturbance'.[32]
This exculpating commentary, however, was insufficient for the Metropolitan Police, who believed that Paramount should not have filmed the
incident in the first place and, as a consequence, denied the facilities that

it requested for filming the Lord Mayor's Show later in the year.[33] Four years later, in a report on the Battle of Cable Street, the commentator for *Universal Talking News* explained that 'Batons and truncheons were drawn, exhibited quite a lot, but used comparatively little'. Then, following a reference to how all foreigners recognised that the English police were 'wonderful', the viewer was invited to 'Watch how this baton doesn't hit!'[34]

In feature films there was an absolute ban on showing any form of police violence. A film script of Walter Greenwood's novel *Love on the Dole* was rejected during the 1930s. The film was made at the beginning of the 1940s when the depression was over and when the unity of war and the hopes of a better society in peace suggested to censors and others that the delicate subject matter of the novel could be portrayed for the general public. It was the first English-made feature film to show English police wielding batons against a crowd.[35] In some instances constables may have adopted, at street level, the hostility towards strikers, socialists, communists and even the unemployed that was manifested by some senior officers. In others they lashed out through fear, through frustration at losing a rest day or time off, or simply as a release after having stood and received abuse and missiles for a period before being given the order to draw batons and disperse a crowd. In Birkenhead in 1932, following crowd trouble over the Means Test, Labour activists alleged that the police embarked on a 'reign of terror' in poor working-class districts, waking people up at night and smashing windows. No enquiry was ever launched into the affair.[36]

There was always a problem of launching enquiries into the behaviour of English provincial police forces. In Parliament the Home Secretary could maintain, correctly, that he had no authority to make enquiries into forces run by standing joint committees of magistrates and county councillors or by borough watch committees. In turn, local committees were usually reluctant to pursue enquiries into their police forces where violence was alleged.[37] No publicity and no serious public debate and exposure meant that there could be no general awareness of any structural or political issue affecting the police. Even though the 1920s, as well as the period immediately before the First World War, witnessed enquiries into the Metropolitan Police following scandals of corruption and, at best, officiousness, there was a general determination to stress the superiority of English institutions and to assign any apparently excessive use of force to the occasional rotten apple. The Royal Commission on Police Powers and Procedures that reported in 1929, for example, emphasised the policeman's exposure to 'physical hardship and ... danger beyond those met with in most occupations'. It did not consider that there was any evidence suggesting that the police were more arbitrary and oppressive in their attitude towards the public than they had been before the war. It concluded with a favourable assessment of the police, suggesting that the 'instinctive and deep-rooted sympathy between the public and the police' was unbroken.[38]

Casualties in violent confrontations between police and demonstrators were very many fewer in England than in the United States or on continental Europe during the nineteenth century and in the first half of the twentieth. The problem is assessing to what extent this lack of casualties was the result of an overall moderation on the part of the English police, which apologists for the institution always stress, to what extent it was the result of the English police being rarely armed with anything other than a short baton,[39] and to what extent it stemmed from political contingency and culture. Some police forces in the United States were strongly tied to business and industrial interests in ways that encouraged them to confront workers, and especially strikers, with considerable violence. In New York during the Progressive period, reformers of the police divided between those whose principal aim was ending corruption and violence and those who felt that the key task of the police should be the eradication of vice and who were prepared to sanction the use of the club on offenders and the axe to smash into 'vice dens'.[40] Many of the European police institutions that had developed in the nineteenth century were military and were armed and equipped as such. They were required to fulfil tasks unlike those required of the English Bobby. In Italy the Carabinieri played a key role in the formation and consolidation of the state itself. In Spain the Guardia Civil helped hold the country together. In France, where this model of policing originated, the Gendarmerie nationale remained the first line of defence for a state where the constitutional structure was continually challenged.[41] The non-military police in these countries, commonly directed by local authorities, probably had rather more opportunities than their English counterparts for annoying all classes because of various police regulations. This was especially apparent in Imperial Germany. It was also possible in Germany for a municipal police officer to be imprisoned for assaulting members of the public, and to return to police duty on his release – something that would not have been countenanced in England.[42] Yet the states of continental Europe increasingly saw themselves as *Rechtsstaats*, states in which officials were answerable to the law, and it would be wrong to assume that the police of these states were seen always as a pressure, or simply as violent, intrusive agents of the state.

Guns and training the police for street and house to house fighting in working-class districts did not in themselves make police officers violent. However, such training appears to have been a key element in the *Blutmai* disaster in Berlin in May 1929. The police had already trained for trouble in particular working-class districts of the city, but the training and expectation of Communist insurrection appears to have turned a minor incident into a massacre by the police. Guns held by the police, the fear of revolutionary action, assumptions about street fighting, and poor command contributed to deaths at the hands of the police in Paris in February 1934 and in the *Affaire de Clichy* in June 1937.[43] Even so, it needs to be stressed that such incidents were not part of the daily routine of policemen in the French Third Republic, in Weimar Germany or even in Nazi Germany. And if violence and terror were part of the armoury of the Gestapo, recent research has shown how much this relatively small organisation depended upon denunciation. Its use of violence and terror was directed almost entirely against those labelled as enemies of the regime and of the idealised national community – the *Volksgemeinschaft*. There was widespread approval for the law and order policies of the Nazis, and it has been noted how, forty years later, people who lived through the 1930s and 1940s looked back with nostalgia to the fact that they 'could leave their bicycles unlocked outside their front doors; and long-haired layabouts were hauled off into Labour Camps'.[44]

This is not an attempt to equate English police behaviour with Nazi police behaviour, a comparison popular with some political radicals during the 1960s and subsequently. The point is rather that political structures and social attitudes tended to conceal the scale of police violence before a more open period that began after the Second World War, though not significantly until 1960s. Aggressive, violent behaviour

by police officers was present after the Second World War. In the early
summer of 1959, for example, R. A. Butler, the Home Secretary, was
given a difficult time in Parliament following the arrest of two men who,
after their interrogation at Hornsey Road Police Station, had to be taken
to the Royal Northern Hospital. Butler reported that the Commissioner
of the Metropolitan Police had investigated his men fully and had found
no grounds for either criminal proceedings or disciplinary action. A
month later, in a completely separate incident, Günter Padola was
arrested for the murder of a police constable. Padola was allegedly
beaten up at Chelsea Police Station and had to be taken to hospital; he
was also held without charge and without being permitted to see a
solicitor. Once again Butler found himself having to talk his way out of
a difficult situation without implying any wrong-doing on the part
of police officers. Towards the end of the year Parliament debated the
payment of £300 by the Commissioner to a civil servant who was suing
a police officer for assault and unlawful imprisonment. The payment, accepted by the plaintiff, did not admit liability; the police officer
concerned had not been disciplined, and there were no plans for a criminal charge. This incident was the direct origin of a Royal Commission
on the Police which, like its predecessor in 1929, gave the police as an
institution a clean bill of health.[45]

But there was also a new degree of openness. In September 1959, the
Commissioner of the Metropolitan Police had an interview with senior
members of the BBC. With the usual statement about things not being
as rough as they had used to be, Sir Joseph Simpson expressed himself
fully prepared to have his officers portrayed as tough and violent in television series. 'We discussed allegations of violence made against the
Police', explained the BBC memo on the meeting,

> and the Commissioner had no doubts at all that on occasion a great deal of
> violence was exerted, and certainly made no bones about the fact that his Fly-
> ing Squad consisted of some of the toughest Policemen in the world ... he
> went on to say that it was his considered opinion that there was ... far less
> violence exerted by the Police these days than had been in his young days on
> the beat.[46]

Within three years the BBC series *Z Cars* was showing policemen who
were violent towards their wives, though significantly in a northern
force rather than in the Metropolitan Police, but it was to be fifteen

years before the hard men of the Flying Squad were to be portrayed in *The Sweeney*. Both of these television series created a stir among sections of the viewing public and the police for portraying English policemen in a rough, tough and violent manner rarely portrayed for a popular cinema or television audience before.

This new openness, and a preparedness to recognise and to accept the existence of tough, aggressive policemen, was fostered by a series of developments during the 1950s and 1960s. Following the Second World War the police in England were poorly paid, undermanned and not always well led. There was, nevertheless, a continuing *esprit de corps*; police officers saw themselves as experts in the pursuit of wrong-doing, as the protectors of citizens, but deserving of greater recognition for their efforts and their difficulties. Circumstances, however, meant that there were now more and more opportunities for these police officers to confront respectable, articulate citizens as 'wrong-doers'. There was the spread of car ownership. The emergence of political demonstrations against nuclear weaponry, against the South African policy of Apartheid and, later, against the war in Vietnam. There was a significant growth in the middle-class student body, now more interested in politics and social change than in student rags, and whose clothing often made them indistinguishable from less articulate working-class youths who might earlier have been labelled as 'police property'. The articulate, politically minded student might also be confronted by the police over the use of recreational drugs. There began to be a growing degree of disquiet among liberal sections of society that police behaviour towards Commonwealth immigrants was not as it might be. Such disquiet was confirmed by Lord Scarman's enquiry into the causes of the rioting in Brixton in 1981.[47] Improved media technology from the 1970s meant that violent confrontations between police and political and industrial protesters could be transmitted into people's homes almost as they happened. And even if NATO helmets, flame-proof overalls, body armour and shields had become necessary during the late twentieth century, the images of such police officers did nothing for the traditional image of the avuncular, non-violent Bobby. Finally, the constant rise in the statistics of crime presented by the annual *Judicial Statistics*, the increasing centrality of these figures and of concerns about violent crime in political debate, combined to suggest to sections of the press and of the public that Dixon of Dock Green might usefully be replaced by Dirty Harry.

In a sense perhaps there was a conspiracy to underplay police violence in England during the nineteenth and early twentieth centuries. But it was not planned as such. Beliefs about English difference and the supremacy of English civilisation were sincerely held. The idealised Bobby was a working-class manifestation of respectable, middle-class Englishness. He may not have been intellectually brilliant, but he spoke civilly to people. Unlike some of his continental European counterparts, he was not required to enforce pettyfogging regulations. Nor did he pry often into people's politics and privacy. But 'people' in this sense were the respectable classes. Admitting that violence and aggression could be used by police officers against individuals in England would undermine the received opinions of Englishness, and arguably this fear became particularly strong with the growth of mass society and the potential of mass entertainment in the form of the cinema. As long as police aggression and violence was directed against those who lacked a strong public voice, it could be ignored or else condoned as a necessary element in civilising the crowd. These ideas probably also had a significant impact on police behaviour. It is easy to recognise that magistrates and others condoning rough police behaviour in the less respectable working-class districts might have encouraged such behaviour. At the same time it is, perhaps, less easy to accept that the constant insistence that the English police were different, and that they were civil and restrained may also have had a profound impact on police behaviour, not just with the respectable but also in their dealings with those on the other side of the tracks.

9

Violence and the State

On 28 January 1953 Derek Bentley, an illiterate nineteen-year-old youth with learning difficulties and epilepsy, was hanged in Wandsworth Prison. Bentley had been found guilty of being an accessory to the murder of PC Sidney Miles during a botched raid on Barlow and Parker's confectionery warehouse in Tamworth Road, Croydon. The events had been as follows. Just after 9.00 p.m. on Sunday 2 November 1952 Bentley, together with sixteen-year-old Christopher Craig, had been seen climbing a gate into the warehouse. The police were telephoned. Two vehicles responded: a van with four officers and a wireless car with two. What happened next was in some ways reminiscent of the courageous, unarmed police pursuit of troopers Vanderberg and Kaye. But on this occasion the pursuit of the offenders was over a rooftop and the consequence was a murder. Craig was armed with a .455 revolver and had no qualms about using it. Detective Constable Frederick Fairfax, an officer with sixteen years in the police interrupted by war service during which he rose to the rank of an infantry captain, was shot and wounded in the shoulder. In spite of his wound Fairfax detained Bentley and handed him over to other officers. Bentley offered no resistance at any point, but Craig continued firing. Constable Miles, a veteran of twenty-two years service, was shot in the head and killed. Fairfax, regardless of his wound and now armed with a police revolver, followed Craig across the roof exchanging shots with him until the latter was out of ammunition. Craig jumped from the roof and, seriously injured, was arrested by the police. Bentley was found to have a knife and a knuckle-duster in his pocket. But he had no gun, had been standing with the police when Miles was shot, and had shown no inclination to resist them or run from them.

The case was a sensation. Reflecting upon it two years later, Sir Harold Scott, who had been Commissioner of the Metropolitan Police at the time, stressed the rarity of lethal shootings and armed robbery in London, and in Britain in general. But there were few such sober counsels at the time. At Constable Miles's funeral the Archdeacon of Croydon, the Venerable C. F. Tonks, raised the well-worn concerns about a changing England and new levels of violence.

> The present wave of robbery and violence is foreign to this country. It is seriously disturbing the minds and consciences of us all. Women go in fear, fear of opening their doors after dark, fear of walking alone in quiet roads.
>
> Single-handed shopkeepers look askance at strange customers and the thought must cross the minds of the police – will they find a gunman where they might expect a petty thief? This is not England, the England we have known and for which men and women have laid down their lives.

The case followed hard on the heels of the arrest of Craig's elder brother, his conviction and sentence to twelve years in prison for the possession of a firearm and armed robbery.[1] On the same day that Craig and Bentley were convicted Norman Parsley, another sixteen-year-old, was sentenced to four years after having pleaded guilty to the armed robbery, in company with Craig, of an elderly couple in their own home.[2] These cases came in the wake of the post-war scares about brutalised war veterans and violent youths. The scares had been mirrored a few years earlier in *The Blue Lamp* and were mirrored again with the premier of a new film, *Cosh Boy*, between Miles's shooting and Bentley's, Craig's and Parsley's appearances in court.[3]

Yet, in spite of these scares, there was considerable disquiet over the way in which the legal system responded to the convictions of Bentley and Craig. The sixteen year old, who had fired the shot that killed Miles and had emptied his gun twice in the direction of the police officers, was too young to be hanged. He was sentenced to be detained at Her Majesty's pleasure. Bentley, however, who had been standing with the police but was not, technically, in their custody at the time of the fatal shot, was sentenced to hang. The jury recognised the problem and recommended mercy in Bentley's case. An appeal was rejected on the grounds that there had been nothing untoward in the trial, and the appeal judges ruled that: 'If two persons went out on a joint adventure and one of them committed part of the joint adventure while the other stood by, as a result of the law each was liable for the consequences of the act of the other.'[4] The Home Secretary, Sir David Maxwell-Fyfe, decided against recommending the exercise of the royal prerogative of mercy and commuting Bentley's sentence to life imprisonment. It has been common to ascribe this decision to the recommendation of the seventy-six-year-old Lord Chief Justice, Rayner Goddard, who had presided at the trial. Lord Goddard was well known for his support for both capital and corporal punishment, and noted for his contempt of criminals and those who interceded for them as psychiatrists, probation officers and social workers. In fact, while the tenor of Goddard's advice may be guessed, precisely what he recommended to Maxwell-Fyfe is unknown. Moreover, Goddard told the jury that he would pass on their recommendation and, in sentencing Craig, he declared him to be 'the more guilty of the two'.[5]

Bentley's execution occasioned outrage in many quarters. Petitions were sent in the hopes of preventing it. There was an attempt in Parliament to persuade Maxwell-Fyfe to reconsider the pardon and a deputation of MPs called on him. In the aftermath of the execution Frederick Fairfax, now promoted to sergeant, received threats in the post. The *Lancet* published an article on the subject: 'To the English ... revenge is seldom a fully satisfying experience; it carries too much guilt with it. In the case of Bentley the public sense of guilt seems to have been strong – far stronger than the desire for vengeance.' The religious journal, *British Weekly*, carried a fierce criticism of Maxwell-Fyfe – 'a Tory minister ... can always be expected to show a proper contempt for the conscience and convictions of the public'. Two members of the editorial board resigned in protest at the statement, and the clergyman editor, who had written it, publicly expressed his 'regret' at his choice of words.[6]

Six months after Bentley's execution, there was further disquiet when the conviction of the multiple murderer John Christie called into question the execution of Timothy Evans, a lorry driver with considerable learning difficulties who had been hanged for the murder of his wife and baby daughter in 1950. In 1955 the execution of Ruth Ellis for the murder of her violent lover provoked another wave of criticism of the death penalty; yet the government remained unmoved and merely advised Parliament to take note of the recent Royal Commission that advised abolition. The Homicide Act of 1957 established distinct categories of capital and non-capital murder, and provided new defences of diminished responsibility and provocation. These would have saved Bentley, and probably Ellis and Evans, but capital punishment remained an option available in British courts for another eight years. There seems to be justification for arguing that Bentley and Ellis were singled out as examples. Bentley was hanged in response to the post-war scare about violent young male offenders and as a warning to others. Ellis, who shot her lover only ten days after a miscarriage brought on by one of his beatings, and who was in a seriously disturbed state at the time of the shooting, was a warning to those labelled as 'good-time girls'. 130 women were sentenced to death in England and Wales between 1900 and 1955, but only fifteen of these, including Ellis, were executed. A strong case can be made that these fifteen were singled out because their life-style and behaviour fell far short of the idealised gender norm for English women during the period.[7] For all its claims to liberalism and restraint, the British state, which in this context can be defined as the executive, the legislature and the judiciary, maintained the option of violent punishments – corporal as well as capital – for much longer than many of its continental counterparts. The changes in capital and corporal punishment have been well chronicled.[8] The intention here is rather to highlight the paradox of a liberal state with a violent penal code, and to underline the way in which English exceptionality was occasionally foregrounded in the debates and developments.

In *Candide* Voltaire commented satirically on the British decision to execute Admiral Byng following his unsuccessful expedition to Minorca in 1757; it had to be done, Voltaire's eponymous hero was told, *pour encourager les autres*.[9] The penal system of eighteenth-century England is commonly referred to as 'the Bloody Code'. There were more than two hundred offences on the statute book that carried the death penalty. This did not mean that there were two hundred distinct, capital offences, since some of the statutes referred to specific offences in specific places and the majority of individuals executed under the Bloody Code were condemned for murder or some form of major larceny. Nevertheless in theory, if not always in practice, a high percentage of property offences ran the risk of a death sentence. From early on in the eighteenth century there were members of the elite who looked for alternatives to execution. Transportation was the principal 'secondary punishment' developed during the century and over the same period some of the more grotesque methods of execution were mitigated. Increasingly, traitors were simply beheaded, rather than being half strangled and having their entrails ripped from their bodies as a precursor to the headsman's axe; and women guilty of petty treason – which could mean the murder of their spouse – were commonly strangled before being burned at the stake. But for most of the eighteenth century execution still meant slow strangulation on a public gallows. There were a set of social ideas about how justice should work that led to many being pardoned – these were usually the young, the old, first offenders, women, those suffering from severe economic distress and those who were employable. There was rarely much mercy for the cruel or the hardened offender, and the execution as a means of discouraging others continued to be staunchly defended. Violence was both a tool of discipline and a way of asserting the authority and power of the state.

A movement for change, spearheaded most notably by Sir Samuel Romilly, gathered pace in the late eighteenth and early nineteenth centuries. The arguments centred on attempts to define the nature of English justice. The defenders of the Bloody Code insisted that the use of judicial discretion and royal clemency had stood the test of time and were deployed with wisdom and humanity by men experienced in the process. They insisted that the system was geared for dealing with individual cases and rejected the idea that a system of mechanical certainty with prescribed categories of punishment for different offences and offenders could be constructed. This, they argued, was something that French thinkers had tried in broad terms in 1789, with disastrous consequences. The reformers, in contrast, were keen to remove any impression that partiality or inequality influenced the law. The growing public demands of the emergent middle and working classes, together with the burgeoning industrial towns and cities that were undermining the personal relations claimed for the old system, gave an added urgency to the reformers' arguments.[10] At the same time, the reformers drew unfavourable comparisons with the situation elsewhere in Europe. Sir James Mackintosh, for example, compared the six capital offences in the French penal code with 223 capital statutes in England, and this at the close of thirty years of wars in which France had been 'twice invaded [and] had disbanded a large army'. The Attorney General responded to

Mackintosh by suggesting that France also had the fearsome police system of Napoleon, and only with such an institution, inimical to English liberties, might change in the capital legislation be considered.[11] Nevertheless, by the third decade of the nineteenth century it was really only judges and the law officers of the Crown who were holding the conservative line. As Tory Home Secretary in the 1820s, Sir Robert Peel commenced a significant reorganisation of the criminal law that began to reduce the number of capital statutes. 'It is impossible to conceal from ourselves', he admitted to the Commons in 1830, 'that Capital Punishments are more frequent, and the criminal law more severe, on the whole, in this country than in any country in the world.'[12] By the early 1840s capital punishment was essentially limited to four offences: high treason, murder, piracy with violence, and the destruction of public arsenals and dockyards. This was confirmed by the Criminal Law Consolidation Act of 1861.

There are several ways of explaining these changes in the death penalty. These are not mutually exclusive but place their emphasis very differently. On the one hand, the changes have been put down to a growing humanitarianism and rationalism that was inspired by the Enlightenment and rejected the 'barbarism' of earlier centuries. Linked with this is the conclusion that, during the eighteenth century, a growing sensibility to the public infliction of pain can be found among the elite. Thus the crowds at executions appear to have been increasingly influenced more by the physical sufferings of the offender than by any intended lesson that shamed him or her and acted as a warning to others. The other principal explanation is centred on state pragmatism. In the early nineteenth century more and more people were being apprehended for, and convicted of, capital offences. There was anxiety that too many executions would be intolerable, and this led to an increase in the number of commutations to transportation or imprisonment. But these commutations, in turn, prompted concerns that the existing law was being undermined by the inability of the system to function as it had been intended. Reducing the number of capital offences provided a solution to the problem; and by the focus on murder it also emphasised the heinous nature of this, the ultimate violent crime.

As early as 1751 the novelist and Bow Street magistrate Henry Fielding had suggested that capital punishment in private would have greater impact than the turbulent scenes and fairground atmosphere around the gallows at Tyburn.

> Foreigners have found fault with the Cruelty of the *English* Drama, in representing frequent murders upon the Stage. In fact, this is not only cruel, but highly injudicious: A Murder behind the Scenes, if the Poet knows how to manage it, will affect the Audience with greater Terror than if it was acted before their Eyes ...
>
> If Executions therefore were so contrived, that few could be present at them, they would be much more shocking and terrible to the Crowd without Doors than at present, as well as much more dreadful to the Criminals themselves, who would thus die in the Presence only of their Enemies ...

He suggested that the solemnity of executions in Holland, in the presence of magistrates, was one reason why they were so rare in that country.[13] The removal of public executions to Newgate Prison in 1783 meant that there were no longer lengthy parades through the streets of London from prison to the execution site at Tyburn, situated near the modern Marble Arch. These parades had disrupted traffic and annoyed respectable individuals with expensive new houses close by the route. On occasions, for offenders with a popular appeal such as a courageous and flamboyant 'gentleman of the road', the parades became triumphal processions before cheering crowds. But for anyone who had roused popular anger, such as a violent and brutal robber or a child murderer, they were horrendous journeys before baying, hostile crowds.

Yet even when the execution site shifted to a scaffold outside Newgate the scene was not necessarily decorous. People paid considerable sums for the 'best' seats in windows overlooking 'the drop', and large crowds gathered in the space before the scaffold ready to sympathise with or execrate the condemned. It was not until 1868 that executions were moved inside prison walls and thus ceased to be public spectacles. The shift was not made without heated debate. There were many who argued that the common people would never believe that a gentleman was hanged unless they saw it for themselves. The public execution thus ensured the impartiality of the legal process and, at the same time, the spectacle was manifestly open rather than furtive and, by implication, foreign.[14]

More powerful, however, appears to have been the growing belief that such public demonstrations of the state's power were indecorous for a

civilised society. This was not least because of the way that, according to
The Times, 'abandoned women and brutal men, met beneath the gallows
to pass the night in drinking and buffoonery; in ruffianly swagger and
obscene jests'.[15] The satirical journal *Tomahawk* made the same point
with a drawing imagining the last sight that the condemned saw from the
scaffold – a crowd of simian-looking brutes drinking, fighting, throwing
sticks and animals (Fig. 10). Yet the privacy of executions did not necessarily ensure that they were any more decorous, or that the proceedings
were any more restrained. A succession of public hangmen during the
1880s, William Marwood, Bartholomew Binns and James Berry, were
often drunk and seriously botched executions. Berry also made the
rounds of public houses on the night before an execution entertaining
large crowds with stories and comic songs. The executioners made mistakes, but botched executions were also a result of cheeseparing over the
construction of gallows, and arguments between the executioner and the
prison doctor over the appropriate length of rope. If the rope was too
short the condemned might strangle slowly; if it was too long, he or she
might be decapitated.[16]

Concerns about the indecorous nature of the public infliction of pain
combined with growing sensitivity, or squeamishness, to bring about
changes in other forms of assault on the bodies of offenders. Less significant, but echoing the increasing opposition to violent games in the
streets and drunken brawls, was the annoyance caused to residents and
the inconvenience to traffic when public space was taken over by such
spectacles. Associated with all of these concerns was the fear that watch-
ing such spectacles encouraged cruelty among the populace, appealed to
the baser passions and inflamed those 'abandoned women and brutal
men' who cavorted at public executions. Branding, which for most of
the eighteenth century, had meant burning a mark on an offender's
thumb, was abolished in 1779. The last burning of a woman was in 1789,
and the practice was abandoned the following year. The pillory had been
designed as a shaming punishment. It was used in the eighteenth century for individuals who had committed moral transgressions with
seditious or religious blasphemies, frauds, homosexual acts, and other
sexual offences such as rape or bestiality. By the eighteenth century the
pillory was presenting problems. On occasions the pilloried person

10. 'Under the Scaffold: or The Hangman's Pupils', published in *Tomahawk*, 26 October 1867. The illustration claims to show the last thing seen by the condemned man on the scaffold at a public execution, just before the execution hood is pulled over his head. It reflects the perception that public executions pandered to the brutalised and least civilised sections of society.

might capture the popular imagination, when the sentence backfired on the authorities. Such was the case when a printer, John Williamson, was pilloried in 1765 for reprinting and selling a pamphlet by John Wilkes that had previously been condemned. The crowds cheered Williamson and made a collection for him. Similarly with Daniel Isaac Eaton, an elderly radical printer, sentenced to be pilloried in 1812 for publishing Tom Paine's *Age of Reason*, deemed by the courts to be a blasphemous libel. As one contemporary put it, 'anyone who had offered him the accustomed insults, would have run a great risk of being torn to pieces'. Other offenders, however, as the last quotation suggests, were violently assaulted in the pillory, and a few were even killed.[17]

Increasingly the pillory appeared to be a punishment that, by encouraging and pandering to the fury of the crowd, served rather to undermine order. Indeed, one critic during the post-Napoleonic period condemned it, with an implicit reference to the French Revolution, as 'of the wildest republican cast'.[18] At the same time there was, as has been noted earlier, an increasing desire to establish a greater decorum on the streets and in public places. Furthermore, as an individual's reputation began to be built less on public show and more on work, voluntary activity and what was disseminated about him (or her) through the printed word, so the notion of shame in the public pillory became less relevant. Concerns that judicial intentions would be undermined by sympathetic crowds appears to have led to a reduction in the use of the pillory for sedition offences from the mid eighteenth century.[19] In 1816 the punishment was limited to those convicted of perjury or subornation of perjury; it was abolished in 1837.

Whipping along the street at a cart's tail or else strapped to a public whipping post was also increasingly restricted. The first moves began among the judiciary in the second half of the eighteenth century as they sought to develop a system by which whippings might appear proportionate to the scale of the offence.[20] The judiciary similarly began, independently, to order private whippings, principally for women but also for some men. This predated statutory approval for private whipping which came in 1779. The public whipping of women was abolished in 1817, and three years later an Act of Parliament decreed that women were not to be whipped at all; though this does not appear to have percolated down to some of the lower courts for some years.[21]

Men continued to be whipped publicly well into the 1830s, and public whipping was not finally abolished by statute until 1862.

Sensitivity and concerns about indecorous behaviour did not combine to abolish the state's desire to employ violent sanctions against criminal offenders. There were moves for the abolition of whipping or flogging that accompanied a decline in the use of such sentences during the 1840s and 1850s. But the garotting attack on James Pilkington prompted a campaign orchestrated by *The Times* and urged vigorously by a clutch of MPs that threw these developments into reverse. In spite of the reservations of Sir George Grey, the Home Secretary, the Security from Violence Act of 1863, popularly known as the Garotters' Act, authorised floggings for those convicted of robbery; offenders aged under sixteen were to suffer up to twenty-five strokes, those over sixteen up to fifty strokes.[22]

The campaign for the abolition of capital punishment followed a similar trajectory. A group of independent MPs and their extra-parliamentary supporters sought to follow up Peel's reforms with the complete abolition of the death penalty. During the 1830s and early 1840s they appear to have considered that history was on their side. They thought in terms of progress, and believed in a growth of humanitarianism and sensibility. They pointed out that the recent abolition of the death penalty for many serious felonies had not led to a massive increase in crime. The advocates of retention recognised the force of these arguments and yielded ground step by step. By the middle of the century both sides were focused on the issue of the sanctity of human life and at this point the abolitionists' confidence seems to have led them to ignore a new vigour that entered their opponent's case.

Capital punishment, its defenders now asserted, demonstrated nothing more than the state's determination to protect the lives of the queen's subjects. Murderers were equated with the worst elements of the criminal classes; they were a threat to civilisation itself. The defenders of the death penalty played upon the fears of the dangerous classes and of garotters, insisting that it was only the threat of the most severe punishment that held them in check. Senior churchmen joined the debate on the side of retention and several significant abolitionists, including Carlyle, Dickens and John Stuart Mill, drifted into the retentionist camp. The Whig Macaulay labelled abolitionists as 'effeminate' and

Mill, in a powerful peroration to the Commons in 1868, urged resistance
to the 'enervation' and 'effeminacy' in the mind of the country that was
fostering an increase in hardened offenders. The removal of executions
from the public gaze appeared to the majority in the Commons to be
sufficient.[23] In the second half of the nineteenth century the campaigns
for the abolition of corporal and capital punishment in England were
muted, and this was at precisely the time when several continental European powers and some states of the United States were legislating for
abolition.

   Herein lies the paradox. The Victorian elite was keen to stress that the
ideal Englishman was controlled, restrained and used violence only in
the last resort. Moreover, when he did so, this violence was administered
in a fair and open manner. Through the courts and the police, these
ideas were enforced with more and more determination as the century
progressed. As the great jurist and essayist James Fitzjames Stephen put
it in a magazine article in 1864: 'Men ought to control their passions,
and if they fail to do so, they ought to suffer for it. The object of the
criminal law is to control the passions which prompt men to break it.'[24]
Towards the close of the eighteenth century it continued to be accepted
that men might physically 'correct' their children, their wives and their
servants. A century later it was only children who might be chastised by
a parent. Wife-beating, like street fighting, was now stigmatised and
identified as behaviour alien to accepted masculine culture, to be found
only among the rougher elements of the working class, and something
that needed to be curbed. In certain circumstances, for the police, the
enforcement of the new social and state norms might be a matter of
negotiation rather than confrontation. In other instances, in the case of
some strikes for example, the police used considerable violence.

   Arguably something of an agreement developed between the state and
the citizens. The latter surrendered to the state and its instruments –
policemen and courts – much of the traditional autonomy of their
neighbourhood in dealing with petty thieves. They also increasingly
reported to these instruments the excessive wife- or child-beater, those
considered as sexual deviants and other offenders who transgressed
against community norms. The state promised to use its monopoly of
violence for the benefit of its citizens, and implicit in this was a determination to limit the use of violence in both public and private places.[25]

Yet, for all its boasted liberalism and restraint, and for all its determination to limit the violence of individual working-class men, the state persevered in using forms of violence that other countries were rejecting. Even Prussia did not restore corporal punishment when an authoritarian regime was re-established after the liberal experiments of 1848. And while in 1871 Bismarck insisted on the resuscitation of the death penalty for the new German Criminal Code, he made no attempt to restore flogging.[26]

It would be convenient, but unhelpful and indeed wrong, to write the Victorians off as hypocrites over this. Recent history had contributed to a cultural perception in Victorian England that fostered a belief in the unique nature of its state and its people. The British state had no revolution at the end of the eighteenth century, and it defeated Napoleon. The storms of Luddism, Captain Swing and Chartism were weathered and there were no revolutionary upheavals like those experienced across continental Europe in 1830 and again in 1848. English commentators and politicians may have worried about such upheavals from time to time, but British success in war and in not experiencing the troubles of continental neighbours was put down to the superiority of the British state and its constitution. As long as Europeans – especially 'Mediterraneans' like the French, Italians or Spanish – could be perceived as volatile and potentially revolutionary, requiring a strong hand, and as long as European states could be perceived as authoritarian, with national, militarised police forces, then the English could see themselves as restrained, level-headed and even more civilised than their continental neighbours, and without the need for a similar firm hand. The view westwards across the Atlantic led to similar conclusions. The Americans were seen as rude and turbulent, and this was put down to their having no natural order of rank to restrain their democracy.

The paternalist English elite considered themselves restrained by their acceptance of the code of the gentleman. They also recognised a natural order in the class structure, and felt themselves justified in seeking to impose civilised English behaviour on the working classes. Most of the witnesses who gave evidence to the Royal Commission on Capital Punishment that deliberated between 1864 and 1866 appear to have assumed that murders were committed principally by the worst section of the working class, the criminal class. They considered that the death penalty was the best deterrent for dissuading burglars and robbers from committing worse crimes. One judge, Sir Samuel Martin, was quite explicit about murderers: 'It very seldom occurs that any person in the middle classes of life is indicted for murder.' He believed that the commission ought to interrogate people who knew the 'lower classes' better, though in his opinion the death penalty 'must be a terror to them'.[27] Yet even the English working classes were perceived as being more sensible and civilised than their continental European counterparts. And while they maintained capital and corporal punishment, successive British governments held rigidly to the idea that their police need not be armed and need not be political in the sense of their continental European counterparts.[28] Englishmen found it difficult to credit that the new Italian state could seriously consider abolishing the death penalty when the country appeared to be alive with brigands.[29] At the same time, and paradoxically, the leaders of the new Italian state were impressed by *il bobby inglese*, but felt that it would be impossible to establish such a body given the volatility of their own working class and peasantry.[30]

While recent history contributed to a particular self-perception among the English that kept the police unarmed and helped to justify the criminal code, the perception of the British soldier helped to maintain a violent military code that provided an uncomfortable contrast with European counterparts. Until well into the First World War the soldiers of the British army were volunteers. The rank and file were recruited from the working class; and many officers appear to have shared the Duke of Wellington's oft-quoted assertion that the soldiery was 'the scum of the earth – the mere scum of the earth'. To the military commanders in Horse Guards, capital punishment and the lash seemed the only sure way to maintain discipline. On occasions, even in the late eighteenth and early nineteenth centuries, what appeared excessive punishment could prompt anger among the populace, in much the same way that a capital conviction in a civilian court could create murmurs and unrest. The floggings ordered by Joseph Wall, when Governor of Goree in West Africa, that resulted in the death of three soldiers, offer the most extreme example. Wall was subsequently prosecuted for murder under the ordinary criminal law at the Old Bailey in 1802 and convicted. Crowds jeered at his execution. 'The barbarous exultation of the populace upon the appearance of Mr Wall on the scaffold resembled the horrid bravoes at the French Guillotine', commented *The Times*. 'It is to be remembered, however, that the inhumanity of the English populace proceeded from their detestation of inhumanity.'[31]

The flogging of a group of militiamen, made worse by the fact that the men were local and that foreign troops from the King's German Legion were deployed to keep the peace, led to serious disorder in Ely in 1810. A newspaper publisher's comparison of the lot of British soldiers with that of the French saw him brought before a carefully selected jury, convicted and sentenced to eighteen months in prison with a £200 fine. Military floggings were far more ferocious than those administered in civilian prisons and were generally carried out in front of the whole regiment *pour encourager les autres*. Following a similar pattern to the civilian situation, the numbers sentenced to military floggings decreased in the early 1830s at the same time that the number of courts martial increased. But when a soldier died, as a result of a flogging at Hounslow in 1846, *The Times* expressed its outrage at the continuing insistence of military officers that such sanction was necessary:

> According to their theory, the English soldier must always remain but a few degrees above the condition of a brute ... It would be dangerous to instruct him, foolish to interfere with his *ménage*, foolish to restrain his fondness for drink. It would mar the discipline and destroy the 'pluck' of the army. Was ever such fudge talked? Was ever such crass ignorance of human nature displayed?

Again the comparison was drawn with France: 'As if the English soldier was only fit for fighting and flogging – as if the French soldier had less courage because he studied the elements of his profession.'[32] Floggings continued and some soldiers continued to die as a result. Another death in 1867 led to restrictions in the punishment, but it was not finally abolished until 1881.

Only in 1871 was the branding of military offenders on the body with a 'D' for deserter and 'BC' for a bad character abolished. The number of brandings followed a similar pattern to the increasing resort to the lash by the civilian criminal law. About 400 military offenders were branded each year in the early 1850s; the numbers increased to some 1500 men a year in the following decade. The reform of 1881 resulted in the British army maintaining a total of twenty-seven capital offences; twelve were punishable by death at any time and a further fifteen only when on active service. There were also harsh field punishments which left the British soldier under a code that was more severe than either that of republican France or imperial Germany. Moreover, any man convicted had no right of appeal to a higher court, something which, at least on paper, was even allowed to soldiers in the authoritarian empires of Austria-Hungary and Russia.

The scale of British military executions during the First World War highlighted the violence of the system. Initially British commanders were inclined to see their men, particularly the regulars, as needing harsh discipline. Eugenic arguments also came into play as it was decided which of the men sentenced to be shot should have the sentence carried out. 'Driver Bell is a determined shirker during a time of war and unworthy of being a soldier and an Englishman', declared a corps commander when required to give his opinion on one such man. Such men were better offered up as examples than being returned to the line, and ministers were prepared to back the demands of the generals that the firing squad was the best way to maintain discipline and to prevent desertion and cowardice. The appearance of conscript soldiers at the front, however, led some commanders to reconsider their attitudes, and within days of the Armistice in 1918 the War Office told its generals that any future executions for cowardice would require ministerial approval. During the 1920s a campaign was fought from the back benches of the parliamentary Labour Party challenging the military establishment's determination to maintain their violent punishments. The campaign was led, not by pacifists, but by men who had fought in the war and who appear to have brought the Labour front bench on side by embarrassing it. In 1923 the campaigners succeeded in having the fearsome Field Punishment No. 1 – popularly known as 'crucifixion' – abolished. In 1930, following a free vote and with the support of large numbers of Conservative MPs, the death penalty was abolished for cowardice and desertion.[33]

The debates about capital and corporal punishment for civilian offenders revived in the aftermath of the First World War. In the case of capital punishment, this was partly the result of the commitment of the Labour Party to reform. But it appears also to have been prompted by some sensational murder cases and controversial executions. In 1923, for example, Edith Thompson and her lover were executed for the murder of her husband. Thompson had played no part in the killing and had immediately sought medical assistance when her lover stabbed her husband. Her critics portrayed her as the evil seductress of a younger man, but this led others to fear that she was being singled out and punished for her adultery. Her execution profoundly affected the chaplain and governor of Holloway Prison. It also prompted the executioner to resign and, allegedly, contributed to his later suicide.[34] In 1925 the National Council for the Abolition of the Death Penalty (NCADP) was established. It linked closely with members of the Labour Party and its campaigning brought about a full-scale parliamentary debate in October 1929. The upshot of the debate was the appointment of a select committee to enquire into capital punishment.

The select committee received passionate, yet detailed and reasoned, evidence from the NCADP. The point was stressed that several European countries and individual American states had abolished the death penalty without any serious and unfavourable results. But twenty-one of the committee's thirty-one witnesses, many of whom held senior official positions within the penal system, favoured the retention of capital punishment, and several of these argued from the point of view of English exceptionalism. 'We are a nation alone ...', declared Captain G. F. Clayton the governor of Dartmoor Prison, 'and there is nobody quite like us.' Sir Archibald Bodkin, the Director of Public Prosecutions, praised English law as 'a stern stable thing based on the experience of centuries'. It could not be a pendulum, swinging one way and then another like some foreign laws. Lieutenant-Colonel Herbert Hales, the governor of Parkhurst Prison, considered that it was only the death penalty that prevented 'a crowd of polyglot undesirables' and the 'fluid population of our seaports' from committing murders with the weapons that they were accustomed to carrying in their own countries. Moreover, he insisted:

> Abolish the death penalty and you must arm the police ... and one can think of nothing more repugnant to the Englishman's sense of law and order than a fusillade in Bond Street between police and (say) motor thieves ... If newspaper reports are to be believed, similar affrays between robbers and Police form part of the daily routine in America where the death penalty is almost a dead letter.[35]

Not all Conservative MPs were retentionists, but all of those on the committee were. The committee divided on party lines with the

Conservative members rejecting the final recommendation that there be an experimental five-year trial period of abolition. The division of the committee, together with the weakness of the Labour government, left the matter unresolved and, as noted above, governments were to remain resistant to proposals for abolition for another thirty years and more.

The state's sanction of corporal punishment followed a rather similar trajectory to that of capital punishment. For a variety of reasons that may be encapsulated in the concept of a 'civilising process' – squeamishness and sensibility, fear of turbulent crowds, annoyance and inconvenience at the unruliness and crowding around indecorous sites in public places – capital and corporal punishment were removed from the public's gaze in the mid nineteenth century. As noted already, it appeared that the penal punishment of beating an adult offender across the back with some sort of cat-of-nine-tails might fall into disuse until the reaction occasioned by the garotting panic of 1862. The 'Garotters' Act' of 1863 made provision for the flogging of street robbers and, over the next half century, other offenders were added to the list of those who might suffer such punishment – armed burglars, sexual offenders, pimps. Flogging also remained a sanction within the prison, and while it ceased to be available to the courts from 1948, it remained an option for prison boards of visitors, subject to confirmation by the Home Secretary, until 1967.[36]

Flogging, whipping or beating with a cane constitute different forms of what has been characterised as *le vice anglais* – the English vice. The assumption behind the notion of this national vice is that some Englishmen developed the masochistic habit of enjoying a beating as a result of their experiences at some of the more superior English schools. The physical chastisement of children and young people, like the physical chastisement of male, criminal offenders, had a much greater longevity in England than in many of the states with which the English generally liked to compare themselves. But not only was it a penal sanction for those who had transgressed the law of the land, it was also widely used in schools. Often those who opposed the flogging of adult offenders supported its use in schools. It was perceived by many as the ideal punishment for the naughty boy; it was short, sharp and, according to the theory, should immediately have followed the offence. Shortly before

the First World War, it was held up by its supporters as a crucial deter-
minant of national character. Like manly, physical sports, it taught pluck
and endurance, encouraged duty and determination, and banished
feebleness and effeminacy.[37]

The beating of naughty boys, however, grew increasingly contentious
in the late nineteenth and early twentieth centuries. Some boys objected,
sometimes violently; some parents objected similarly. This appears to
have been particularly the case with children and parents from sections
of the working class.[38] The contentious nature of the penal sanction
meant that, since it was ordered by local and often lay magistrates, there
were wide variations across the country. Some benches of magistrates,
and some individual magistrates, favoured the use of the punishment;
others opposed it. There was a broad increase in the use of the birch as
a result of the scare about juvenile delinquency during the First World
War, but thereafter the numbers of boys sentenced to a birching
declined. When the Recorder of Leicester sentenced a fifteen-year-old
boy to twelve strokes of the birch for housebreaking in January 1938,
it was the first time that such a sentence had been passed in the city
for twenty years.[39] There was an outcry in the city and the police, who
were charged with carrying out the birching, were concerned because
they had no birch and no officer with the experience of using one
(Figure 11). The Departmental Committee on Corporal Punishment that
was established in 1938 found no evidence that corporal punishment
acted as a deterrent, and there was increasing disquiet among legislators
and others that other countries appeared to be getting rid of the sanction with no adverse effect. The Second World War delayed the
introduction of legislation that would have abolished such punishment,
and the war-time scare about delinquents saw another increase in its
use. But, apart from a flurry in the House of Lords with Lord Goddard
at its centre, there was no serious opposition in Parliament to the clauses
of the Criminal Justice Act that abolished corporal punishment as a
penal sanction in 1948.[40]

Various individuals, newspapers and public bodies lamented the abolition and, from time to time, usually in the wake of a serious robbery
or assault, they urged reintroduction. The Home Office even thought it
worthwhile to open a file on public reactions to the abolition, collecting
press reports and journal articles to set alongside its own assessments.[41]

11. 'This nasty little job of whipping boys should not be left to police officers
... but should be carried out by parents or guardians.' Bert Thomas took these
words from the Chief Constable of Northampton as the caption for this cartoon,
published in the *Evening News* of 17 March 1939, which contrasts a reluctant,
sweating police officer in a magistrates' court with a small, nervous father.
Neither policeman nor father seems best placed to cane the large offender.

In February 1953 an amendment to the Criminal Justice Bill proposing the reintroduction of corporal punishment was debated in the Commons and rejected by 159 votes to 63.[42] Six years later Cyril Osborne raised the matter in a question to the Home Secretary. The minister's written response referred back to the conclusion of the 1938 committee that 'the evidence … does not indicate that when flogging and birching were available as judicial penalties that they had an especially effective influence as deterrents'. He stressed that 'more constructive measures' were being developed.[43] However, while the legislative elite set its face against the reintroduction of corporal punishment as a penal sanction, it was not until 1987 that the ability of a teacher to beat an offending schoolchild was finally abolished.

During the nineteenth century the British state had been run by patricians with an eye for what was best for state and society, and with a profound belief in the superiority of British institutions. Many of the men running the British state in the first half of the twentieth century had been schooled in this environment. The Victorians had sensibility, but not, perhaps, quite the same Enlightenment ideals and rationalism as their European counterparts, especially those who had reformed and reorganised their states in the wake of the Napoleonic Wars and the revolutions of 1830 and 1848. But then the leaders of the British state had no practical need of such reorganisations; they did not think in terms of an *ancien régime* that had recently been replaced, of a church and gentry that needed to have their judicial authority subjugated to that of the state. There was an assumption that the British ways were best and that there was little to be learned from continental European practices. The law, the organisation of the legal, police and penal systems were seen as having unique characteristics, and as being part of the successful arrangement of the British constitution. 'We are not the converts of Rousseau,' thundered Burke in his *Reflections on the Revolution in France*,

we are not the disciples of Voltaire; Helvétius has made no progress amongst us. Atheists are not our preachers; madmen are not our lawgivers. We know that *we* have made no discoveries, and we think that no discoveries are to be made, in morality; nor many in the great principles of government, nor in the ideas of liberty, which were understood long before we were born, altogether as well as they will be after the grave has heaped its mould upon our

168   HARD MEN

presumption, and the silent tomb shall have imposed its law on our pert loquacity.[44]

These words encapsulate much nineteenth-century English thinking among both conservatives and liberals.

In the aftermath of the First World War, the British elite could maintain that their overall system had triumphed again. They might fret that events during and immediately after the war had brought them close to employing the violent methods of Prussian militarism. Yet, to their own satisfaction, they seemed able to apply a brake to this in the inter-war years, and at a time while many states on continental Europe appeared to be lurching again into authoritarianism and militarism. There was a gradual change with the increasing reluctance on the part of magistrates to order birching as a judicial punishment. This was in line with a general liberalisation of the government's penal policy that saw prisons closed and a greater use of probation and other sanctions; it may also have been linked with a belief that penal corporal punishment should not be necessary in a progressive, liberal democratic society. Beatings in schools, however, remained different; these continued to be understood as a tried and trusted means of disciplining and civilising the unruly boy and, to a much lesser extent, the unruly girl. Moreover the 'pluck' necessary for accepting and taking such punishment continued to be perceived as part of the moulding of Englishness. The revival of the campaign to abolish capital punishment in the aftermath of the First World War can be linked with beliefs that led to the overall liberalisation of penal policy. As with the sentences of birching, the numbers of individuals executed by the state showed a slight decline during the 1930s, though they picked up again in the following decade (Table 3). But, in contrast to the moves to abolish corporal punishment, the state, in the form of the judges and the Home Secretaries, appears to have gone along with belief that capital punishment was just, that errors were unlikely – if not impossible – and that the punishment was a successful deterrent. They were supported in these beliefs by the leadership of the Anglican Church, and these views probably reflected those of the majority of the population.

This chapter has focused largely on the elite that directed and managed the state and its penal policy. The evidence of popular attitudes is a little more difficult to glean. It may be indicative of popular feeling

Table 3
Numbers hanged in England and Wales, 1900–1964

Years	Men	Women
1900–1909	154	6
1910–1919	120	0
1920–1929	139	2
1930–1939	80	3
1940–1949	133	1
1950–1959	104	3
1960–1964	17	0

that, when the public executioner died in 1883, a surprised Home Office received some 1400 unsolicited applications for the post in about three weeks.[45] It is also clear that there were offenders during the eighteenth and nineteenth centuries who were loathed and who the populace were delighted to see whipped or hanged. In other instances, however, the crowd showed its displeasure. The popular hostility to the execution of a twenty-two-year-old servant girl, Eliza Fenning, on a dubious charge of attempted murder in 1815,[46] for example, was as manifest as the condemnation of the execution of Derek Bentley a century and a half later. Similarly, parents who objected to the corporal punishment of their children by the state or by a teacher did not necessarily object to corporal punishment itself, but only to a particular instance of its use, possibly ordered by a notorious magistrate or inflicted by a bullying teacher. The contemporary assumption appears to be that the majority of the population of England favours capital punishment and also, perhaps, a degree of corporal punishment. It is now the state, in the form of the legislature and the executive, which prevents such punishment. The new ruling elite has thus assumed a stance much closer to that of the Enlightenment-inspired elites of nineteenth-century continental Europe and their successors in the post Second World War period. Conservatives in the United States, the only liberal democracy to perpetuate capital punishment, are now confident in lumping the British state with the rest of old Europe in such matters.[47]

Even though the British state maintained capital and corporal

punishment until the second half of the twentieth century, the overall
thrust of penal policy from the late Victorian period was for the treatment and rehabilitation of offenders. The phrase 'penal-welfarism' has
been coined as characterising the policies in both Britain and the United
States until roughly the last quarter of the twentieth century. But a series
of problems whittled away at these policies from the 1960s.[48] First, there
were the ever-rising statistics of crime. At the same time experts working within the system began to express anxieties that rehabilitation as it
had evolved simply was not working, while criminologists observing
from outside began publicly to lament the failure of their subject to
produce any convincing causal explanations for criminal offending.
Together with these lamentations academics began to demonstrate that
criminal offences could be the result of ambiguous behaviour. The
motives and behaviour of protest and political crowds discussed in previous chapters can be situated within this critique, undermining the
explanations of the old positivism as to who committed themselves to
violent protest and why. It is always difficult to pinpoint shifts in social
awareness, yet most commentators seem to agree that there was a new
celebration of individualism and, perhaps also, of hedonism that gathered pace from the 1960s, undermining the old moral restraints. Finally,
the growth of the electronic media ensured that local events, broadcast
into people's homes almost as they happened, could make even a relatively isolated picket-line disturbance a national event and hence a
national problem.

   In spite of the rising crime statistics and the occasional sensational,
violent crime, the broad consensus of penal welfarism was maintained
among politicians and political commentators until the end of the
1960s. Politicians did not see crime and violence as an issue for election manifestos, and did not use these issues as weapons with which to
criticise their opponents and woo the electorate. Then, in 1970, the Conservative manifesto stressed the need to deal with offences 'connected
to public order – peculiar to the age of demonstration and disruption'.
It is something of an irony that this manifesto appeared in the same
year that the former Home Office civil servant, T. A. Critchley, published his book arguing that the English had succeeded in conquering
violence. From then on the 'law and order' debate became central to
political discourse and more shrill.[49] Neither Margaret Thatcher, nor

her American soulmate Ronald Reagan, had fully developed their new right economic policies when they came to power, but both articulated concerns about crime and the breakdown of law and order, and this contributed to their success at the polls. That said, and in the political climate of the early twenty-first century when crime and penal policy are issues at the forefront of political discourse, the reintroduction of capital and corporal punishment is not on the agenda of any mainstream political party in Britain. To this extent at least, the facility for physical violence to be inflicted as a normal punishment on a citizen or on a visitor to Britain has been removed.

10

The Present

On 12 July 2002 Dr Tim Brown, a research fellow at the University of Portsmouth, went out for a drink with his brother-in-law in London. At the end of the evening, in Trafalgar Square, they debated whether to take a taxi or to catch a night bus. Briefly alone for a moment, standing on the plinth at the bottom of Nelson's Column, Tim Brown was approached by two youths, who asked for a cigarette. His brother-in-law rejoined him, but the next thing that Brown remembered was being on the ground at the foot of the plinth, his glasses broken and his right eye closing. He looked round for his brother-in-law and found him, also on the ground but now on the other side of the plinth and being kicked and stamped on by half a dozen or more youths. Finding it difficult to see without his glasses and with one eye almost closed, he went to help his brother-in-law, and was knocked unconscious for a second time. When he came round there was a group of Asian youths standing over him. He remembers them saying something like: 'Are you alright? You've just had a real kicking!' These youths, or someone else, had called for the police and an ambulance. Brown and his brother-in-law were taken to St Thomas's Hospital. The injuries to his brother-in-law's right leg were so serious that there were concerns for several days that it might have to be amputated below the knee. Brown had a fractured cheekbone, a gash on his forehead and severe bruising across his upper right arm and back caused by a blow from some sort of blunt instrument. The police wanted descriptions, but neither Tim Brown nor his brother-in-law could give them.

They were not the only victims of the gang that attacked them. According to the police the gang had moved down Charing Cross Road seriously assaulting several other young men, possibly as many as a dozen. One suspect had been apprehended for an earlier assault, but would give no information. The suspect was subsequently identified as being from a respectable family in a respectable suburban district. But there was no clear evidence against him or anyone else, and no charges were ever brought. A year later Tim Brown and his brother-in-law received a compensation payment from the Criminal Injuries Board. Tim Brown continues his university career, but his brother-in-law, who used to work as a builder, has had to find a desk job. The details of the attack on Tim Brown were recorded by the Metropolitan Police, and Crime Number CX 6210198/02/AA was, no doubt, duly entered among the assaults known to the police in the criminal statistics for 2002. However, but for the fact that Tim Brown's wife happens to work in the same department as me, the details would have been lost to the historian. The incident was not reported in the press, on the radio or on television. But it is the kind of incident that has come to be used by sections of the contemporary media to illustrate the claims that England's streets are more unsafe at the beginning of the twenty-first century than in earlier times.

Tim Brown's attackers were white youths. Robbery does not appear to have been a motive; no property was taken and no attempt was made to take anything. The attack may have been drink or drug fuelled. The social origin of the attackers is unknown, though there is some evidence of 'respectability' to suggest that they were not from a so-called 'sink estate' or from the 'underclass' identified by Charles Murray and that has been stigmatised as the group responsible for so much recent offending.[1] The assailants may have considered themselves as a fighting gang, but they do not appear to have been the sort of fighting gang present in nineteenth- and early twentieth-century towns and cities who fought, with similar gangs, over territory. It might be convenient to label the assault as 'motiveless'. Yet the members of the gang that moved down Charing Cross Road on the night of 12 July 2002 were working together, acting together and knew what they were doing. In the relaxed and tranquil surroundings of a study or an armchair these actions might appear 'motiveless', but it is meaningless to superimpose the thoughts of one context on to another that is quite different.

Incidents like the attack on Tim Brown might be used to substantiate arguments about 'the decline of order, justice and liberty', and about an inexorable increase in violence within English society. Comparisons are made with a simultaneous decline in the statistics of violence and an apparent increase in security in the United States. Blame is situated with liberals of the 1960s, the determination of successive British governments to disarm their citizenry, and the relative ineffectiveness of the British police in comparison with their American counterparts.[2] Violent incidents in England appear to be more common. Some are given big headlines and wide coverage in the press or on the television. Some, like the attack on Tim Brown, never become public. It was the same in the past. The level of violence in English society in the past cannot be recaptured and such statistics as we have cannot be set against the equally uncertain contemporary statistics so as to make precise assessments. A noted historian of American criminal statistics has queried whether the ten-year alteration that is currently focused upon is sufficient for the big claims made about the direction of violence in the United States. 'How long of a time period do we need to apprehend in order to call upward and downward drifts [in violent crime] a trend?'[3] The American decline over ten years is a pretty slender one when set against a much longer pattern of violence in the United States. These are equally slender statistics to draw comparisons with the English experience in which the statistical levels of violent crime over the long term were proportionately so much lower. At the close of the twentieth century the homicide rate in London was rising and that in cities in the United States was falling, but London and other major European cities still had a much lower rates than, for example, New York and Washington DC (Table 4). Perhaps, indeed probably, violence is higher in England today than in, say, the inter-war period. But it is also the case that there has always been a steady undercurrent of violence in English society, much of which was excused by contemporaries as rough, sportsmanlike behaviour, or behaviour by those not yet brought into the civilised English community. The majority of English people have never been exposed to criminal violence, police violence or violent public disorder. They probably have rarely perceived any physical violence in which they have been involved, or which they have suffered – being smacked by a parent, beaten by a teacher, experiencing rough play in hockey, rugby or soccer, or fast bowling in cricket – as being serious physical violence. Moreover, the violence of one decade can be perceived very differently in later years. In his memoirs Sir Robert Mark, former Commissioner of the Metropolitan Police, could note with relief the distinction between

the response to his violent behaviour as a PC armed with an unautho-
rised truncheon in the 1930s and the probable response to such
behaviour forty years later.[4]

Table 4

Homicides per 100,000 of the population, 1996–2000

City	1996	1997	1998	1999	2000
Amsterdam	5.85	5.59	5.27	3.03	3.97
Berlin	3.49	4.34	2.83	2.53	2.2
London	1.85	2.51	2.09	2.47	2.59
Paris	2.96	2.16	2.44	2.02	4.10
Rome	1.24	1.32	1.25	1.1	1.36
New York	13.39	10.51	8.6	9.03	8.69
Washington DC	73.11	56.89	49.15	46.44	41.78

Source: Gordon Barclay and Cynthia Tavares, *International Comparisons of
Criminal Justice Statistics* (London, Home Office, 2002), table 1.2.

Cultural attitudes are never static and they interrelate with each other.
The changes in social organisation, in the public use of space, in the perceptions of class and gender have all had an impact on the evolving
understanding of violence.[5] In the late eighteenth and nineteenth centuries this understanding contributed to the notion of what it was to be
English, and this notion, in turn, was fed back into the understanding by
the English of violence within their society. There were new, very significant shifts in the aftermath of the Second World War. The expansion
of higher education in the 1960s led to more people being educated to a
level at which they were prepared to challenge received opinion about
England and the unique or special qualities of its inhabitants. The concept
of the English gentleman was always an ideal type, but its popularity and
its position as a role model declined significantly in the post-war world.
These changes linked with, and contributed to, a decline in deference.

Again the significance of deference in the respective pre-war and post-
war worlds is difficult to assess or measure with any precision, but after
1945 there appears to have been something of a step change in attitudes

and a move towards a greater egalitarianism. The universal uniform adopted by young people from the 1960s meant that the police were no longer able to differentiate readily between classes. An articulate, educated youth in blue jeans and a tee-shirt looks much like an inarticulate, poorly educated youth in blue jeans and a tee-shirt – until he has been spoken to. But by the time of a policeman's challenge there may be no going back on either side. From the 1960s the articulate young could be found participating in demonstrations in support of CND, against Apartheid and against the war in Vietnam. Confrontations with the police in such demonstrations were common. Young demonstrators were fired by youthful passions for righting political wrongs. The police were under-strength, underpaid and had generally poor leadership. The increasing popularity and use of recreational drugs such as cannabis further increased the likelihood of confrontations between articulate youth and the police.

A series of other elements also fused to raise awareness of, and perhaps sensibility towards, violence from the late twentieth century. The use of drugs, both recreational and 'hard', probably accentuated a rise in crime, and notably violent crime, as users sought goods to provide cash for their habit and suppliers clashed with each other over territory. The major suppliers were increasingly identified with armed gangs that had originated in the Caribbean. While this may have been true, it also conveniently enabled much of the violence to be stigmatised as 'other'. During the 1970s, for reasons that are still debated, law and order was pushed to the top of various media and political agendas. Violent crime has always made good copy for the former, but increasingly it was used as a stick with which to beat the opposition party or any government that could be accused of providing insufficient funds for the courts, the police or the prison and probation services. At the same time elements within the media took it upon themselves to usurp the role of politicians by insisting, for example, that if politicians were not prepared to distribute information to the public on the whereabouts of convicted paedophiles, then they, the media, would do so. The growth of the Feminist movement contributed significantly to an awareness of the extent of rape, violent sexual abuse and domestic violence. This increasing awareness alleviated some of the stigma previously attached to victims, and appears to have encouraged more reporting

and more understanding police and court responses to victims. It has
also encouraged historians to investigate the topic. Finally, since the
1970s attempts to regenerate towns and cities have resulted in a night-
time economy based on consumption and hedonism in which the
leisure industry targets an audience of young high-spenders. The product is an alcohol-fuelled 'good-time' that also fosters clashes between
intoxicated strangers as well as between acquaintances, with the whole
presided over not by the public police, whose numbers are far too small,
but by bouncers who stem from the tradition of the working-class hard
man. Evidence from a variety of town and city experiences at the turn
of the millennium points to a very close relationship between the
increased number of licensed premises established as part of this new
night-time economy and the increased number of assaults and public
order offences.[6] Considerable media attention has been devoted to these
problems, again fostering both public concern and serious academic
investigation.

This book has focused on a few specific events and extrapolated from
these. I have no intention of entering the lists for a joust with my post-
modernist colleagues. These events happened; and I have tried to
explain how they fit with other events and with the understanding of
what it was to be English. For the people who experienced these events,
they were a momentary present, and for many who experienced them a
frightening, painful present, sometimes with a long aftermath of trauma
and recuperation. By putting these events together I have constructed a
narrative of violence; and I have stressed how this narrative of violence
occurred within a society whose commentators from the mid nineteenth
to the mid twentieth centuries appear to have considered increasingly
that they lived in a non-violent society. But this poses a problem, the
key problem that I have sought to address. Were these commentators
mistaken? Were they hypocritical? Were they conspirators? They
thought of themselves as belonging to a civilised nation in which the
male role model was restrained. The English gentleman was someone
who held his aggression in check, and in some respects this may well
have become a self-fulfilling narrative.

The English murder rate began to decline before the eighteenth century, and, according to the available statistics, throughout the period of
this study it has remained low. In general terms the decline might be

related to changing weapon use, improved medical and surgical practice, and shifting ideas of honour and masculinity. But these changes can be found in other countries and can only partially explain the English decline. It is impossible to assess the rate of non-lethal violence, but this was something that, increasingly, was disapproved of by judges, magistrates and, probably with a slight time lag, by jurors. The state violence inflicted by the courts, among others, was not perceived as 'violence' but as a means to preserve the state and society in war, and to civilise, domesticate, punish or warn others likely to participate in violent criminal behaviour. The perception of the non-violent English was a narrative for the respectable classes, and a narrative to convince the non-respectable, the uncivilised, and the uneducated; it was a model to which all were expected to aspire. From the perspective of the early twenty-first century it is easy to disparage the idea of the English gentleman. But the Victorian, Edwardian and inter-war present of the people who accepted and aspired to the model was not our present. And there are few today who would dispute that a non-violent society – whatever that might look like – would be a good thing. While the concept of the non-violent English may have been an idea that evolved within, and was pressed by an elite, it was nevertheless an idea that had appeal way beyond that elite. The idea was the perception of an idealised political entity rather than of an observed social community. Nevertheless, the repeated belief may well have had an impact on action and encouraged some actors to step back from a physical assault or an immediate physical response to an affront. But the proof of this, like the broader proof of the English as a non-violent people, remains beyond the reach of either the historian or other social scientists.

It is always difficult to be sure what people think and of the extent to which the members of a past society shared attitudes to concepts such as violence. Nevertheless, the Victorians (or those who spoke for the Victorians as politicians, social commentators, social reformers and so forth) stressed their 'civilisation' and their society's 'progress' in constitutional and moral, as well as technological, fields. Part of their civilisation and moral progress involved the regulation of those sports that they believed engendered the virtues of pluck and team spirit. In soccer it became illegal to trip an opponent; in rugby it was illegal to tackle high; in boxing gloves were worn to limit injury and punching below the belt was outlawed. At the same time it was stressed that the important thing was 'playing', and thus demonstrating manliness and physical commitment, rather than simply 'winning'. The Victorians and their immediate successors insisted upon the control of emotions and on non-violent behaviour, except when compelled to go to war, or when there was a clear need to 'correct' the less civilised, in the sense of children, who were not yet civilised, and 'primitive' peoples, such as some members of the working class and the indigenous peoples of the empire. The Victorians and their successors in the first half of the twentieth century could laugh at some 'primitive' behaviour. Children's violence, that of 'savages' in the empire, sometimes even that of parts of the working class could be reported with humour as well as with disapproval and, on occasions, with fury and outrage. Moreover the faith that such groups could become civilised, if necessary by the deployment of severe, but ultimately kind, punishment, could lead to less stigmatisation and less media hysteria than today, even in the most dreadful instances.

In 1855 two ten-year-old boys beat seven-year-old James Fleeson with a brick and then drowned him in the Leeds-Liverpool canal. Initially the community of the street where they lived alongside their victim shielded the perpetrators from the authorities. When they were caught they were sentenced to one year's imprisonment for manslaughter and in prison they were taught to read and write. In Stockport six years later two-year-old James Burgess was murdered by two eight-year-olds. After initial shock and outrage, both press and people appear to have been prepared to let judicial process and the penal system deal with the offenders. The judge spoke of 'babyish mischief' and sentenced the boys to a month in gaol after which they were to be transferred to a reformatory for five years. In neither of these cases, unlike the more recent Jamie Bulger murder, were there condemnations of 'unparalleled evil and barbarity', labelling of the offenders as 'monsters', or crusading journalists determined to re-expose them 'in the national interest' when they had served their sentence. The sentences were not condemned publicly as 'too short' and the parents of the murdered boys were not singled out as additional victims with any 'rights' in the affair. There was almost something of an assumption that boys would be violent until disciplined and civilised, and that prisons and reformatory schools were, in exceptional circumstances, ways of achieving this.[7] As a corollary, since children and 'native peoples' were 'primitive' and not yet formed in the mould of the mature Englishman, there was also a need to ensure that they did not receive too much stimulation that would excite violent behaviour. This fostered concern about the literature of 'penny dreadfuls' and subsequently about cinema violence; the latter had to be censored, partly because it would 'frighten', but also because it might 'encourage' or 'stimulate'.

Violence was consistently described as 'un-English'. The savage in the empire was violent because he was primitive. The continental European was violent in his politics because he lacked the measured constitution that had evolved in Britain over preceding centuries. The citizen of the United States was violent because his country had too much licence, too much of what might best be defined as 'democracy'. There was no hierarchical structure within American society, and the American police were tied into this democratic structure and closely linked with local politicians. English self-perception in the nineteenth century owed much to Burke's characterisation of an organic, improving constitution, as mediated by Macaulay's Whiggism. Politics in England no longer depended on king and elite conspiring in factions with killings, coups and civil wars. The latter had been left behind in 1688–89, with some minor problems recurring in 1715 and 1745. England's politics, so the English maintained, were never at the mercy of mob rule, unlike those of Europe, particularly France, which erupted in revolution in 1789, 1830, 1848, and 1871, with much of Europe following her in 1830 and 1848. The waves of political exiles who came to England in the aftermath of these upheavals, and particularly after 1848, might not have had anywhere else to go, but their arrival and residence was taken by many as a further demonstration of both the existence of liberty and the unique stability of politics in England.[8] The rough and tumble of English elections also was seen as a mere reflection of English liberty giving candidates the opportunity to show their pluck. After the First World War many among the elite expressed concerns about violence in the empire and in Ireland, and, in the 1930s, among the un-English political ideologies of communism and fascism. But they could still find satisfaction in what they saw as a general moderation in England's politics: the English had no March on Rome, no insurrection like that in Paris in 1934, no civil war like Spain, no Nazi street fighters, with all their attendant political violence and political murder. Today much of this would be attributed to good luck and contingency, but in the context of the time the most persuasive explanation for this lack of violence was found in assumptions about the 'good sense', 'moderation' and 'restraint' of the English people or 'race'.

It was but a short step from this understanding of English politics to dismiss rioters and other violent individuals as members of the residuum situated at the bottom of the working class. The more recent attempts of social historians to find 'faces in the crowds' and to understand crowd motivation can, at times, be a mirror image of this. The explanation that appears to absolve one set of violent protesters can be in danger of absolving all violent protesters. If eighteenth-century crowds demonstrating against food shortages, press gangs, enclosures, changing work practices and so forth had comprehensible 'legitimising notions' underpinning their actions, then why not anti-Catholic, anti-Jacobin, anti-German, anti-Black, anti-police, anti-*The Satanic Verses*, anti-paedophile, anti-Muslim rioters?

In the riot on the north London estate of Broadwater Farm in October 1985 a police officer was hacked to death. Some contemporaries labelled the riot as the work of 'Trotskyites, social extremists, Revolutionary Communists, Marxists and black militants from as far away as Toxteth'.[9] Today the temptation might be to write them off simply as 'the underclass', as previous offenders were written off as the 'criminal class' or the 'residuum', but this neither explains nor suggests solutions to real problems. Shortly after the riot John Bohstedt, one of the most significant historians of eighteenth-century crowds, wrote a letter to *The Times* suggesting that a variant of what he had defined as 'community politics' had been at work on the estate. Alienated young people were drawing their problems and their anger to the attention of the authorities, and were focusing on the police as the physical presence and 'the face of an alien power structure'.[10] There is much in this, even if some individuals who were involved in the killing of the police officer had been involved in criminality and in drug trafficking and use. This is not an attempt to condone rioting and murder, but to emphasise that the young people of an identifiable community were the participants in the riot. Labelling their behaviour as 'mindless', or insisting that they were whipped up by outside political agitators (who, if they existed, have never been publicly identified), is not an explanation of that behaviour.

Rather more easy to explain are the anti-paedophile demonstrations and rioting in the summer of 2000. In July that year the *News of the World* 'pledged' to 'name and shame' the 110,000 'proven paedophiles' in the United Kingdom. In the aftermath of the kidnapping and murder of eight-year-old Sarah Payne, the newspaper declared its aim to change the law: 'child sex perverts jailed for life must NEVER be released. They must NEVER get parole. Life MUST mean life.' Somewhat disingenuously it announced that its identification of paedophiles 'is ABSOLUTELY NOT a charter for vigilantes'.[11] Not surprisingly, however, it became an incitement to vigilantism and the innocent, wrongly identified as a result of the newspaper's actions, as well as 'proven paedophiles', were attacked and driven from their homes. The best publicised, and the longest running, demonstrations and disorders were in the Paulsgrove district of Portsmouth, supposedly where several convicted sex offenders had been housed by the local council. One liberal journalist confessed to being terrified of 'Paulsgrove woman':

> faces studded, shoulders tattooed, too small pink singlets worn over shell-suit bottoms, pallid faces under peroxided hair telling tales of a diet of hamburgers, cigarettes and pesticides. And they'd taught their three-year old kids (on whose behalf all this was supposedly being done) to chant slogans about hanging and killing.

But he also acknowledged the rationality of their cause and the fact that they felt, for a brief moment only perhaps, empowered with people listening to them and their complaints.[12]

Violence is not un-English and the English have never 'conquered' it. Conceivably the level of violence is greater in England at the beginning of the twenty-first century than it has been at certain times over the last two hundred years. But in the end this is a statistical question that the statistics are insufficient to answer. Often those who lament what they detect as a clear increase in violence also lament the fact that the state itself is less violent towards offenders. They assume that the former is a direct result of the latter, though this assumption is also ultimately incapable of proof. Probably, at the beginning of the twenty-first century, the English are more sensitive to violence than they were a hundred years ago, but also probably aware of its different manifestations as a result of other developments. First, media coverage can relay events in, for example, Paulsgrove across the country in a fashion unknown before the Second World War. The national community thus became as aware of the murders of Jamie Bulger and Sarah Payne as the local communities of Liverpool and Hampshire. Mary Ann Cotton, whose murders were in the north east, was never a national figure in the same way. There were never any images of James Fleeson and George Burgess being lured to their deaths as in the case of the painful, but repeated *ad nauseam*, CCTV film of Jamie Bulger. Secondly, the media has taken upon itself the right to pursue offenders and to challenge legal decisions in ways that were scarcely known in earlier times. At the same time violence and violent crime have been elevated to a new prominence in political discourse and politicians themselves seem fully prepared to employ populist rhetoric and to undermine still further a legal system in which many have lost faith.

I am conscious that I have no solution to violence in contemporary English society and no explanation for many violent incidents. I can offer an explanation for the Broadwater Farm riot and the Paulsgrove disorders, but that does not mean that I condone them. Nor does it mean that I am not scared of such incidents and of those who participated in them. I can suggest explanations for the actions of Lieutenant Malcolm and PC Ashworth, but this again is not to condone. I cannot provide explanations for the murder of Jamie Bulger or of James Fleeson and George Burgess, or for the attack on Tim Brown, but I resist strongly the explanation that goes no further than to call the attackers 'monsters' or 'mindless', or labels them as members of an incorrigible, self-perpetuating underclass. These are not explanations for why individuals behave in particular ways either individually or in groups. If nothing else, I hope that I have shown that while violence may often have been attributed to such a class, it was never behaviour restricted to one class alone. Moreover, while it is tempting to smirk at the idea of the English gentleman and the ideas of self-control and restraint – especially in a society where people are encouraged more and more to show their feelings, 'be themselves' and indulge in mass outpourings of emotion – perhaps that aspiration and those ideas did keep some violence in check.

Notes

Notes to Chapter 1: A Violent Society?

1. PRO, MEPO 3/905, armed army absentees, 1938; *Police Review*, 25 March 1938, p. 281. The quotations in the following two paragraphs are all drawn either from the PRO file or from *The Times* reports of the trial, *Times*, 31 March, p. 11, 1 April, p. 13, and 2 April 1938, p. 9.

2. V. A. C. Gatrell, 'The Decline of Theft and Violence in Victorian and Edwardian England', in V. A. C. Gatrell, Bruce Lenman and Geoffrey Parker, eds, *Crime and the Law: The Social History of Crime in Western Europe since 1500* (London: Europa, 1980).

3. See, inter alia, George Orwell, 'The Lion and the Unicorn: Socialism and the English Genius' (first published, December 1940); 'The English People' (written in 1944; first published in 1947); 'The Decline of the English Murder' (*Tribune*, 14 February 1946). These may be found in Sonia Orwell and Ian Angus, eds, *The Collected Essays, Journalism and Letters of George Orwell*, 4 vols (London: Secker and Warburg, 1968), especially ii, pp. 79 and 81; iii, pp. 16–17 and 24; iv, pp. 124–28.

4. Geoffrey Gorer, *Exploring English Character* (London: Cresset Press, 1955), pp. 13–15; T. A. Critchley, *The Conquest of Violence: Order and Liberty in Britain* (London: Constable, 1970) p. 25. While Critchley's book has 'Britain' in the title, he admits in the text that he is mainly concerned with England and Wales.

5. MPA, Refused Charge Book, 'J' Division, Chingford, 27 December 1921. The ticket collector did not press charges but told the police that he intended to report the matter to his superiors with a view to a summons.

6. Bedfordshire RO, QSD 50 and QSM 49, fol. 609; *Bedfordshire Standard*, 4 January 1918, p. 3.

7. Bedfordshire RO, PSL 3/9, no. 137, PSL 3/10, nos 22–23, 56 and 60, PSL 1/19; QSM 49, fol. 529, case of Ernest Jeffs, 1 July 1914; QSM 50, fol. 102, case of Ernest Jeffs, 8 April 1925; *Bedfordshire Standard*, 3 July 1914, p. 5.

8. Bedfordshire RO, PSL 3/10, nos 166, 186 and 191.

9. Nottinghamshire RO, C/QSM 1.57, fos 791 and 797, 2 April 1906. Holgate was given two nine month sentences with hard labour for the assaults on Amelia and Helenor, the sentences to run concurrently, and a sentence of one day's hard labour for the assault on PC Button.

10. See, inter alia, Nottinghamshire RO, C/QSM 1.58, fos 304, 338 and 340, cases of Arthur Antcliffe, 23 October 1916 and George Henry Hall, 7 April 1919.

11. *Judicial Statistics, 1923*, Cmd 2385 (London: HMSO, 1925) p. 8.

12. Nottinghamshire RO, C/QSM 1/58, fos 551 and 665, cases of John Knight, 9 April 1928 and John Alfred Riley, 4 October 1928.

13. Bedfordshire RO, QSM 49, fos 26, 282–83 and 664, cases of William Wooding, 16 January 1901, George Benson, 16 October 1907, and Alfred Cooper, 7 April 1920; Nottinghamshire RO, C/QSM 1/58, fol 329, case of Joseph Woolley, 14 October 1918.

14. MPA, Refused Charge Book, 'J' Division, Chingford, 20 June 1901 (rape); 29 and 30 August 1904 (robbery and assault); 21 September 1908 (grievous bodily harm); 7 May 1935 (attempted murder); 28 February 1936 (indecent exposure); 6 November 1939 (indecent assault).

15. Buckinghamshire RO, BC/5/1 Brill Station Occurrence Book, 1859–1932.

16. MPA, Refused Charge Book, 'K' Division, Isle of Dogs, 6 August 1935.

17. MPA, Refused Charge Book, 'K' Division, Isle of Dogs, 26 December 1935; MPA, Refused Charge Book, 'Y' Division, Highgate, 22 May 1907; MPA, Refused Charge Book, 'J' Division, Chingford, 2 August 1936.

18. See, for example, Jonathan Shepherd, 'Violent Crime in Bristol: An Accident and Emergency Perspective', *British Journal of Criminology*, 30 (1990) pp. 289–305.

19. John E. Archer, '"The Violence We Have Lost"? Body Counts, Historians and Interpersonal Violence in England', *Memoria y Civilización*, 2 (1999) pp. 171–90, at pp. 186–87.

20. Bedfordshire RO, Bedford Hospital, Surgical Notes, Mr Nash (30 August to 5 December 1930); Bedford Hospital, Surgical Notes, Mr Storrs (27 April to 13 September 1945).

21. Quoted in L. Perry Curtis Jr, *Jack the Ripper and the London Press* (New Haven and London: Yale University Press, 2002) p. 264.

22. Stuart Hall, Charles Critcher, Tony Jefferson, John Clarke and Brian Roberts, *Policing the Crisis: Mugging, the State, and Law and Order* (London: Macmillan, 1978). In fact the word 'mugging' does not appear to have been particularly new; see below, p. 16.

23. Kenneth Baker, 'How We Can Fight Britain's New Heart of Darkness',

Evening Standard, 16 February 1993, p. 4; Martin Kettle, 'Less and Less to Say More and More', *Guardian*, 20 February 1993, p. 21; Jeff Powell, 'Soccer Should Lament Symbol of Lost Values', *Daily Mail*, 22 February 1993; Fay Weldon, 'The Grief that Could Redeem a Nation', *Evening Standard*, 1 March 1993, p. 9.

24. See, for example, the press treatment of the annual crime statistics released in January 2001. While newspapers showed some awareness that there could be problems with the statistics, the overall decline in crime was overshadowed in the coverage by a stress on an increase in violent offences. The *Daily Mail* wrote of a 'tide of violence' (p. 19); the *Sun* reported that the 'streets were more dangerous' (p. 8); the *Daily Express* visited a small Suffolk town where, even though it was peaceful, people were afraid of violence (p. 13). Broadsheets like the *Daily Telegraph* (p. 6) and the *Times* (p. 6) also opted to stress the violence figures. All references to the editions of 17 January 2001. BBC Radio 4 broadcast a four-part series about violence in modern Britain, 'The Violence Files', in January 1995 and a similar two-part series, 'Violent Britain', in November 2000. Peter Hitchens, *A Brief History of Crime: The Decline of Order, Justice and Liberty in England* (London: Atlantic Books, 2003), is a polemic with a similar thrust.

25. See, inter alia, Michael Levi with Mike Maguire, 'Violent Crime', in Mike Maguire, Rod Morgan and Robert Reiner, eds, *The Oxford Handbook of Criminology* (3rd edn, Oxford: Clarendon Press, 2002).

26. Manuel Eisner, 'Modernization, Self-Control and Lethal Violence: The Long-Term Dynamics of European Homicide Rates in Theoretical Perspective', *British Journal of Criminology*, 41 (2001) pp. 618–38; idem, 'Long-Term Historical Trends in Violent Crime', *Crime and Justice: A Review of Research*, 30 (2003) pp. 83–142.

27. Norbert Elias, *The Civilizing Process*, 2 vols (Oxford: Oxford University Press, 1978).

28. See, inter alia, Michel Foucault, *Discipline and Punish: The Birth of the Prison* (London: Allen Lane, 1977); Ronnie Po-Chia Hsia, *Social Discipline and the Reformation: Central Europe, 1550–1750* (London: Routledge, 1992); Gerhard Oestreich, *Neostoicism and the Early Modern State* (Cambridge University Press, 1982).

29. Eisner, 'Modernization, Self-Control and Lethal Violence', pp. 621–23; Randolph Roth, 'Homicide in Early Modern England, 1549–1800: The Need for a Quantitative Synthesis', *Crime, Histoire et Sociétés / Crime, History and Societies*, 5 (2001), pp. 33–67.

30. Quoted in Paul Langford, *Englishness Identified: Manners and Character,*

1650–1850 (Oxford: Oxford University Press, 2000), pp. 142–43, and for the broad shift from the barbarous beef eater to the upholder of 'fair play' see pp. 137–57.

31. J. Carter Wood, *Violence and Crime in Nineteenth-Century England: The Shadow of Our Refinement* (London, Routledge, 2004).

32. Englishness has generated a considerable amount of work, both academic and popular, over the last decade or so. In addition to Langford, *Englishness Identified*, see, for example, Robert Colls, *Identity of England* (Oxford: Oxford University Press, 2002), and Jeremy Paxman, *The English: A Portrait of a People* (London: Michael Joseph, 1998). For an analysis of the English gentleman, and particularly his demise, see Marcus Collins, 'The Fall of the English Gentleman: The National Character in Decline, 1918–1970', *Historical Research*, 75 (2002), pp. 90–111.

Notes to Chapter 2: Garotters, Gangsters and Perverts

1. *Times*, 18 July 1862, pp. 5 and 6. The panic is dealt with in Jennifer Davis, 'The London Garotting Panic of 1862: A Moral Panic and the Creation of a Criminal Class in Mid-Victorian England', in V. A. C. Gatrell, Bruce Lenman and Geoffey Parker, eds, *Crime and the Law: The Social History of Crime in Western Europe since 1500* (London: Europa, 1980), and Rob Sindall, *Street Violence in the Nineteenth Century: Media Panic or Real Danger?* (Leicester: Leicester University Press, 1990), especially chap. 4.

2. [Henry W. Holland] 'The Science of Garotting and Housebreaking', *Cornhill Magazine*, 7 (1863), pp. 79–92.

3. Mark Brown, 'Crime, Governance and the Company Raj: The Discovery of Thugee', *British Journal of Criminology*, 42 (2002), pp. 77–95. The British Library Catalogue contains different editions of Meadows Taylor's novel dated 1839, 1840, 1858, 1873 and 1879.

4. *Times*, 17 July 1851, p. 4, 19 July 1851, p. 5, and 21 July 1851, p. 8.

5. *Times*, 22 October 1850, p. 4.

6. *CCCSP*, 57 (November 1862), p. 41.

7. *CCCSP*, 57 (November 1862), p. 42; and for police accusations of other accused associating with thieves see p. 44 (case of John Redwood); p. 47 (case of James Mowatt); and p. 50 (case of Charles Jones).

8. Peter King, 'Newspaper Reporting, Prosecution Practice and Perceptions of Urban Crime: The Colchester Crime Wave of 1765', *Continuity and Change*, 2 (1987) pp. 423–54.

9. The two men charged with the offence against Pilkington, Roberts and Anderson, were acquitted on this charge at Great Marlborough Street

Police Court (Davis, 'London Garotting Panic' p. 204 and Sindal, *Street Violence*, p. 51). They were prosecuted in November 1862 for a different attack.

10. Peter King, 'Moral Panics and Violent Street Crime, 1750–2000: A Comparative Perspective', in Barry Godfrey, Clive Emsley and Graeme Dunstall, eds, *Comparative Histories of Crime* (Cullompton: Willan Publishing, 2003).

11. Howard Taylor, 'Rationing Crime: The Political Economy of Criminal Statistics since the 1850s', *Economic History Review*, 51 (1998) pp. 569–90; idem, 'The Politics of the Rising Crime Statistics of England and Wales, 1914–1960', *Crime, Histoire et Sociétés / Crime, History and Societies*, 2 (1998), pp. 5–28; idem, 'Forging the Job: A Crisis of "Modernization" or Redundancy for the Police in England and Wales, 1900–1939', *British Journal of Criminology*, 39 (1999), pp. 113–35; Robert M. Morris, '"Lies, Damned Lies and Criminal Statistics": Reinterpreting the Criminal Statistics in England and Wales', *Crime, Histoire et Sociétés / Crime, History and Societies*, 5 (2001), pp. 111–27.

12. Robert Anderson, 'Our Absurd System of Punishing Crime', *The Nineteenth Century*, 49 (1901), pp. 268–84 (at p. 269).

13. V. A. C. Gatrell, 'The Decline of Theft and Violence in Victorian and Edwardian England', in V. A. C. Gatrell, Bruce Lenman and Geoffrey Parker, eds, *Crime and the Law: The Social History of Crime in Western Europe since 1500* (London: Europa, 1980).

14. Leon Radzinowicz and Roger Hood, *The Emergence of Penal Policy in Victorian and Edwardian England* (Oxford: Clarendon Press, 1990), chapter 5.

15. Sir John Moylan, *Scotland Yard and the Metropolitan Police* (2nd edn, London: Putnam, 1934), pp. 204–6.

16. *Times*, 21 January 1920, p. 12, for example, has the headline 'Crime Wave', followed by 'Murder, Robbery, and Theft. Two Post-Office Raids Yesterday. Old Man Killed by Burglar'.

17. Thorsten Sellin, 'Is Crime Increasing in Europe?', *Annals of the American Academy of Political and Social Science*, 126 (1926) pp. 29–34. Sellin had a certain amount of difficulty in making England and Wales fit his model. More recently the idea of the First World War's brutalising effect on soldiers was discussed in George L. Mosse, *Fallen Soldiers: Reshaping the Memory of the World Wars* (Oxford: Oxford University Press, 1990), chapter 8. This chapter focuses primarily on the German experience arguing that 'England [sic] and France ... were able to keep the process of brutalisation largely, if not entirely, under control', p. 159.

18. Jon Lawrence, 'Forging a Peaceable Kingdom: War, Violence, and Fear of

Brutalization in Post-First World War Britain', *Journal of Modern History*, 75 (2003), pp. 557–89; Charles E. Leach, *On Top of the Underworld: The Personal Reminiscences of Ex Divisional Detective Inspector Leach* (London: Sampson Low, Marston & Co., 1933), p. 3.

19. John E. Horwell, *Horwell of the Yard* (London: Andrew Melrose, 1947), p. 68, insisted that the razor-slashing gangs at the end of the First World War victimised 'our brave lads who had for nearly five years been risking their lives for us' and were mainly composed of 'men of military age and fitness who systematically and successfully evaded military service'.

20. *Judicial Statistics of England and Wales for 1924*, Cmd 2494 (London: HMSO, 1926), p. 2.

21. Sir Harold Scott, *Scotland Yard* (Harmondsworth: Penguin, 1957), p. 62. The idea of commando brutalisation also appeared in novels of the time, see Nevil Shute, *The Chequer Board* (London: Heinemann, 1947).

22. *Judicial Statistics, 1948*, Cmd 7733 (London: HMSO, 1949), p. viii.

23. Taylor, 'Forging the Job'.

24. Hermann Mannheim, *Social Aspects of Crime in England between the Wars* (London: George Allen and Unwin, 1940), p. 48.

25. Taylor, 'Rationing Crime'.

26. Mannheim, *Social Aspects of Crime*, pp. 65 and 122. Maria Tatar, *Lustmord: Sexual Murder in Weimar Germany* (Princeton, New Jersey: Princeton University Press, 1995), draws attention to the fascination with sexual murder in Weimar Germany and suggests links between the cultural representations of such murder and the notions of sacrifice and of suffering as victims which developed in Germany during the First World War.

27. Susan Kingsley Kent, *Making Peace: The Reconstruction of Gender in Interwar Britain* (Princeton New Jersey: Princeton University Press, 1993), pp. 97–101.

28. *Judicial Statistics, 1933*, Cmd 4977 (London: HMSO, 1935), p. xiv; *Judicial Statistics, 1946*, Cmd 7428 (London: HMSO, 1948), p. vii. The Occurrence Book for Brill Police Station in Buckinghamshire recorded twelve 'indecent assaults' between 1900 and 1932; of these only one involved two males; two others involved, respectively, an elderly man and a girl, and an elderly man and a boy; the ages of the offenders in the other instances were 12 (1), 13 (1), 15 (3), 17 (1), 19 (2), 20 (1). Buckinghamshire RO, BC/5/1.

29. Carolyn A. Conley, *The Unwritten Law: Criminal Justice in Victorian Kent* (New York: Oxford University Press, 1991), chapter 3 (quotation at p. 95).

30. MPA, Refused Charge Book, 'K' Division, Isle of Dogs, 4 July 1928.

31. Buckinghamshire RO, BC/5/1, Brill Occurrence Book 1859–1932, cases in 1902, 1907, 1916 and 1924.

32. MPA, Refused Charge Book, 'R' Division, Sidcup, 10 September 1933. The problems for women victims in similar cases during the 1980s and 1990s are explored in Gerry Chambers and Ann Millar, 'Proving Sexual Assault: Prosecuting the Offender or Persecuting the Victim', in Pat Carlen and Anne Worrall, eds, *Gender, Crime and Justice* (Milton Keynes: Open University Press, 1987), and Sue Lees, *Ruling Passions: Sexual Violence, Reputation and the Law* (Milton Keynes: Open University Press, 1997).

33. MPA, Refused Charge Book, 'J' Division, Chingford, 8 August 1907; Refused Charge Book, 'Y' Division, Highgate, 26 March 1912, 30 August 1928, 16 May 1931, 21 April 1938.

34. MPA, Refused Charge Book, 'J' Division, Chingford, 18 August 1908.

35. PRO, MEPO 3/347, see, in particular, Wontner & Sons to Assistant Commissioner CID, 17 August 1921; PRO, MEPO 3/904; Hansard, 203, col. 1382, 10 March 1927. But in Ancoats, Manchester, the cutting off of long, plaited hair appears to have been the trademark of a teenage gang in the early years of the First World War. The gang, calling itself the Napoo, took the hair as a trophy, possibly inspired by stories of scalping by native Americans. Stephen Humphries, *Hooligans or Rebels? An Oral History of Working-Class Childhood and Youth, 1889–1939* (Oxford: Basil Blackwell, 1981), p. 191.

36. Mannheim, *Social Aspects of Crime*, pp. 77–78; for the early years of the NSPCC and its activities in the courts see Louise A. Jackson, *Child Sexual Abuse in Victorian England* (London: Routledge, 2000), chapter 3.

37. Nottinghamshire RO, C/QSM 1/59, fos 219 and 227–29, QSC/N6 (no pagination), case of Leonard and Florrie Lawrence, 12 June 1933.

38. Robert Roberts, *The Classic Slum: Salford Life in the First Quarter of the Century* (Harmondsworth: Penguin, 1973), p. 45.

39. Harry Ferguson, 'Cleveland in History: The Abused Child and Child Protection, 1880–1914', in Roger Cooter, ed., *In the Name of the Child: Health and Welfare, 1880–1940* (London: Routledge, 1992). Some NSPCC cases can, of course, be found in court books: see, for example, Nottinghamsire RO, C/QSM 1.57, fos 851 and 853–54, case of Arnold and Elizabeth Turgoose, 15 April 1907; C/QSM 1.58, fos 51–52, 56, 58, 98, 100 and 350–52, cases of George and Mary Hartley, 19 October 1908; Joseph and Mary Jane Dixon, 4 January 1909; and Joseph and Elizabeth Buttery, 4 April 1910.

40. Gillian Spraggs, *Outlaws and Highwaymen: The Cult of the Robber in England from the Middle Ages to the Nineteenth Century* (London: Pimlico, 2001).

41. Frank McLynn, *Crime and Punishment in Eighteenth-Century England* (London: Routledge, 1989), p. 74. In July 1753 John Stockdale and Christopher Johnson were tried at the Old Bailey for the highway robbery and murder of Zachariah Gardiner. Stockdale and Johnson both blamed the other for firing the shot that killed Gardiner. There is no information on Johnson, but Stockdale was aged eighteen years and had recently come from Leicester to take up the post of a clerk in Doctors' Commons. The whole incident appears to have been two young men engaged in a stupid attempt to get money. Whoever fired the shot appears to have done so after Gardiner's property had been taken. The motive for the shooting is impossible to assess, and both Stockdale (in spite of very good character references) and Johnson were executed. OBSP ref: 17530718–33.

42. Spraggs, *Outlaws and Highwaymen*, pp. 1–2 and 156–57; Paul Langford, *Englishness Identified: Manners and Character, 1650–1850* (Oxford: Oxford University Press, 2000), p. 145; Anon, 'Paris in 1828', *London Magazine*, 3 (1829), pp. 137–39; Anon, 'The State of the Empire: Police, Press, Popery and Foreign Relations', *Monthly Magazine*, 8 (October 1829), pp. 361–69 (at pp. 362–63).

43. Paul Muskett, 'English Smuggling in the Eighteenth Century' (unpublished Ph.D., Open University, 1997), especially chapter 3.

44. Patrice Peveri, ' "Cette ville était comme un bois": criminalité et opinion public à Paris dans les années qui précédèrent l'affaire Cartouche (1715–1721)', *Crime, Histoire et Sociétés / Crime, History and Societies*, 1 (1997), pp. 51–73; Bernard Lesueur, *Le vrai Mandrin* (Paris: Editions Spéciales, 1971); T. C. W. Blanning, *The French Revolution in Germany: Occupation and Resistance in the Rhineland, 1792–1802* (Oxford: Clarendon Press, 1983), pp. 292–300.

45. Clive Emsley, *Crime and Society in England, 1750–1900* (3rd edn, London: Longman, 2004), chapter 3; Martin J. Weiner, *Reconstructing the Criminal: Culture, Law and Policy in England, 1830–1914* (Cambridge: Cambridge University Press, 1990).

46. See, for example, *News of the World*, 11 January 1880, p. 4, and *Daily Telegraph*, 15 January 1884, p. 2.

47. See, for example, the panic in Shoreditch in 1908 that 'hooligans' were robbing people in the streets when the police were changing over their beats. *East London Observer*, 5 September 1908, p. 6.

48. Clive Emsley, ' "The Thump of Wood on a Swede Turnip": Police Violence in Nineteenth-Century England', *Criminal Justice History*, 6 (1985), pp. 125–49, at pp. 135–41.

49. *Times*, 25 January 1909, pp. 9 and 11.

50. Donald A. Rumbelow, *The Houndsditch Murders and the Siege of Sidney Street* (London: W. H. Allen, 1988). For correspondence and debates about the arming of the police see *The Times*, 20 December 1910, p. 10; 21 December 1910, p. 10; 23 December 1910, p. 8; 27 December 1910, p. 3; and 28 December 1910, p. 8.

51. PRO, MEPO 3/894, Philip Jaeger: sentenced and died in hospital, 1933–34.

52. Billy Hill, *Boss of Britain's Underworld* (London: Naldrett Press, 1955) pp. 27–28; see also pp. 19 and 77.

53. James Morton, *East End Gangland* (London: Little Brown and Company, 2000), chapter 6; Raphael Samuel, ed., *East End Underworld: Chapters in the Life of Arthur Harding* (London: Routledge & Kegan Paul, 1981).

54. PRO, MEPO 3/346, The Epsom Hold-Up. Sergeant Dawson was armed with a revolver and, in his statement, declared that he had threatened to shoot anyone who tried to escape.

55. PRO, MEPO 3/352, Race Gang Affray in Waterloo Road, 1925.

56. J. P. Bean, *The Sheffield Gang Wars* (Sheffield: D. & D. Publications, 1981).

57. Geoffrey Pearson, *Hooligan: A History of Respectable Fears* (London: Macmillan, 1983), chapter 5 (for the hooligan's clothing, see pp. 92–101; for the use of firearms, see pp. 102–6).

58. Andrew Davies, 'Youth Gangs, Masculinity and Violence in Late Victorian Manchester and Salford', *Journal of Social History*, 32 (1998), pp. 349–69; idem, '"These Viragoes are no Less Cruel than the Lads": Young Women, Gangs and Violence in Late Victorian Manchester and Salford, *British Journal of Criminology*, 39 (1999), pp. 72–89; idem, 'Youth Gangs, Gender and Violence, 1870–1900', in Shani D'Cruze, ed., *Everyday Violence in Britain: Gender and Class* (Harlow: Longman, 2000).

59. Andrew Spicer, 'The Emergence of the British Tough Guy: Stanley Baker, Masculinity and the Crime Thriller', in Steve Chibnall and Robert Murphy, eds, *British Crime Cinema* (London: Routledge, 1999), p. 84n.; Jerry White, *The Worst Street in North London: Campbell Bunk, Islington, between the Wars* (London: Routledge, 1986), p. 166.

Notes to Chapter 3: Play the Game

1. PRO, HO 42.46.128, Messrs Bytherwood, Cook and Bradshaw to Duke of Portland, 24 February 1797; quoted in Robert W. Malcolmson, *Popular Recreations in English Society, 1700–1850* (Cambridge: Cambridge University Press, 1973), pp. 139–40.

2. William Hone, *The Every-Day Book*, 2 vols (London, 1826), i, cols 244–45.

3. *Times*, 2 March 1840, p. 5.

4. Macolmson, *Popular Recreations*, pp. 138–45. Neal Garnham, 'Patronage, Politics and the Modernization of Leisure in Northern England: The Case of Alnwick's Shrove Tuesday Football Match', *English Historical Review*, 474 (2002), pp. 228–46, is an interesting case study revealing how a 'traditional' football match (possibly dating back only to 1788) was revived by the Duke of Northumberland in the mid nineteenth century as a way of celebrating his local position. Thereafter it was gradually domesticated by the middle class.

5. Mark Traugott, ed. *The French Worker: Autobiographies from the Early Industrial Era* (Berkeley, California: University of California Press, 1993), p. 138, and see also pp. 147–48, 150 and 171–73.

6. W. Litt, *Wrestliana: or An Historical Account of Ancient and Modern Wrestling* (Whitehaven, 1823), pp. 18–21 and p. 38.

7. Pierce Egan, *Boxiana: or Sketches of Antient and Modern Pugilism*, 4 vols (London, 1818–24), i, pp. 13–14.

8. Paul Langford, *Englishness Identified: Manners and Character, 1650–1850* (Oxford: Oxford University Press, 2000), p. 46.

9. Martin J. Wiener, *Men of Blood: Violence, Manliness and Criminal Justice in Victorian England* (Cambridge: Cambridge University Press, 2004), p. 42.

10. *Sheffield and Rotherham Independent*, 13 November 1841, p. 3. For the availability and use of knives see David Philips, *Crime and Authority in Victorian England* (London: Croom Helm, 1977), pp. 265–66.

11. Malcolmson, *Popular Recreations*, chapter 7.

12. For an excellent discussion of the value of Elias and for the developments in sport in late eighteenth- and early nineteenth-century Britain, see Richard Holt, *Sport and the British: A Modern History* (Oxford: Clarendon Press, 1989), chapter 1.

13. Emma Griffin, 'Sport and Celebration in English Towns, 1660–1750', *Historical Research*, 75 (2002), pp. 188–208.

14. Hone, *Every-Day Book*, i, col. 245.

15. Robert Shoemaker, 'Male Honour and the Decline of Public Violence in Eighteenth-Century London', *Social History*, 26 (2001), pp. 190–208.

16. Antony E. Simpson, 'Dandelions on the Field of Honor: Duelling, the Middle Classes and the Law in Nineteenth-Century England', *Criminal Justice History*, 9 (1988), pp. 99–155; Robert Shoemaker, 'The Taming of the Duel: Masculinity, Honour and Ritual Violence in London, 1600–1800', *Historical Journal*, 45 (2002), pp. 525–45.

17. Wiener, *Men of Blood*, pp. 40–41.

18. See the essays of Ute Frevert, Steven Hughes and Robert Nye that consti-tute part one of Pieter Spierenburg, ed., *Men and Violence: Gender, Honor, and Rituals in Modern Europe and America* (Columbus, Ohio: Ohio State University Press, 1998).

19. Current medical opinion, generally opposed to boxing, suggests that the introduction of the boxing glove, the abolition of wrestling throws, and the limits on rest periods may have intensified the violent intensity of the sport by reducing the impact of a punch on a boxer's hand and knuckles and redirecting the focus of the boxer's assault to his opponent's head. See, inter alia, articles in *Physician and Sports Medecine*, 11 (1983), p. 49, and 20 (1992), p. 29.

20. *Justice of the Peace*, 62, 24 April 1898, pp. 825–26.

21. Sir Percy Sillitoe, *Cloak without Dagger* (London: Cassell, 1955), pp. 84–85; A. W. Cockerill, *Sir Percy Sillitoe* (London: W. H. Allen, 1975), pp. 81–82.

22. *Times*, 30 July 1906, p. 11. The damage might have been greater but for the fact that Knox was 'lame' for part of one of Yorkshire's innings.

23. Holt, *Sport and the British*, pp. 233–36.

24. *Cheltonian*, 20 (October 1895), p. 11, quoted in J. A. Mangan, *The Games Ethic and Imperialism: Aspects of the Diffusion of an Ideal* (Har-mondsworth: Viking, 1986), p. 46; see also p. 45.

25. J. A. Mangan, 'Duty unto Death: English Masculinity and Militarism in the Age of the New Imperialism', in J. A. Mangan, ed., *Tribal Identities: Nationalism, Europe, Sport* (London: Frank Cass, 1996), p. 25.

26. CBOA, B346, pp. 74–77 (Carter, 1 June, 1897).

27. Holt, *Sport and the British*, pp. 331–35. For late nineteenth-century criti-cism of the roughness of the game see, inter alia, C. Edwardes, 'The New Football Mania', *Nineteenth Century*, 32 (1892), and Ernest Ensor, 'The Football Madness', *Contemporary Review*, 74 (1898), pp. 750–60. Ensor lamented the decline of the idea of 'fair play'. 'Englishmen seem converted to French or American methods of sport' (p. 760).

28. Robert D. Storch, '"Please to Remember the Fifth of November": Conflict, Solidarity and Public Order in Southern England, 1815–1900', in Robert D. Storch, ed., *Popular Culture and Custom in Nineteenth-Century England* (London: Croom Helm, 1982).

29. *Cambridge Daily News*, 6 November, 1934; and see also 6 November, 1926, 6 November, 1928, and 14 November, 1931.

30. MPA, MS 105.87, Charles Hanslow, 'Anecdotes: Memories of Charles Hanslow', fol. 19 (copy also in OUPA).

31. *Justice of the Peace*, 94 (1930), 15 November, p. 706. In this instance the *Jus-tice of the Peace* suggested that magistrates in the East End may have dealt

particularly leniently with two young teenagers arrested for similar behaviour to students, precisely because of the lenience offered to the students. See also, *Justice of the Peace*, 90 (1926), 25 December, p. 756.

32. *Times*, 9 November, 1953, p. 9. For the trouble, and the trials a Bow Street, see *Times*, 6 November, p. 8, 7 November, p. 3, and 9 November, p. 4. The rest of the press reported the violence, if not the court proceedings; see, inter alia, *Daily Herald*, 6 November, p. 1, and *Daily Sketch*, 6 November, pp. 1 and 16.

33. *Times*, 10 November, 1953, p. 9.

34. *Times*, 14 November, 1953, p. 7; for other letters, for and against, see *Times*, 11 November, p. 9, 12 November, p. 9, and 13 November, p. 9.

35. *Daily Sketch*, 6 November, 1953, p. 2, and 7 November, p. 4.

36. Holt, *Sport and the British*, p. 78.

37. Wiener, *Men of Blood*, pp. 51, 53 and 55–59.

38. Jerry White, *The Worst Street in North London: Campbell Bunk, Islington, between the Wars* (London: Routledge & Kegan Paul, 1986), p. 99.

Notes to Chapter 4: Family and Home

1. Arthur Appleton, *Mary Ann Cotton: Her Story and her Trial* (London: Michael Joseph, 1973), quotations at pp. 103–4.

2. Appleton, *Mary Ann Cotton*, p. 1.

3. Katherine Watson, *Poisoned Lives: English Poisoners and their Victims* (London: Hambledon and London, 2004), pp. 87–92 and 94.

4. Robert Roberts, *The Classic Slum: Salford Life in the First Quarter of the Century* (Harmondsworth: Penguin, 1973), pp. 121–22.

5. M. Loane, *The Queen's Poor: Life as They Find it in Town and Country*, first published 1905, new edition with introduction by Susan Cohen and Clive Fleay (London: Middlesex University Press, 1998), p. 1.

6. Jerry White, *Rothschild Buildings: Life in an East End Tenement Block, 1887–1920* (London: Routledge & Kegan Paul, 1980), p. 126; idem, *The Worst Street in North London: Campbell Bunk, Islington, between the Wars* (London: Routledge & Kegan Paul, 1986), pp. 96–97 and 140–45.

7. *Sheffield Mail*, 1 January 1930, p. 1.

8. Pat Ayers and Jan Lambertz, 'Marriage Relations, Money, and Domestic Violence in Working-Class Liverpool, 1919–39', in Jane Lewis, ed., *Labour and Love: Women's Experience of Home and Family, 1850–1940* (Oxford: Basil Blackwell, 1986).

9. Shani D'Cruze, *Crimes of Outrage: Sex, Violence and Victorian Working Women* (London: UCL Press, 1998), p. 66.

10. *Times*, 27 March 1867, p. 11.

11. Mabel Sharman Crawford, 'Maltreatment of Wives', *Westminster Review*, 139 (1893) pp. 292–303; quotation at p. 303.

12. Martin J. Wiener, 'The Sad Story of George Hall: Adultery, Murder and the Politics of Mercy in Mid-Victorian England', *Social History*, 24 (1999), pp. 174–95; idem, 'Judges v. Jurors: Courtroom Tensions in Murder Trials and the Law of Criminal Responsibility in Nineteenth-Century England', *Law and History Review*, 17 (1999), pp. 467–506. More generally see his *Men of Blood: Violence, Manliness and Criminal Justice in Victorian England* (Cambridge: Cambridge University Press, 2004).

13. Pamela J. Walker, *Pulling the Devil's Kingdom Down: The Salvation Army in Victorian Britain* (Berkeley, California: University of California Press, 2001), p. 125.

14. *Southwark and Bermondsey Recorder*, 20 September 1912, p. 7.

15. *Times*, 7 November 1856, p. 10.

16. E. P. Thompson, 'Rough Music', in E. P. Thompson, *Customs in Common* (London: Merlin Press, 1991), especially pp. 505, 510–12 and 526–30.

17. *South London Observer*, 2 January and 5 January 1884.

18. Julie English Early, 'Keeping Ourselves to Ourselves: Violence in the Edwardian Suburb', in Shani D'Cruze, ed., *Everyday Violence in Britain, 1850–1950: Gender and Class* (London: Longman, 2000), quotations at pp. 179 and 180.

19. MPA, Refused Charge Book, 'K' Division, Isle of Dogs, 1 January, 13 March and 19 July 1910.

20. MPA, Refused Charge Book, 'K' Division, Isle of Dogs, 17 April 1932. For similar instances in inter-war Liverpool see Mike Brogden, *On the Mersey Beat: Policing Liverpool Between the Wars* (Oxford: Oxford University Press, 1991), pp. 142–43.

21. MPA, Refused Charge Book, 'Y' Division, Highgate, 31 July 1948.

22. D'Cruze, *Crimes of Outrage*, pp. 70–71.

23. Galleries of Justice, Nottingham, Rainer Foundation Archive, Associated Societies for the Protection of Women and Children Council Minute Book, 1904–1911, fol. 420.

24. CBOA, B367 (Wyborn, 16 March 1900).

25. *Southwark and Bermondsey Recorder*, 14 June 1912, p. 3, and 20 September 1912, p. 3.

26. *Sheffield Mail*, 7 January 1926, p. 3.

27. Jacky Burnett, 'Exposing the "Inner Life": The Women's Co-operative Guild's Attitude to "Cruelty",' in D'Cruze, ed., *Everyday Violence in Britain*, p. 144.

28. Quoted in John E. Archer, '"The Violence We Have Lost"? Body Counts, Historians and Interpersonal Violence in England', *Memoria y Civilización*, 2 (1999), pp. 171–90 (at p. 186).

29. Sir Howard Vincent, *The Police Code* (14th edn, London, 1907), p. 124.

30. Sir Howard Vincent, *The Police Code* (16th edn, London, 1924), pp. 119 and xiii. Precisely the same words are to be found in the seventeenth edition published in 1931, pp. 121 and ix. The police instructions distributed to other forces in the late nineteenth and early twentieth centuries were similar, see Alan Bourlet, *Police Intervention in Marital Violence* (Milton Keynes: Open University Press, 1990), p. 15. Bourlet, himself a serving police officer, considered that there was still a reluctance among many police officers to get involved in 'domestics' at the time of his research and writing.

31. MPA, Edward Lyscom, 'London Policeman' (copy also in OUPA), fol. 25, and see also fos 67–68.

32. Lyscom, 'London Policeman', fol. 32.

33. Lyscom, 'London Policeman', fos. 87–88.

34. See, inter alia, Lynn Abrams, 'Crime against Marriage? Wife-Beating, the Law and Divorce in Nineteenth-Century Hamburg', in Margaret L. Arnot and Cornelie Usborne, eds, *Gender and Crime in Modern Europe* (London: UCL Press, 1999); Linda Gordon, *Heroes of their Own Lives: The Politics and History of Family Violence, Boston, 1880–1960* (London: Virago, 1989).

35. Burnett, 'Exposing the "Inner Life"', p. 146.

36. Bedfordshire RO, QSI 21, Minutes of S. H. Whitbread at Quarter Sessions, 1903–14; QSM 49, fol. 366.

37. *Sheffield Mail*, 8 January 1926, p. 1.

38. Louise A. Jackson, *Child Sexual Abuse in Victorian England* (London: Routledge, 2000), pp. 46–50.

39. Carolyn A. Conley, *The Unwritten Law: Criminal Justice in Victorian Kent* (New York: Oxford University Press, 1991), pp. 105–7.

40. White, *The Worst Street*, pp. 153–54.

41. George K. Behlmer, *Friends of the Family: The English Home and its Guardians, 1850–1940* (Stanford, California: Stanford University Press, 1998), p. 111.

42. D'Cruze, *Crimes of Outrage*, pp. 60–61.

43. Roberts, *Classic Slum*, p. 45.

44. Behlmer, *Friends of the Family*, pp. 104–16.

45. George K. Behlmer, 'Deadly Motherhood: Infanticide and Medical Opinion in Mid-Victorian England', *Journal of the History of Medicine and Allied Science*, 34 (1979) pp. 403–27: at pp. 424–25.

46. Quoted in Lionel Rose, *Massacre of the Innocents: Infanticide in Great Britain, 1800–1939* (London: Routledge & Kegan Paul, 1986), p. 39. See also Archer, '"The Violence We Have Lost"?', pp. 179–83. For a general introduction to the weakness of the coroner system during the nineteenth century see Mary Beth Emmerichs, 'Getting Away with Murder? Homicide and the Coroners in Nineteenth-Century London', *Social Science History*, 25 (2001), pp. 93–100.

47. Louis Chevalier, *Labouring Classes and Dangerous Classes in Paris during the First Half of the Nineteenth Century* (London: Routledge and Kegan Paul, 1973), pp. 275–76; Eugen Weber, *Peasants into Frenchmen: The Modernization of Rural France, 1870–1914* (Stanford California: Stanford University Press, 1976), pp. 182–83.

48. Richard J. Evans, *Death in Hamburg: Society and Politics in the Cholera Years, 1830–1910* (London: Penguin Books, 1987), pp. 215–16.

49. Howard Taylor, 'Rationing Crime: The Political Economy of the Criminal Statistics since the 1850s', *Economic History Review*, 51 (1998), pp. 569–90.

50. Robert M. Morris, '"Lies, Damned Lies and Criminal Statistics": Reinterpreting the Criminal Statistics of England and Wales', *Crime, Histoire et Sociétés/Crime, History and Societies*, 5 (2001), pp. 111–27.

51. Bedfordshire RO, PSL 3/8, nos 99–104.

52. MPA, MS 175.88, Arthur Battle, 'This Job's Not What it Used to Be', fos 39–40 (copy also in OUPA); White, *The Worst Street*, pp. 87–88, 97 and 99.

Notes to Chapter 5: Foreign Passions: English Laws

1. *Times*, 27 August 1917, p. 4.

2. *Times*, 11 September 1917, p. 4. For full details of the trial, from which the following quotations are taken, see the *Times* reports of 11 September, p. 4, and 12 September, p. 4.

3. *Daily Mirror*, 12 September 1917, p. 2; *Daily Sketch*, 12 September, p. 2.

4. *Daily Sketch*, 11 September 1917, p. 2.

5. *Daily Mirror*, 12 September 1917, p. 2.

6. *Daily Sketch*, 12 September 1917, p. 2.

7. *Times*, 12 September 1917, p. 7.

8. *Daily Sketch*, 15 August 1917, p. 2.

9. See above pp. 63–64.

10. M. Dorothy George, *London Life in the Eighteenth Century* (2nd edn, Harmondsworth: Penguin), 1965, pp. 138–39 and 353–54.

11. Hereward Senior, *Orangism in Ireland and Britain, 1795–1836* (London: Routledge and Kegan Paul, 1966).

12. Frank Neal, *Sectarian Violence: The Liverpool Experience, 1819–1914* (Manchester: Manchester University Press, 1988).

13. W. L. Arnstein, 'The Murphy Riots: A Victorian Dilemma', *Victorian Studies*, 19 (1975), pp. 55–71; Sheridan Gilley, 'The Garibaldi Riots of 1862', *Historical Journal*, 16 (1973), pp. 697–732.

14. CBOA, B346, pp. 31–33 (Carter, 31 May 1897); B371, pp. 158–59 (Clyne, 16 May 1900); B351 pp. 17–18 (Reid, 7 March 1898).

15. Quotations in Kristina Jeffes, 'The Irish: An Outcast Community', in Roger Swift, ed., *Victorian Chester* (Liverpool: Liverpool University Press, 1996), p. 105, and Donald M. MacRaild, 'William Murphy, the Orange Order and Communal Violence: The Irish in West Cumberland, 1871–1884', in Panikos Panayi, ed., *Racial Violence in Britain in the Nineteenth and Twentieth Centuries* (revised edn, London: Leiceister University Press, 1996), p. 52. See in general, Roger Swift, 'Crime and the Irish in Nineteenth-Century Britain', in Roger Swift and Sheridan Gilley, eds, *The Irish in Britain, 1815–1939* (London: Pinter, 1989); and idem, 'Anti-Irish Violence in Victorian England: Some Perspectives', *Criminal Justice History*, 15 (1994), pp. 127–39.

16. *Times*, 27 November 1866, p. 8.

17. J. Carter Wood, *Violence and Crime in Nineteenth-Century England: The Shadow of our Refinement* (London: Routledge, 2004), pp. 128–29; Alan O'Day, 'Varieties of Anti-Irish Behaviour in Britain 1846–1922', in Panayi, ed., *Racial Violence in Britain.*

18. Geoffrey Pearson, *Hooligan: A History of Respectable Fears* (London: Macmillan, 1983) pp. 74–75 and pp. 253n.

19. Pamela J. Walker, *Pulling the Devil's Kingdom Down: The Salvation Army in Victorian Britain* (Berkeley, California: University of California Press, 2001), especially pp. 217–18.

20. George, *London Life*, pp. 131–38.

21. CBOA, B350, pp. 64–65 (Drew, 18 January 1898) and B351, pp. 86–87 (Reid, 15 March 1898). According to Police Sergeant Charles Horatio French in Whitechapel there was no trouble with the police 'because the Jews are not men enough to be rough'; B351, pp. 150–51 (21 March 1898).

22. L. Perry Curtis, Jr, *Jack the Ripper and the London Press* (New Haven, Connecticut and London: Yale University Press, 2001), pp. 162–63, 170–71 and 236–37. The quotation from the *Daily News* is cited in Jerry White, *Rothschild Buildings: Life in an East End Tenement Building, 1887–1920* (London: Routledge and Kegan Paul, 1980), p. 25.

23. See, inter alia, David Englander, ed., *A Documentary History of Jewish*

Immigrants in Britain, 1840–1920 (Leicester, London and New York: Leicester University Press, 1994), pp. 94, 255–57, 262–71, and 288–89.

24. *Times*, 25 January 1909, p. 11, and 20 December 1910, p. 10.

25. *Standard*, 25, 26, 27 and 28 January 1911. These articles were forwarded to the Home Office with a refutation drafted by the President of the London Committee of Deputies of British Jews, 9 February 1911. See, HO 45.24610. My thanks to Jim Whitfield for this information.

26. Englander, ed., *Documentary History of Jewish Immigrants*, pp. 289–98.

27. James Morton, *East End Gangland* (London: Little Brown and Company, 2000), chapter 7; Philip Jenkins and Gary W. Potter, 'Before the Krays: Organised Crime in London, 1920–1960', *Criminal Justice History*, 9 (1988), pp. 209–30.

28. Herbert T. Fitch, *Traitors Within: The Adventures of Detective Inspector Herbert T. Fitch* (London: Hurst and Blackett, 1933) pp. 321–22.

29. *John Bull*, 8 February 1936. My thanks to Stefan Slater for this reference.

30. *Times*, 4 April 1921, p. 10.

31. James Morton, *East End Gangland* (London: Little Brown and Company, 2000), chapter 6; Raphael Samuel, ed., *East End Underworld: Chapters in the Life of Arthur Harding* (London: Routledge and Kegan Paul, 1981), pp. 182–86: quotation, from Cecil Chapman, at p. 329.

32. CBOA, B350, pp. 42–43 (7 January 1898).

33. David Philips, *Crime and Authority in Victorian England: The Black Country, 1835–1860* (London: Croom Helm, 1977), pp. 246–52; Carolyn Conley, *The Unwritten Law; Criminal Justice in Victorian Kent* (New York: Oxford University Press, 1991), p. 52.

34. *Times*, 2 November 1843, p. 6.

35. John E. Archer, '"Men Behaving Badly"? Masculinity and the Uses of Violence, 1850–1900', in Shani D'Cruze, ed., *Everyday Violence in Britain, 1850–1950: Gender and Class* (London: Longman, 2000), pp. 44–45; Martin J. Wiener, *Men of Blood: Violence, Manliness and Criminal Justice in Victorian England* (Cambridge: Cambridge University Press, 2004), pp. 58–59.

36. Phillip Thurmond Smith, *Policing Victorian London: Political Policing, Public Order and the London Metropolitan Police* (Westport, Connecticut: Greenwood Press, 1985), pp. 153 and 155.

37. *Times*, 6 October 1875, p. 8; see also, 19 June 1865, p. 8, 14 October 1875, p. 4, 25 October 1885, p. 10. For the violence of Italian policemen, worst of all against an Englishman, see William Mercer, *How the Police Manage Italy* (Rome: Italo-American School Press, 1876).

38. *Times*, 9 January 1885, p. 5 and 10 January, p. 5. The French response to Madame Clovis-Hughes's acquittal was rather more ambivalent than *The*

Times implied. See Ruth Harris, *Murders and Madness: Medicine, Law, and Society in the Fin de Siècle* (Oxford: Clarendon Press, 1989), pp. 213–14.

39. J. P. Bean, *The Sheffield Gang Wars* (Sheffield: D. & D. Publications, 1981), p. 21.

40. Archer, '"Men Behaving Badly"?', p. 45.

41. George Orwell, 'Raffles and Miss Blandish', *Horizon*, October 1944; 'The Decline of the English Murder', *Tribune*, 14 February 1946. These may be found in Sonia Orwell and Ian Angus, eds, *The Collected Essays, Journalism and Letters of George Orwell*, 4 vols (London: Secker and Warburg, 1968), iii, pp. 246–60, and iv, pp. 124–28. For other examples of concerns about the impact of Hollywood during the interwar years see Geoffrey Pearson, *Hooligan: A History of Respectable Fears* (London: Macmillan, 1983), pp. 31–33.

42. Jeffrey Richards, 'The British Board of Film Censors and Content Control in the 1930s: Images of Britain', *Historical Journal of Film, Radio and Television*, 1 (1981), pp. 95–116; Tom Dewe Mathews, *Censored* (London: Chatto and Windus, 1994), pp. 52–53.

43. *Report, by Mr Herbert du Parcq, KC, on the Circumstances Connected with the Recent Disorder at Dartmoor Convict Prison*, Cmd 4010 (London: HMSO, 1932). Seven prisoners received gunshot wounds, twenty-three were injured with batons and an unknown number by fellow prisoners. One prison officer was seriously injured in the run up to the injury; four were put on the sick list as a result of their injuries; fifteen to twenty continued to report for duty although injured.

44. Mathews, *Censored*, p. 54.

45. James Chapman, '"Sordidness, Corruption and Violence Almost Unrelieved": Critics, Censors and the Post-War British Crime Film', paper presented at the European Social Science History Conference, Berlin, 23–27 March 2004.

46. J. R. Seeley, *The Expansion of England* (2nd edn, London: Macmillan, 1895), pp. 8, 282–87 and 318–20.

47. *Times*, 13 August 1857, p. 8.

48. *Times*, 4 November 1865, p. 7.

49. *Times*, 13 November 1865, p. 8.

50. Geoffrey Dutton, *The Hero as Murderer: The Life of Edward John Eyre, Australian Explorer and Governor of Jamaica, 1815–1901* (London: Collins, 1967).

51. Derek Sayer, 'British Reaction to the Amritsar Massacre, 1919–1920', *Past and Present*, 131 (1991), pp. 130–64. For a near contemporary, direct parallel drawn between the actions of Eyre and Dyer see Lord Olivier, *The Myth*

of Governor Eyre (London: Hogarth Press, 1933). Olivier's book was published with the assistance of Leonard and Virginia Woolf.

52. Archer, '"Men Behaving Badly"?', p. 45.

53. Jacqueline Jenkinson, 'The 1919 Riots', in Panayi, ed,, *Racial Violence in Britain*, quotation at p. 102; Michael Rowe, 'Sex, "Race" and Riot in Liverpool, 1919', *Immigrants and Minorities*, 19 (2000), pp. 53–70.

54. Edward Pilkington, *Beyond the Mother Country: West Indians and the Notting Hill White Riots* (London: I. B. Tauris, 1988), pp. 129–33.

Notes to Chapter 6: Violent Protest

1. *Leighton Buzzard Observer*, 11 August 1914, p. 5.

2. Bedfordshire RO, SJV 11

3. *Leighton Buzzard Observer*, 18 August 1914, p. 7.

4. For a similar incident at Hitchin a few days earlier see *Bedfordshire Standard*, 7 August 1914, p. 6; and for similar problems in northern towns see Robert Roberts, *The Classic Slum: Salford Life in the First Quarter of the Century* (Harmondsworth: Penguin, 1973), pp. 186–87.

5. Anthony Babington, *Military Intervention in Britain: From the Gordon Riots to the Gibraltar Incident* (London: Routledge, 1990), p. 147.

6. In Chapter 7.

7. Mark Harrison, *Crowds and History: Mass Phenomena in English Towns, 1790–1835* (Cambridge: Cambridge University Press, 1988).

8. George Rudé, 'The Gordon Riots: A Study of the Rioters and their Victims', *Transactions of the Royal Historical Society*, 5th series, 6 (1956) pp. 93–114.

9. E. P. Thompson, 'The Moral Economy of the English Crowd in the Eighteenth Century', in E. P. Thompson, *Customs in Common* (London: Merlin Press, 1991), p. 188. The essay first appeared in *Past and Present*, 50 (1971).

10. E. P. Thompson, 'The Moral Economy Reviewed', in Thompson, *Customs in Common*.

11. Nicholas Rogers, *Crowds, Culture and Politics in Georgian Britain* (Oxford: Clarendon Press, 1998), chapter 2.

12. John Bohstedt, *Riots and Community Politics in England and Wales, 1790–1810* (Cambridge, Massachusetts: Harvard University Press, 1983).

13. Cynthia A. Bouton, *The Flour War: Class, Gender and Community in Late Ancien Régime French Society* (University Park, Pennsylvania: Pennsylvania State University Press, 1993); for the disorders of 1789 the best book is still Georges Lefebvre, *The Great Fear of 1789: Rural Panic in Revolutionary*

France (London: NLB, 1973), first published in French as *La grande peur* (1932).

14. See, in general, Peter Jupp and Eoin Magennis, eds, *Crowds in Ireland, c. 1720–1920* (Houndmills, Basingstoke: Macmillan, 2000). Thompson, 'Moral Economy Reviewed', p. 302, makes a comparison between England and Ireland, and discusses also the example of India, where something of a food riot tradition began to emerge in the last quarter of the nineteenth century.

15. Jennifer Davis, '"A Poor Man's System of Justice": The London Police Courts in the Second Half of the Nineteenth Century', *Historical Journal*, 27 (1984) pp. 309–35; Barry Godfrey, 'Judicial Impartiality and the Use of Criminal Law against Labour: The Sentencing of Workplace Appropriators in Northen England, 1840–1880', *Crime, Histoire et Sociétés / Crime, History and Societies*, 3 (1999) pp. 57–72.

16. Norma Landau, *The Justices of the Peace, 1679–1760* (Berkeley, California: University of California Press, 1984).

17. This elision was found, for example, in history books focused at the popular market. Christopher Hibbert, *King Mob: The Story of Lord George Gordon and the London Riots of 1780* (London: Longmans, 1958); Babington, *Military Intervention*, pp. 27–28, in his discussion of the Gordon Riots, juxtaposes the conclusions of M. Dorothy George with those of George Rudé, after having already written about 'the rabble' having its ranks swelled with 'newly liberated convicts and … criminals who had poured into the capital from the counties nearby' (p. 26).

18. J. M. Neeson, 'The Opponents of Enclosure in Eighteenth-Century Northamptonshire', *Past and Present*, 105 (1984), pp. 114–39.

19. David Eastwood, 'Communities, Protest and Police in Early Nineteenth-Century Oxfordshire: The Enclosure of Otmoor Reconsidered', *Agricultural History Review*, 44 (1996) pp. 35–46.

20. John E. Archer, *'By a Flash and a Scare': Arson, Animal Maiming and Poaching in East Anglia, 1815–1870* (Oxford: Clarendon Press, 1990); and for the Swing Riots see E. J. Hobsbawm and George Rudé, *Captain Swing* (London: Lawrence & Wishart, 1969).

21. Peter Sahlins, *Forest Rights: The War of the Demoiselles in Nineteenth-Century France* (Cambridge, Massachusetts: Harvard University Press, 1994); for an introduction to the French Revolution's attempt to deal with the issue of common land see P. M. Jones, *The Peasantry in the French Revolution* (Cambridge: Cambridge University Press, 1988), pp. 137–54.

22. Rogers, *Crowds, Culture and Politics*, chapter 3 passim; idem, 'Impressment and the Law in Eighteenth-Century Britain', in Norma Landau, ed., *Law,*

Crime and English Society, 1660–1830 (Cambridge: Cambridge University Press, 2002).

23. Clive Emsley, *British Society and the French Wars, 1793–1815* (London: Macmillan, 1979), pp. 27, 35–37 and 56.

24. Isser Woloch, 'Napoleonic Conscription: State Power and Civil Society', *Past and Present*, 111 (1986), pp. 101–29; Alan Forrest, *Conscripts and Deserters: The Army and French Society during the Revolution and Empire* (Oxford: Oxford University Press, 1989); Clive Emsley, *Gendarmes and the State in Nineteenth-Century Europe* (Oxford: Oxford University Press, 1999), pp. 70–72, 93, 111 and 156–57.

25. Adrian Randall, 'The Industrial Moral Economy of the Gloucestershire Weavers in Eighteenth-Century England', in John Rule, ed., *British Trade Unionism, 1750–1850: The Formative Years* (London: Longman, 1988).

26. For Luddism see, inter alia, F. O. Darvall, *Popular Disturbances and Public Order in Regency England* (2nd edn, Oxford: Oxford University Press, 1969), M. I. Thomis, *The Luddites* (Newton Abbott: David and Charles, 1970), and E. P. Thompson, *The Making of the English Working Class* (2nd edn, Harmondsworth: Penguin, 1968).

27. Thompson, 'Moral Economy Reviewed', p. 341.

28. Maxime Berg, 'Workers and Machinery in Eighteenth-Century England', and Michael Hayes, 'Employers and Trade Unions, 1824–1850', in Rule, ed., *British Trade Unionism*, pp. 259–61; Clive Behagg, 'Secrecy, Ritual and Folk Violence: The Opacity of the Workplace in the First Half of the Nineteenth Century', in Robert D. Storch, ed., *Popular Culture and Custom in Nineteenth-Century England* (London: Croom Helm, 1982).

29. E. J. Hobsbawm, 'The Machine Breakers', in E. J. Hobsbawm, *Labouring Men* (London: Weidenfeld and Nicholson, 1964).

30. J. Carter Wood, *Violence and Crime in Nineteenth-Century England: The Shadow of our Refinement* (London: Routledge, 2004) p. 32.

31. John Archer, '"Men Behaving Badly?": Masculinity and the Uses of Violence, 1850–1900', in Shani D'Cruze, ed., *Everyday Violence in Britain: Gender and Class* (Harlow: Longman, 2000), p. 51.

32. Sidney Pollard, 'The Ethics of the Sheffield Outrages', *Transactions of the Hunter Archaeological Society*, 7 (1953–54), pp. 118–39; Richard N. Price, 'The Other Face of Respectability: Violence in the Manchester Brickmaking Trades', *Past and Present*, 66 (1975), pp. 110–32.

33. J. E. King, '"We Could Eat the Police!" Popular Violence in the North Lancashire Cotton Strike of 1878', *Victorian Studies*, 28 (1985), pp. 439–71.

34. See, inter alia, *Daily Herald*, 31 May 1912, p. 1; 12 July, p. 1; 1 August, pp. 1

and 4; *Southwark and Bermondsey Recorder*, 14 June 1912, p. 3; 21 June, p. 5; 28 June, p. 6; and 23 August, p. 7.

35. PRO, HO 45.10666.216733, Volunteer Police Force, 1911–14.

36. Jon Lawrence, 'Forging a Peaceable Kingdom: War, Violence, and Fear of Brutalization in Post-First World War Britain', *Journal of Modern History*, 75 (2003), pp. 557–89, at pp. 582–83.

37. Jane Morgan, *Conflict and Order: The Police and Labour Disputes in England and Wales, 1900–1939* (Oxford: Clarendon Press, 1987), pp. 103–4 and 127–28; Barbara Weinberger, *Keeping the Peace? Policing Strikes in Britain, 1906–1926* (New York and Oxford: Berg, 1991), pp. 175, 177, 182 and 200.

38. Quoted in Weinberger, *Keeping the Peace?*, p. 201.

39. Hermann Mannheim, *Social Aspects of Crime in England between the Wars* (London: George Allen and Unwin, 1940) pp. 158–59.

40. Morgan, *Conflict and Order*, pp. 199–200; Roger Geary, *Policing Industrial Disputes, 1893 to 1985* (Cambridge: Cambridge University Press, 1985), pp. 61–66.

41. Geary, *Policing Industrial Disputes*. For the debate over police tactics see Tony Jefferson, *The Case against Paramilitary Policing* (Buckingham: Open University Press, 1990), and P. A. J. Waddington, *The Strong Arm of the Law: Armed Police and Public Order Policing* (Oxford: Clarendon Press, 1991).

42. Karl Marx, 'Critical Notes on the Article "The King of Prussia and Social Reform" by a Prussian', *Marx: Early Writings* (Harmondsworth: Penguin, 1975), p. 414. For the two uprisings see Maurice Moissonier, *Les canuts: 'vivre en travaillant ou mourir en combattant'* (4th edn, Paris: Messidor / Editions sociales, 1988), and Robert J. Bezucha, *The Lyon Uprising of 1834: Social and Political Conflict in the Early July Monarchy* (Cambridge, Massachusetts: Harvard University Press, 1974).

43. Gwyn A. Williams, *The Merthyr Rising* (London: Croom Helm, 1978).

44. Michelle Perrot, *Workers on Strike: France, 1871–1890* (Leamington Spa: Berg, 1984), pp. 166–87; Edward Shorter and Charles Tilly, *Strikes in France, 1830–1968* (Cambridge: Cambridge University Press, 1974), especially p. 81.

45. Clive Emsley, 'Police and Industrial Disputes in England and North America, 1880–1970', and Ira Katznelson, 'Working Class Formation and the State: Nineteenth-Century England in American Perspective', both in David Englander, ed., *Britain and America: Studies in Comparative History, 1760–1970* (New Haven, Connecticut and London: Yale University Press, 1997).

Notes to Chapter 7: Stones and Fisticuffs

1. John Thelwall, *An Appeal to Popular Opinon against Kidnapping and Murder: Including a Narrative of the Late Atrocious Proceedings at Yarmouth* (London, 1796), quotation at p. 25; idem, *A Particular Account of the Late Outrages at Lynn and Wisbeach, being a Postscript to the Appeal to Popular Opinion against Kidnapping and Murder* (London, 1796), quotation at p. 15; E. P. Thompson, 'Hunting the Jacobin Fox', *Past and Present*, 142 (1994), pp. 94–140.

2. Albert Goodwin, *The Friends of Liberty: The English Democratic Movement in the Age of the French Revolution* (London: Hutchinson, 1979), p. 367. The minister was William Windham, Secretary at War and MP for Norwich.

3. Thomas Hardy, *Memoir of Thomas Hardy* (London, 1832), pp. 36–38 and 79–87.

4. *Stratford upon Avon Herald*, 1901, 28 June, p. 2; 12 July, p. 2; 19 July, p. 2; *Warwick and Warwickshire Advertiser*, 1901, 13 July p. 6; 20 July, p. 5; Richard Price, *An Imperial War and the British Working Class* (London: Routledge, 1972), pp. 141–42 and 145.

5. Quoted in Brock Millman, *Managing Domestic Dissent in First World War Britain* (London: Frank Cass, 2000), p. 159.

6. E. P. Thompson, *The Making of the English Working Class* (2nd edn, London: Victor Gollancz, 1980) p. 85.

7. Price, *An Imperial War*, p. 147.

8. J. A. Hobson, *The Psychology of Jingoism* (London, 1901) and C. F. G. Masterman, *From the Abyss* (London, 1902), both quoted in Price, *An Imperial War*, p. 134.

9. Alexis de Tocqueville, *Journeys to England and Ireland*, ed, J. P. Mayer (New York: Doubleday, 1968), p. 11.

10. Frank O'Gorman, *Voters, Patrons and Parties: The Unreformed Electoral System of Hanoverian England, 1734–1832* (Oxford: Clarendon Press, 1999), pp. 255–59.

11. Nicholas Rogers, *Crowds, Culture, and Politics in Georgian Britain* (Oxford: Clarendon Press, 1998).

12. Tony Hayter, *The Army and the Crowd in Mid-Georgian England* (London: Macmillan, 1978), chapter 12.

13. Rogers, *Crowds, Culture, and Politics*, chapter 5.

14. There are many published editions of Thomas Carlyle, *The French Revolution*. The quotations are take from, respectively, part 3, book 7, chapter 5, and part 2, book 4, chapter 7.

15. See especially, Roger Wells, *Insurrection: The British Experience, 1795–1803* (Gloucester: Alan Sutton, 1983).

16. Clive Emsley, *The English Police: A Political and Social History* (2nd edn, London: Longman, 1996), pp. 57–59. For governments urging restraint in the aftermath of Peterloo see, inter alia, John Saville, '1848: Britain and Europe', in Sabine Freitag, ed., *Exiles from European Revolutions: Refugees in Mid-Victorian Britain* (New York and London: Berghahn, 2003), pp. 26–27.

17. F. C. Mather, *Public Order in the Age of the Chartists* (Manchester: Manchester University Press, 1959), for example, could write that 'the disturbances of the Chartist period were far less destructive than those of a previous generation' (p. 12), and that 'the urge to wanton destruction had been considerably weakened by the time of the Chartist disturbances' (p. 13).

18. F. C. Mather, 'The General Strike of 1842: A Study in Leadership, Organisation and the Threat of Revolution during the Plug Plot Disturbances', in John Stevenson and Roland Quinault, eds, *Popular Protest and Public Order: Six Studies in British History, 1790–1920* (London: Allen and Unwin, 1974); Mick Jenkins, *The General Strike of 1842* (London: Lawrence and Wishart, 1980); Robert Fyson, 'The Crisis of 1842: Chartism, the Colliers' Strike and the Outbreak in the Potteries', in James Epstein and Dorothy Thompson, eds, *The Chartist Experience: Studies in Working-Class Radicalism and Culture, 1830–1860* (London: Macmillan, 1982).

19. Brian Harrison, 'The Sunday Trading Riots of 1855', *Historical Journal*, 8 (1965), pp. 219–45.

20. Philip Thurmond Smith, *Policing Victorian London: Political Policing, Public Order and the London Metropolitan Police* (Westport, Connecticut: Greenwood Press, 1985), chapter 8.

21. Victor Bailey, 'The Metropolitan Police, the Home Office and the Threat of Outcast London', in Victor Bailey, ed., *Policing and Punishment in Nineteenth-Century Britain* (London: Croom Helm, 1981).

22. *Times*, 7 September 1850, p. 4, 12 September, p. 5; Jasper Ridley, *Lord Palmerston* (London: Constable, 1970), p. 395. *The Times* also reported European reactions to the event. There were some in France who put the attack down to German 'democrats' and others who believed that it was the result of German 'socialists' winning English converts (17 September, p. 6). The press in the Austrian Empire was, understandably, outraged and suggested that intellectual agitators, England's liberal press and even Lord Palmerston had a hand in stirring up the crowd (18 September, p. 7).

23. Donald C. Richter, *Riotous Victorians* (Athens, Ohio: Ohio University Press, 1981), chapter 5.

24. Raphael Samuel, ed., *East End Underworld: Chapters in the Life of Arthur Harding* (London: Routledge and Kegan Paul, 1981), p. 266.

25. Jon Lawrence, *Speaking for the People: Party, Language and Popular Politics in England, 1867–1914* (Cambridge: Cambridge University Press, 1998), pp 181–93.

26. *Hansard*, vol. 198, cols 2169 and 2331 (17 and 19 December 1908). Thorne went back to his 'awful bashing' at Camborne in the debate that centred on Mosley's Olympia Rally a quarter of a century later. *Hansard*, vol. 209, col. 1947 (14 June 1934). Again it was to defend free speech, not the violence of the Blackshirt stewards.

27. *Report of the Departmental Committee on the Duties of the Police with Respect to the Preservation of Order at Public Meetings*, ii, *Minutes of Evidence*, Cmd 4674 (London: HMSO, 1909), q. 1174; see also (q. 573) the comments of Leonard Dunning, Head Constable of Liverpool (and subsequently one of His Majesty's Inspectors of Constabulary): 'If you consider that your meeting is going to be disturbed by fifty roughs you must have seventy-five roughs who can throw them out.'

28. *Report of the Departmental Committee on the Duties of Police*, i, *Report and Appendices*, Cmd 4673 (London: HMSO), pp. 14–15.

29. Jon Lawrence, 'Contesting the Male Polity: The Suffragettes and the Politics of Disruption in Edwardian Britain', in Amanda Vickery, ed., *Women, Privilege and Power: British Politics, 1750 to the Present* (Stanford, California: Stanford University Press, 2001).

30. The following paragraphs draw heavily on two important articles by Jon Lawrence, 'Forging a Peaceable Kingdom: War, Violence, and Fear of Brutalization in Post-First World War Britain', *Journal of Modern History*, 75 (2003), pp. 557–89; and 'Fascist Violence and the Politics of Public Order in Inter-War Britain: The Olympia Debate Revisited', *Historical Research*, 76 (2003), pp. 238–67.

31. Sir Oswald Mosley, *My Life* (London: Nelson, 1968), pp. 296 and 301. For the Olympia meeting in general see Robert Skidelsky, *Oswald Mosley* (London: Macmillan, 1975), chapter 19.

32. Quoted in Skidelsky, *Oswald Mosley*, p. 377.

33. *Hansard*, vol. 290, col. 2004 (14 June 1934).

34. Lawrence, 'Fascist Violence and the Politics of Public Order'.

Notes to Chapter 8: Violent Policemen

1. *Report of the Royal Commission upon the Duties of the Metropolitan Police*, Cmd 4185 (London: HMSO, 1908), pp. 388–410; CCCSP, 149, pp. 840–53 (23–26 October 1908); *Metropolitan Police Orders 1908*, 7 October (p. 1019) and 28 October (p. 1076); Raphael Samuel, ed., *East End Underworld: Chapters in the Life of Arthur Harding* (London: Routledge & Kegan Paul, 1981), pp. 190–94. Harding claimed that both Sheedy and Ashworth were dismissed from the police. I have been unable to find any record of disciplinary action against PS Sheedy in the *Orders*.

2. The description of the event in Martin Fido and Keith Skinner, *The Official Encyclopedia of Scotland Yard* (London: Virgin, 1999), p. 229, suggests that this sort of behaviour was common in the East End, but goes on to denigrate Gamble and Griffiths ('a streetwalker's favourite punter') and to argue that, while Ashworth's behaviour had been 'improper', he 'had not meant to inflict quite so serious an injury'. According to this version the 'less tolerant view' of the police hierarchy and the court resulted in gaol sentences for both Ashworth and Sheedy. But Sheedy was not tried at the Old Bailey.

3. Max Weber, *The Theory of Social and Economic Organisation*, edited and introduced by Talcott Parsons (London: Collier-Macmillan, 1964), p. 156; David H. Bayley, *Patterns of Policing: A Comparative International Analysis* (New Brunswick, New Jersey: Rutgers University Press, 1985), pp. 7–13. Egon Bittner, *The Functions of the Police in Modern Society* (Chevy Chase, Maryland: National Institute of Mental Health, 1970). A powerful criticism of Bayley's and Bittner's views, stressing that as the police so rarely use force it should not therefore be used as a defining characteristic, is to be found in Jean-Paul Brodeur, 'Police et Coercition', *Revue Française de Sociologie*, 35 (1994), pp. 457–85.

4. David Taylor, *Policing the Victorian Town: The Development of the Police in Middlesbrough, c. 1840–1914* (Houndmills: Palgrave Macmillan, 2002), p. 87.

5. *PP*, 1875 (352), xiii, *Select Committee on Police Superannuation Funds*, q. 1614.

6. Clive Emsley, '"The Thump of Wood on a Swede Turnip": Police Violence in Nineteenth-Century England', *Criminal Justice History*, 6 (1985), 125–49; Mark Clapson and Clive Emsley, 'Street, Beat and Respectability: The Culture and Self-Image of the Late Victorian and Edwardian Urban Policeman', in Louis A. Knafla, ed., *Policing and War in Europe: Criminal Justice History*, 16 (2002), pp. 107–31, at pp. 119–24.

7. *Illustrated London News*, 15 November 1873; anon, 'The Metropolitan Police System', *Westminster Review*, 101 (old series), 45 (new series) (1874), pp. 31–56, at p. 45.

8. *Times*, 12 March 1870, p. 9, and 24 March, p. 11.

9. *Daily Telegraph*, 9 January 1884, p. 7.

10. *Times*, 28 December 1908, p. 6.

11. Hugh R. P. Gamon, *The London Police Court Today and Tomorrow* (London: J. M. Dent, for the Toynbee Trust, 1907), pp. 26–27.

12. *Justice of the Peace*, 86 (1922), 18 March, p. 126.

13. *Justice of the Peace*, 89 (1925), 7 November, p. 637. *Times*, 31 August 1920, p. 7, reported two policemen stating that when they arrested a young soldier in Camberwell, South East London, for disorderly conduct, 'a hostile crowd of 300 persons surrounded them, throwing bricks, stones, glass bottles and other missiles'.

14. *Justice of the Peace*, 91 (1927), 25 June, p. 489; and see also, 23 April p. 308 and 15 October p. 776.

15. Jerry White, *The Worst Street in North London: Campbell Bunk, Islington, between the Wars* (London: Routledge and Kegan Paul, 1986), p. 280 n. 62. James Morton, *East End Gangland* (London: Warner Books, 2001), pp. 27–28, reports an interview with a PC whose grandfather claimed to have received a certificate for rescuing a constable thrust into a man hole.

16. White, *The Worst Street in North London*, p. 115. Ted Lyscom recalled Mullins rescuing him from a fight with three drunks armed with bottles. Mullins did not strike a blow; his presence and personal authority were sufficient to make the drunks leave peaceably. MPA, Edward Lyscom, 'London Policeman', fos 36–37 (copy also in OUPA).

17. OUPA, Fred Hall, 'The Saga of a Practical Copper', fol. 23.

18. Mike Brogden, *On the Mersey Beat: Policing Liverpool Between the Wars* (Oxford: Oxford University Press, 1991), p. 107, and see in general pp. 104–10.

19. *Justice of the Peace*, 89 (1925), 7 November, p. 637.

20. John Wainwright, *Wainwrights's Beat: Twenty Years with the West Yorkshire Police Force* (London: Macmillan, 1987), pp. 174–75; see also pp. 183 and 198–201 for the effect of the beat on Wainwright and his wife.

21. Victor Meek, *Cops and Bobbies* (London: Gerald Duckworth, 1962), p. 15.

22. Harry Daley, *This Small Cloud: A Personal Memoir* (London: Weidenfeld and Nicolson, 1986), pp. 82–83 and 120–21.

23. See, inter alia, *Times*, 11 July 1868, p. 11; Charles Tempest Clarkson and J. Hall Richardson, *Police!* (London: Field and Tuer, 1889), pp. 363–64.

24. Buckinghamshire RO, BC 4/7, Constabulary Casualty Book, 1870–1965, records a constable dismissed in November 1902 for being 'drunk and assaulting people on [the] highway'. Greater Manchester Police Museum, Lancashire Police, Manchester Division Misconduct Book, 1912–35, fol. 33, a constable called upon to resign for assaulting his wife and frequently quarrelling with her (1917); fol. 89, a constable 'ordered to resign' for fighting with his wife (1924); and fol. 78, a constable transferred to the Warrington Division for 'conduct to his wife which was likely to bring discredit on the reputation of the Force' (1923). MPA, Defaulters' Book, 'R' Division, 1927–35, a constable dismissed for indecently assaulting a woman 'by placing his hand under her clothing and touching her leg' (1929); a constable fined two days' pay, severely reprimanded and cautioned for assaulting a private person while off duty and in plain clothes (1931). See also Taylor, *Policing the Victorian Town*, pp. 177–79.

25. *Tomahawk*, 1 February 1868; for a similar complaint about a young gentleman who was assaulted by the police see Anon, 'The Metropolitan Police System', *Westminster Review*, 55 (1874), pp. 31–54 (at p. 40).

26. *Fun*, 21 July 1866, p. 196; see also 2 June 1866, p. 116, and 13 October 1866, p. 51.

27. William McAdoo, 'The London Police from a New York Point of View', *Century Magazine*, 78 (September 1909), p. 661.

28. *East London Observer*, 5 December 1868; *Report of the Royal Commission upon the Duties of the Metropolitan Police, 1908*, p. 66. One East End magistrate who gave evidence to the Royal Commission, Arthur Cluer, stands out for taking a more critical view of police behaviour.

29. *Times*, 12 February 1929, p. 5; see also 5 February, p. 11.

30. Clive Emsley, *The English Police: A Political and Social History* (2nd edn, London: Longman, 1996), pp. 69 and 112.

31. My thanks to my colleague Bernard Waites for information on this point.

32. *British Paramount News*, 175, 31 October 1932.

33. Kevin Williams, *Get Me a Murder a Day: A History of Mass Communication in Britain* (London: Arnold, 1998), pp. 122–23. The offence was compounded in police eyes by Paramount's decision to distribute the film in the USA.

34. Quoted in Clive Emsley, 'Police Forces in England and France during the Interwar Years', in Clive Emsley and Barbara Weinberger, eds, *Policing Western Europe: Politics, Professionalism and Public Order, 1850–1940* (Westport, Connecticut: Greenwood Press, 1991), p. 169.

35. James C. Robertson, *The British Board of Film Censors: Film Censorship in Britain, 1896–1950* (London: Croom Helm, 1985), p. 137.

36. Emsley, 'Police Forces in England and France', especially pp. 169–72.

37. See for example, Barbara Weinberger, 'Police Perceptions of Labour in the Inter-War Period: The Case of the Unemployed and of Miners on Strike', in Francis Snyder and Douglas Hay, eds, *Labour, Law and Crime: An Historical Perspective* (London: Tavistock, 1987), pp. 158–60.

38. Emsley, *The English Police*, p. 144; *Report of the Royal Commission on Police Powers and Procedure*, Cmd 3297 (London: HMSO, 1929), pp. 111–12.

39. *Justice of the Peace*, 92, 28 January 1928, p. 54, for example, declared that 'the English policeman prefers generally to carry nothing more lethal than a truncheon, and to use it sparingly'. See also, *Justice of the Peace*, 93, 12 January 1929, pp. 18–19; 94, 29 March 1930, p. 198; and 95, 5 December 1931, p. 756.

40. Clive Emsley, 'Police and Industrial Disputes in Britain and the United States', in David Englander, ed., *Britain and America: Studies in Comparative History, 1760–1970* (New Haven, Connecticut, and London: Yale University Press, 1997); Allen Steinberg, 'The Strange Case of Police Brutality and Progressive Reform in New York', paper presented at the Social Science History Association Conference, St Louis, October 2002.

41. Clive Emsley, *Gendarmes and the State in Nineteenth-Century Europe* (Oxford: Oxford University Press, 1999).

42. Elaine Glovka Spencer, *Police and the Social Order in German Cities: The Düsseldorf District, 1848–1914* (DeKalb, Illinois: Northern Illinois University Press, 1992), p. 85.

43. Peter Leßmann-Faust, 'Blood May: The Case of Berlin, 1929', and Simon Kitson, 'The Police and the Clichy Massacre, March 1937', in Richard Bessel and Clive Emsley, eds, *Patterns of Provocation* (New York and Oxford: Berghahn, 2000).

44. Detlev J. K. Peukert, *Inside Nazi Germany: Conformity, Opposition and Racism in Everyday Life* (London: Penguin Books, 1987), p. 198. For recent research on the Gestapo see Robert Gellately, *The Gestapo and German Society: Enforcing Racial Policy, 1933–1945* (Oxford: Clarendon Press, 1990), and Eric Johnson, *The Nazi Terror: The Gestapo, Jews and Ordinary Germans* (London: John Murray, 2000). They take rather different perspectives on the scale of denunciation to the Gestapo. The best account of the French Police is Jean-Marc Berlière, *Polices et policiers en France, XIXe-XXe siècles* (Brussels: Complexe, 1996).

45. *Hansard*, vol. 607, cols 621–31 (8 June 1959), vol. 609, cols 873–82 (20 July 1959), vol. 613, cols 1239–1303 (18 November 1959); *Final Report of the Royal Commission on the Police 1962*, Cmd 1782 (London: HMSO 1962), especially chapter 9.

46. Quoted in Susan Sydney-Smith, *Beyond Dixon of Dock Green: Early British Police Series* (London: I. B. Tauris, 2002), pp. 143–44.

47. *The Brixton Disorders, 10–12 April 1982* (Cmd 8427, London: HMSO, 1981), reprinted as *The Scarman Report* (Harmondsworth: Penguin, 1982).

Notes to Chapter 9: Violence and the State

1. Sir Harold Scott, *Scotland Yard* (Harmondsworth: Penguin, 1954), pp. 84–89; *Evening News*, 6 November 1952.

2. *Times*, 12 December 1952, p. 2.

3. Tony Aldgate, 'Women of Twilight, *Cosh Boy* and the Advent of the "X" Certificate', *Journal of British Popular Cinema*, 3 (2000), pp. 59–68.

4. *Times*, 14 January 1953, p. 4.

5. *Times*, 12 December 1952, p. 2.

6. *Times*, 27 January 1953, p. 8; 28 January, p. 6; 31 January, p. 6; 6 February, p. 3; and 23 February, p. 2. The Bentley and Craig case has been the subject of several books: see, inter alia, David Yallop, *To Encourage the Others* (London: W. H. Allen, 1971); M. J. Trow, *Let Him Have It Chris* (London: Constable, 1990); Francis Selwyn, *Nothing But Revenge: The Case of Craig and Bentley* (Harmondsworth: Penguin, 1991). On 30 July 1998 the Court of Appeal ruled that Bentley's conviction was unsafe.

7. Anette Ballinger, *Dead Woman Walking: Executed Women in England and Wales, 1900–1955* (Dartmouth: Ashgate, 2000).

8. See, for example, J. B. Christoph, *Capital Punishment and British Politics: The British Movement to Abolish the Death Penalty, 1945–1957* (London: Allen and Unwin, 1962); Harry Potter, *Hanging in Judgement: Religion and the Death Penalty in England* (London: SCM Press, 1993); E. O. Tuttle, *The Crusade Against Capital Punishment* (London: Stevens and Sons, 1961); Victor Bailey, 'The Shadow of the Gallows: The Death Penalty and the British Labour Government, 1945–1951', *Law and History Review*, 18 (2000), pp. 305–49.

9. Voltaire, *Candide* (Harmondsworth: Penguin, 1947), p. 111.

10. Randall McGowen, 'The Image of Justice and Reform of the Criminal Law in Early Nineteenth-Century England', *Buffalo Law Review*, 32 (1983), pp. 89–125.

11. *Hansard*, 7 (4 June, 1822), cols 796–800; and for a similar comparison before the French Revolution see *Times*, 20 September 1785, p. 2: 'The whole continent of Europe does not execute as many criminals in four years, as England and Ireland do in one'.

12. *Hansard*, 23 (1 April, 1830), col. 1179.

13. Henry Fielding, *An Enquiry into the Causes of the Late Increase of Robbers* (first published, 1751; edited by Marvin R. Zirker, Oxford: Clarendon Press, 1988), pp. 169–71.

14. David D. Cooper, *The Lessons of the Scaffold* (London: Allen Lane, 1974), pp. 90–92.

15. *Times*, 14 August 1868, p. 6.

16. Seán McConville, *English Local Prisons, 1860–1900: Next Only to Death* (London: Routledge, 1995), pp. 409–31.

17. John Wardroper, *Kings, Lords and Wicked Libellers: Satire and Protest, 1760–1837* (London: John Murray, 1973), pp. 48–49; Michael T. Davis, '"I Can Bear Punishment": Daniel Isaac Eaton, Radical Culture and the Rule of Law', in Louis A. Knafla, ed., *Crime, Punishment and Reform in Europe: Criminal Justice History*, 18 (2003), pp. 89–106, quotation at p. 101.

18. Quoted in Greg T. Smith, 'Civilized People Don't Want to See that Kind of Thing: The Decline of Public Physical Punishment in London, 1760–1840', in Carolyn Strange, ed., *Qualities of Mercy: Justice, Punishment and Discretion* (Vancouver, British Columbia: UBC Press, 1996), p. 35.

19. Robert Shoemaker, 'Streets of Shame? The Crowd and Public Punishments in London, 1700–1820', in Simon Devereaux and Paul Griffiths, eds, *Penal Practice and Culture, 1500–1900: Punishing the English* (London: Palgrave, 2004).

20. J. S. Cockburn, 'Punishment and Brutalization in the English Enlightenment', *Law and History Review*, 12 (1994), pp. 155–79, at p. 172.

21. *Times*, 4 December 1822, for example, reported the case of Matilda Dunn, described as aged under ten years and thirteen years, being sentenced at the Surrey Quarter Sessions for the theft of some cloth. The chairman of the bench, after consulting with his colleagues, directed that she be 'imprisoned for three months in the House of Correction at Brixton, there to be kept to hard labour, and to be twice during that time privately whipped'.

22. Rob Sindall, *Street Violence in the Nineteenth Century: Media Panic or Real Danger?* (Leicester: Leicester University Press, 1990), especially pp. 140–43.

23. Randall McGowan, 'History, Culture and the Death Penalty: The British Debates, 1840–1870', *Historical Reflections / Réflexions Historiques*, 29 (2003), pp. 229–49. V. A. C. Gatrell, *The Hanging Tree: Execution and the English People, 1770–1868* (Oxford: Oxford University Press, 1994), pp. 22–23 and 591–94. Gatrell provides an important interpretation of changing attitudes to capital punishment and challenges the idea that an increasing sensibility brought about its decline and its removal from the public arena. The change, he argues, was less to do with sensibility and

humanitarianism than squeamishness and a refusal on the part of the elite to face up to the reality of the violence inflicted upon the condemned. His arguments are critically reassessed in Randall McGowan, 'Revisiting the Hanging Tree', *British Journal of Criminology*, 40 (2000), pp. 1–13. The shifting attitude of English churches towards capital punishment is discussed in Harry Potter, *Hanging in Judgement: Religion and the Death Penalty in England* (London: SCM, 1993).

24. James Fitzjames Stephen, 'Capital Punishment', *Fraser's Magazine*, 69 (1864), pp. 753–72, at pp. 753–54.

25. John Carter Wood, 'Self-Policing and the Policing of the Self: Violence, Protection and the Civilizing Bargain in Britain', *Crime, Histoire et Sociétés / Crime, History and Societies*, 7 (2003), pp. 109–28; idem, *Violence and Crime in Nineteenth-Century England: The Shadow of Our Refinement* (London: Routledge, 2004).

26. Richard J. Evans, *Rituals of Retribution: Capital Punishment in Germany, 1600–1987* (Oxford: Oxford University Press, 1996), pp. 329–47; idem, *Tales from the German Underworld* (New Haven and London: Yale University Press, 1998), pp. 105–14.

27. *Royal Commission on Capital Punishment* (London: Eyre and Spottiswoode, 1866), q. 245, and appendix, p. 618. J. H. Parry, serjeant at law, was an exception among the witnesses in declaring 'that the majority of murderers are persons who do not belong to the criminal classes' (q. 2506).

28. Bernard Porter, *The Origins of the Vigiland State: The London Metropolitan Police Special Branch before the First World War* (London: Weidenfeld and Nicholson, 1987), p. 10, for Victorian comments on the good sense of the English working class; Clive Emsley, *The English Police: A Political and Social History* (2nd edn, London: Longman, 1996), pp. 248–61.

29. See above p. 87.

30. Steven C. Hughes, 'Poliziotti, Carabinieri e "Policemens": il bobby inglese nella polizia italiana', *Le Carte e la Storia*, 2 (1996), pp. 22–31.

31. *Times*, 1 February 1802, p. 3. See also, *Times*, 29 January 1802, p. 3. For a general discussion of these issues and for information not otherwise footnoted in this and the following paragraph, see John Dinwiddy, 'The Early Nineteenth-Century Campaign against Flogging in the Army', *English Historical Review*, 97 (1982), pp. 308–31; Peter Burroughs, 'Crime and Punishment in the British Army, 1815–1870', *English Historical Review*, 100 (1985), pp. 545–71.

32. *Times*, 29 July 1846, p. 5. At about the same time Lord Brougham also noted the fact the British soldiers were subject to the lash 'alone of all the

European soldiery', see Smith, 'Civilized People Don't Want to See That Kind of Thing', p. 40.

33. Gerard Oram, *Worthless Men: Race, Eugenics and the Death Penalty in the British Army during the First World War* (London: Francis Boutle, 1998), quotation at pp. 90; idem, ' "The Administration of Discipline by the English is Very Rigid": British Military Law and the Death Penalty, 1868–1918', *Crime, Histoire et Sociétés / Crime, History and Societies*, 5 (2001), pp. 93–110; idem, *Military Executions during World War I* (Houndmills: Palgrave, 2003); John McHugh, 'The Labour Party and the Parliamentary Campaign to Abolish the Military Death Penalty', *Historical Journal*, 42 (1999), pp. 233–49.

34. For the case of Edith Thompson, see Ballinger, *Dead Woman Walking*, pp. 221–57.

35. *Report (and Minutes of Evidence) from the Select Committee on Capital Punishment* (London: HMSO, 1931), col. 573; the other quotations are at cols 2993 and 3144.

36. Leon Radzinowicz and Roger Hood, *The Emergence of Penal Policy in Victorian and Edwardian England* (Oxford: Clarendon Press, 1990), pp. 689–711. As far as sentences of flogging for recalcitrant prisoners were concerned, although the sanction remained available until 1967, no such sentence was confirmed after 1962.

37. Radzinowicz and Hood, *The Emergence of Penal Policy*, pp. 711–19; Deborah Thom, 'The Healthy Citizen of Empire or Juvenile Delinquent: Beating and Mental Health in the UK', in Marijke Gijswijt-Hofstra and Hilary Marland, eds, *Cultures of Child Health in Britain and the Netherlands in the Twentieth Century* (Amsterdam and New York: Editions Rodopi, 2003), p. 191.

38. Stephen Humphries, *Hooligans or Rebels? An Oral History of Working-Class Childhood and Youth, 1889–1939* (Oxford: Basil Blackwell, 1981), pp. 74–75 and 82–87.

39. George Ryley Scott, *The History of Corporal Punishment: A Survey of Flagellation in its Historical Anthropological and Sociological Aspects* (first published 1938; 10th impression, London: Torchstream Books, 1954), pp. 63–64. The title page of the 1954 edition carries the direction: 'The sale of this book is restricted to members of the Medical and Legal Professions, Scientists, Anthropologists, Psychologists, Sociologists, Criminologists and Social Workers.'

40. Thom, 'The Healthy Citizen of Empire'; Victor Bailey, *Delinquency and Citizenship: Reclaiming the Young Offender, 1914–1948* (Oxford: Clarendon Press, 1997), pp. 277–78 and 300–1.

41. PRO, HO 45/25066.

42. *Hansard*, 519 (13 February, 1953), cols 754–63.

43. *Hansard*, 600 (26 February, 1959), col. 190.

44. Edmund Burke, *Reflections on the Revolution in France* (first published 1790; quotation from London: Dent, Everyman Edition, 1910), p. 83.

45. Greg T. Smith, ' "I Could Hang Anything You Can Bring Before Me": England's Willing Executioners', in Devereaux and Griffiths, eds, *Penal Practice and Culture*.

46. Gatrell, *The Hanging Tree*, pp. 353–67.

47. Jonah Micah Marshall, 'Europe's Death Penalty Elitism: Death in Venice', *New Republic*, 15 December 2003. My thanks to Martin Wiener for this reference.

48. David Garland, *The Culture of Control: Crime and Social Order in Contemporary Society* (Oxford: Oxford University Press, 2001).

49. David Downes and Rod Morgan, 'The Skeletons in the Cupboard: The Politics of Law and Order at the Turn of the Millenium', in Mike Maguire, Rod Morgan and Roberts Reiner, eds, *The Oxford Handbook of Criminology* (3rd edn, Oxford: Oxford University Press, 2002), p. 289.

Notes to Chapter 10: The Present

1. Ruth Lister, ed., *Charles Murray and the Underclass: The Developing Debate* (London: IEA Health and Welfare Unit/Sunday Times, 1996), which includes Murray's original (1990 and 1994) essays.

2. Peter Hitchens, *A Brief History of Crime: The Decline of Order, Justice and Liberty in England* (London: Atlantic Books, 2003); Joyce Lee Malcolm, *Guns and Violence: The English Experience* (Cambridge, Massachusetts: Harvard University Press, 2002); Norman Dennis, George Erdos, David Robinson, *The Failure of Britain's Police: London and New York Compared* (London: Civitas, Institute for the Study of Civil Society, 2003).

3. Eric Monkkonen, *Crime, Justice, History* (Columbus, Ohio: Ohio State University Press, 2002), p. 54.

4. Sir Robert Mark, *In the Office of Constable* (London: Collins, 1978), pp. 28–29.

5. John Carter Wood, *Violence and Crime in Nineteenth-Century England: The Shadow of Our Refinement* (London: Routledge, 2004).

6. Dick Hobbs, Philip Hadfield, Stuart Lister and Simon Winlow, *Bouncers: Violence, and Governance in the Night-Time Economy* (Oxford: Oxford University Press, 2003).

7. I am indebted to John Archer for information on the Fleeson case, see

Liverpool Mercury, 24 July 1855, *Liverpool Daily Post*, 21 and 23 July 1855, and John Archer and Jo Jones, 'Headlines from History: Violence in the Press, 1850–1914', in Elizabeth A. Stanko, ed., *The Meanings of Violence* (London, Routledge, 2003); Judith Rowbotham, Kim Stevenson and Samantha Pegg, 'Children of Misfortune: Parallels in the Cases of Child Murderers Thompson and Venables, Barratt and Bradley', *Howard Journal of Criminal Justice*, 42 (2003), pp. 107–22.

8. Sabine Freitag, ed., *Exiles from European Revolutions: Refugees in Mid-Victorian England* (New York and London: Berghahn Books, 2003).

9. *Daily Telegraph*, 10 October 1985; *Times*, 10 October 1985.

10. *Times*, 4 November 1985, p. 13.

11. *News of the World*, 23 July 2000.

12. David Aaronovitch, 'Why I am so Scared of Paulsgrove Woman', *Independent*, 11 August 2000, p. 3.

Index